Shanghai Sanctuary

Shanghai Sanctuary

*Chinese and Japanese Policy
toward European Jewish Refugees
during World War II*

Gao Bei

OXFORD
UNIVERSITY PRESS

OXFORD
UNIVERSITY PRESS

Oxford University Press is a department of the University of Oxford.
It furthers the University's objective of excellence in research, scholarship,
and education by publishing worldwide.

Oxford   New York

Auckland   Cape Town   Dar es Salaam   Hong Kong   Karachi
Kuala Lumpur   Madrid   Melbourne   Mexico City   Nairobi
New Delhi   Shanghai   Taipei   Toronto

With offices in

Argentina   Austria   Brazil   Chile   Czech Republic   France   Greece
Guatemala   Hungary   Italy   Japan   Poland   Portugal   Singapore
South Korea   Switzerland   Thailand   Turkey   Ukraine   Vietnam

Oxford is a registered trade mark of Oxford University Press
in the UK and certain other countries.

Published in the United States of America by
Oxford University Press
198 Madison Avenue, New York, NY 10016

Library of Congress Cataloging-in-Publication Data
Gao, Bei.
Shanghai sanctuary : Chinese and Japanese policy toward European Jewish
refugees during World War II / Gao Bei.
p.   cm.
Includes bibliographical references and index.
ISBN 978–0–19–984090–8 (hardback : alk. paper); 978–0–19–049158–1 (paperback : alk. paper)
1. Jews—China—Shanghai—History—20th century.
2. Jewish refugees—China—Shanghai—History—20th century.
3. World War, 1939–1945—Refugees—China—Shanghai.
4. China—Politics and government—1937–1945.
5. Shanghai (China)—Ethnic relations. I. Title.
DS135.C5G36   2013
940.53´181420951132—dc23   2012013153

CONTENTS

ACKNOWLEDGMENTS

I am delighted to use this opportunity to express my appreciation to the many institutions and individuals who made this book possible. In particular, I would like to thank Professor Chen Jian, my dissertation director at the University of Virginia and mentor throughout my graduate studies. I began corresponding with Professor Chen in 1997 when I was still a master's student at the University of Kitakyushu, Japan, and his invitation to study with him in the United States changed my life. I deeply appreciate the time he has devoted to me and to my work over the past decade. He has shown me what it means to be a scholar.

I would also like to thank warmly the members of my dissertation committee, Professors Bradly Reed, Ronald Dimberg, and Brantly Womack, for their thoughtful comments on my work. Professor Reed first introduced me to the story of the Shanghai Jews, and I am grateful for his encouragement and support over the years. Professor Dimberg, director of graduate studies at the University of Virginia's history department during most of the time I was a student, offered me sound guidance on both academic and nonacademic matters. Professor Gabriel Finder also deserves my special thanks. His willingness to discuss with me key aspects of Jewish history and his invitation to participate in Virginia's Jewish Studies Workshop gave me new insights and fresh perspectives on my research topic.

My classmates and fellow graduate students at Virginia gave me good counsel and helpful advice as we presented our dissertation proposals and learned together what it means to be historians. I treasure their help and support. I would also like to thank the librarians, particularly the interlibrary loan staff, at Alderman Library, University of Virginia, and Randall Library, University of North Carolina Wilmington, for their patience and constant help.

It would have been impossible for me to finish my book without financial support from many sources. As a graduate student, summer research funds from the history department at the University of Virginia, two Ellen Bayard Weedon Travel Grants from Virginia's East Asia Center, and a

Graduate Research Award from the Tauber Institute for the Study of European Jewry at Brandeis University made my trips to Asia possible. A Dumas Malone Fellowship for Graduate Research from the University of Virginia's College of Arts and Sciences enabled me to devote myself fully to writing. At my professional home, the College of Charleston, faculty research funds from the history department, the School of Humanities and Social Sciences, and the college made it possible for me to finish and revise my manuscript.

My book would have been quite different had I not received a Charles H. Revson Foundation Fellowship for Archival Research from the Center for Advanced Holocaust Studies at the United States Holocaust Memorial Museum. Steven Sage, the center's staff, and my fellow scholars in residence during the fall of 2004 offered constant support and intellectual stimulation. While in Washington, D.C., I was also fortunate enough to work with the late John Taylor at the U.S. National Archives, as well as Marcia Ristaino and the librarians of the Asian Division at the Library of Congress.

Professor Pan Guang and his fellow scholars at the Center for Jewish Studies at the Shanghai Academy of Social Sciences welcomed me and introduced me to valuable resources. Professors Shen Zhihua and Li Danhui of the Chinese Academy of Social Sciences also helped me to collect vital research materials. I am forever grateful for their scholarly support and kindness. Professor Chang Li of the Institute of Modern History at the Academia Sinica in Taipei also deserves special thanks. Professor Chang not only made possible my two research trips to Taipei but also devoted his time to helping me collect materials and make contacts during my stay.

Professor Tamura Keiko, my graduate adviser at the University of Kitakyushu, Japan, lent me moral support and collected valuable Japanese materials for me. Her encouragement and friendship have been precious to me, and she inspired me to pursue my dream of becoming a scholar. I am fortunate to have her as a role model. I also owe a special debt of gratitude to Professor Sasaguri Junko. Twenty years ago she began teaching me Japanese, and her help in translating difficult Japanese sources was especially important as I wrote this book. Professor Chikuma Yoshiki at the College of Charleston also helped confirm the Romanization of Japanese titles and names.

I would also like to thank friends and colleagues who have provided endless friendship and encouragement throughout the completion of this book: Kathleen Berkeley, Yixin Chen, Chen Yue, Tim Coates, Jim Keller, Laura Witten-Keller, Susan McCaffray, Amy McCandless, Mark Spaulding, Tian Feng, and Wang Shurong. In addition, my department chairs, Bill

Olejniczak and Richard Bodek, have been extremely supportive of my research since I arrived at the College of Charleston.

My editors at Oxford University Press, Nancy Toff and Sonia Tycko, also deserve my gratitude for capably shepherding this project to completion. My thanks also go to Sage Publications, Professor Kathryn Bernhardt, and the editorial staff of the journal *Modern China*. Chapter 2 of this book was adapted as an article, which appeared as "The Chinese Nationalist Government's Policy toward European Jewish Refugees during World War II," published in *Modern China* 37, no. 2 (Spring 2011): 203–237 (http://online.sagepub.com).

Most important, I want to thank my families in China, Japan, and the United States: my father Gao Yuqing, mother Wang Hui, and sister Gao Yi; my Japanese host parents Itō Tetsuo and Itō Shizue; and my mother-in-law Clara Ann Fain. I appreciate all their support and encouragement during my years of research and writing. My daughter, Mika Catherine, was born during the final stages of this project. She has been a further inspiration to me, and her quiet, cooperative good nature made it possible for me to finish reviewing the copyedited manuscript in a timely manner. Finally, I dedicate this book to my husband and best friend, Taylor Fain. His love and support carried me on from the beginning to the end. I could never imagine myself finishing this work without him by my side.

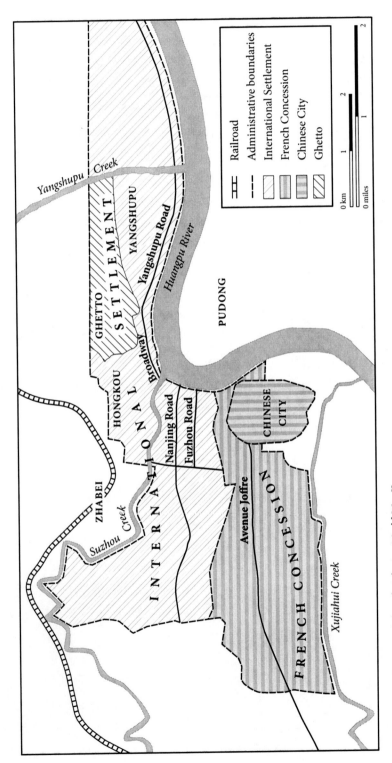

Administrative Districts of Shanghai during World War II

Shanghai Sanctuary

Introduction

When German anti-Semitism turned to widespread terror in 1938, the world and most persecuted Jews realized that flight offered the only hope. For three years that hope remained a possibility. Then the Nazis blocked the exits. If, in the crucial years from 1938 to 1941, the world had opened its doors to the victims of persecution, the history of Europe's Jews from 1942 to 1945 would have been significantly different. Instead, the barriers held firm and relatively few refugees found asylum.
  —David S. Wyman, *Paper Walls: America and the Refugee Crisis 1938–1941*

When David Wyman wrote these words in 1968, he neglected to mention that when the world closed its borders to the desperate Jews of Europe, Shanghai, an open port in East Asia, which could be entered without visas or any documents, became an unexpected last haven for Jewish refugees. Between 1938 and 1941, nearly twenty thousand European Jews fled to Shanghai, and the great majority survived the war.

Nazi Germany's persecution of the Jews is one of the most exhaustively documented tragedies of the twentieth century. However, the story of the European Jewish refugees in China during the Second World War is still not well known and has been explored almost exclusively by Western scholars. The purpose of this book is to examine the story of these wartime Jews from the Chinese and Japanese perspectives. This approach is important because the story of the Jewish refugees in China not only involved tens of thousands of European Jews struggling for survival in a time of great chaos, but also reflects the complicated relationships among China, Japan, Germany, and the United States before and during World War II. The Great Powers' policies toward the Jewish refugee issue reveal much about their national priorities, their international agendas, and their perceptions of the global balance of power.

Shanghai had served as a beacon to Jewish immigrants since the previous century. As early as the second half of the nineteenth century, Jews from Baghdad had come to the city. Some of them flourished in business. Notable Jewish families such as the Sassoons, the Hardoons, and the Kadoories almost dominated Shanghai's economy.[1] After the beginning of the twentieth century, Russian Jews began to settle in Shanghai. The majority of them came to the city because of the Bolshevik Revolution in 1917 and the unstable social conditions caused by Japan's invasion of Manchuria in the early 1930s.[2] However, the European Jews who escaped to Shanghai during the late 1930s did so for very different reasons.

After Hitler came to power in 1933, the Nazi regime decided to force Jews to emigrate from Germany and, later, Europe.[3] By the end of the decade, the *Anschluss* with Austria, the anti-Semitic brutality of *Kristallnacht*, and the invasion of Poland created a flood of European Jewish refugees. But after the annexation of Austria, European Jews found it increasingly difficult to flee to neighboring countries or elsewhere in the world because it became almost impossible for them to obtain entry visas.[4] A great number attempted to escape to the United States, but often they had to wait, sometimes as long as a year, for their quota numbers to come up to enter the country.[5] Even the neutral state of Switzerland was not willing to take in the Jews.[6] From July 6 to 14, 1938, thirty-two countries, including the United States, Great Britain, France, Canada, and Australia, sent delegates to France to participate in the Evian Conference. The conference, convened at the request of U.S. president Franklin Delano Roosevelt, aimed to resolve Europe's growing Jewish refugee crisis. Nevertheless, "no country, America not excepted, declared itself ready to accept unconditionally any number of Jews."[7]

The open port of Shanghai became the last haven for many European Jews. A young Austrian doctor, Samuel Didner, came to Shanghai at the end of 1938. Like thousands of his Austrian coreligionists, Didner had to leave his home country but was unable to find a place of refuge. He first tried the United States, but the American consulate told him that since he was Polish-born, the smaller Polish quota applied to him; it would take a year, at least, until he would be able to obtain a U.S. visa. Time, however, was limited for Didner. The European countries were closing their borders to Jews. He went to the Viennese cafes to collect information about emigration. In the cafes Shanghai was mentioned in discussions, but no one said anything positive about it. "China, they said, was a terrible place to live and thousands of miles away." But Didner was fascinated. "This will be my last resort," he recalled later to Professor James R. Ross of Northeastern University, "at any rate, it doesn't hurt to be on the safe side." As the people in the cafes had foreseen, Didner was told when he visited the Chinese consulate that he would be welcomed in Shanghai. He obtained a visa, although it was not required, and on November 17, 1938, Didner boarded a ship in Italy bound for China.[8]

Shanghai was also the last and only chance for Horst Levin. Levin's family was from a small German town in East Prussia and had moved to Berlin in 1935. In November 1938, Horst's father was arrested by the Gestapo. Afraid for his father's life, Horst went to the Gestapo's office and tried to rescue him. However, he was arrested as well and put into a concentration camp. After a week, the Levins received a notice from the Gestapo that they would release Horst if his family sent him out of the country. Meanwhile, Horst believed he had no chance to obtain a visa as thousands of Jews had been leaving since November. The only place he could travel without a visa was Shanghai. Horst returned home in January 1939, a week after his family had purchased him a ticket to Shanghai. Although the stories about the Chinese city alarmed the family, they knew that this was his only opportunity.[9]

Jewish refugees could go to Shanghai without visas because of its unique status as a city under the control of foreign powers. It had become a treaty port and opened its doors to the Western nations after the first Opium War in 1842. Before the first European Jewish refugees escaped to Shanghai in 1938, the city was ruled by fourteen different countries and divided into four separate administrative units: the "Chinese City" was controlled by Chiang Kai-shek's Nationalist government. A municipal council representing eleven Western powers was in charge of Shanghai's International Settlement. The eastern side of the International Settlement, Hongkou (Hongkew),[10] was exclusively dominated by the Japanese, who had occupied that area after August 1937. Finally, the French Concession was governed by the French consul. Chiang's regime directed passport control in Shanghai until the outbreak of the hostilities between China and Japan in July 1937. However, after the Japanese defeated the Nationalists and drove them out of the city in late 1937, no other country with a presence in Shanghai was given authority to take charge of passport control.[11] In short, the chaos created by the war in China made the Jewish refugees' flight to Shanghai possible.

As this book assesses this turbulent era in the history of East Asia, it aims, first, to examine the Chinese government's policy toward the Shanghai Jewish refugee issue. In early 1939, as China struggled to fend off the invading Japanese, Sun Ke (Sun Fo), president of the Legislative Yuan

and son of Sun Yat-sen, formulated a plan to settle European Jewish refugees in China's southwestern Yunnan Province, which had a small
population and a great deal of uncultivated land. The plan was a humanitarian one, but it was also intended to attract Jewish capital from abroad,
since many leading Nationalist officials believed that Jewish communities
throughout the world, and particularly in the United States, financially
supported the Shanghai Jews. At the same time, the Nationalist government
wanted to favorably impress the British and U.S. governments, which they
hoped would aid China in its war against Japan.

However, although Germany recalled its ambassador to China in June
1938 and the two countries officially severed diplomatic relations in July
1941, China at this point was still nominally an ally of Germany. As a result,
the Chinese also had to be sensitive to the plan's reception by Berlin. China
could not afford to make Germany another enemy. Therefore, China's
settlement plan initially aimed to assist "stateless" Jews—non-German or
Austrian Jews. After American Jewish leaders enthusiastically participated
in the settlement plan and promised to convince the Roosevelt
administration to support China financially, Chinese officials gradually
abandoned their concerns about Germany. China's highest priority during
this period was to win international assistance in its war against Japan.
Meanwhile, the U.S. government was restricting immigration by European
Jews and was unwilling to provide financial assistance to China's Jewish
settlement plan. Without funds, the Nationalist government simply could
not implement the scheme.

This study also intends to shed new light on Japan's Jewish policy. By
ousting the Chinese Nationalist government from Shanghai in late 1937,
Japan became a major power controlling the city along with twelve Western
countries. Although an ally of Germany, Japan treated the Jewish refugees
in Shanghai less harshly than Berlin would have wished. It did so for
pragmatic reasons. Instead of adopting Nazi Germany's policy of exterminating the Jews, the Japanese military "Jewish experts," army colonel Yasue
Norihiro and naval captain Inuzuka Koreshige, key players in formulating
Japan's official Jewish policies in the late 1930s, attempted to exploit the
Jews' purported financial and political power in the service of Japan's war in
East Asia. With the Shanghai Jews under their control, the Japanese believed
that the international Jewish community would not be able to involve itself
in anti-Japanese activities, and American Jewish leaders would work to
pressure the Roosevelt administration on Japan's behalf. However, after the
conclusion of the Tripartite Pact with Germany and Italy in September
1940, the pro-German faction in the military and the government gained
power and demanded that Japan change its policy toward the Shanghai

Jewish refugees. After the Pearl Harbor attack on December 7, 1941, the Shanghai Jews lost any remaining value they may have had to the Japanese, and the Japanese eventually forced them into a ghetto.

The existing literature on this subject is scarce and essentially Eurocentric. This is because of the limited source materials available from the Asian, especially the Chinese, side and Western scholars' apparent inability to interpret fully the documentary record in East Asian languages. There are a number of memoirs by Shanghai survivors and a very few studies of the community life of the Jewish refugees in the city. A few scholars have examined the flight of the European Jews to Shanghai in the context of Japan's wartime foreign policy. Yet, despite the fact that this was a story that unfolded in wartime China, the Chinese are almost completely absent from these histories.

David Kranzler examines the unique role that the Japanese played in saving Jews in East Asia. In *Japanese, Nazis and Jews: The Jewish Refugee Community of Shanghai, 1938–1945*, Kranzler correctly argues that Japanese anti-Semitism was "sui generis." The Japanese were not interested in "eliminating the allegedly powerful and wealthy Jews, but rather in utilizing their great wealth and influence for Japan's 'Greater East Asia Co-Prosperity Policy.'"[12] However, he also contends that Japan's first official Jewish policy of December 1938, in which the Japanese government claimed that it would not persecute Jews but would treat them as they did all other foreigners, was a "pro-Jewish policy."[13] In reality, Japan's Jewish policy in late 1938 was rooted in its own wartime needs and was designed to exploit Jews financially. In addition, the Japanese controlled the fate of the Jews in occupied China, and they made it clear that cooperation with Japan was the only choice left for the Jews if they wished to survive. Therefore, Japan's policy was never "pro-Jewish."

Pamela Rotner Sakamoto explores the story of the Japanese officials, diplomats in particular, and the Jewish refugees who escaped Nazi Europe to East Asia within the framework of a diplomatic history. In her 1998 volume *Japanese Diplomats and Jewish Refugees: A World War II Dilemma*, Sakamoto emphasizes that "Japanese policy saved Jews not out of humanitarianism, but rather as a haphazard response to external conditions."[14] However, Japan's Jewish policy during the Second World War was not "haphazard," and the Japanese government made its decisions after careful consideration. For instance, Japan's first official Jewish policy of late 1938 was initiated after a thorough investigation of Jewish matters by the South Manchurian Railway Company (the SMR or "Mantetsu," short for Minami Manshū Tetsudō Kabushiki Kaisha), Japan's biggest and most comprehensive wartime research institute in and about China.

Marcia Ristaino's *Port of Last Resort: The Diaspora Communities of Shanghai* focuses on both the White Russian community and the European Jewish refugees in Shanghai. Ristaino argues that "the Japanese policy toward the European Jews especially can best be characterized as highly ambivalent. On the one hand, the Japanese felt gratitude to Jews in general.... On the other hand, the Japanese had been exposed to the anti-Semitism of White Russians...and...had translated and digested the contents of the infamous *Protocols of the Elders of Zion*."[15] She points out that it was American Jewish banker Jacob Schiff's loans that helped make possible Japan's victory in the Russo-Japanese War, and that the Japanese also admired "Jewish talent and accomplishments."[16] It is true that the "Jewish experts," Colonel Yasue and Captain Inuzuka, were first exposed to anti-Semitism during the Siberian Expedition in 1918. However, Yasue and Inuzuka did not merely follow the White Russians' anti-Semitic ideas. Instead, they did intensive research on Jewish-related matters both in Japan and in Europe, and they had actual experience meeting Jews on different continents. Yasue and Inuzuka's anti-Semitic theories went beyond the tenets of traditional anti-Semitism. They attempted to attract as many Jews as possible to Japanese-occupied China in order to exploit them ruthlessly. To obtain the cooperation of the Jews in East Asia, the "experts" threatened regularly to stop providing Jews with protection. Thus, Japan's plan to take advantage of Jewish wealth was rooted deeply in anti-Semitic prejudices; no sense of "gratitude" or admiration played a role in saving the Jews.

A thorough examination of this subject requires a transnational and multiarchival approach. This study is firmly grounded in primary sources housed in archives throughout the People's Republic of China, Taiwan, Japan, the United States, Britain, and Israel. It makes use of documents from the Shanghai Municipal Archives, the National Archives of Taiwan, the Archives of the Chinese Nationalist Party in Taiwan, the Ministries of the Army and Navy of Japan, the Diplomatic Record Office of the Ministry of Foreign Affairs of Japan, the files of the U.S. Department of State, and the Shanghai Municipal Police Files from the British authority in Shanghai.

Documents from Taiwan and Shanghai for the first time allow a comprehensive analysis of the Chinese Nationalist government's Jewish policy. The Chinese government's retreat from the city after late 1937 left Shanghai survivors, as well as scholars, with the impression that the Chinese had not been actively concerned with the Jewish refugee issue. However, these documents demonstrate that China at the time had a carefully formulated Jewish policy. Most important, the Chinese attempted to use the European

Jews to win international support for its war against the Japanese. The story of the Jewish refugees in China thus provides a completely new and different perspective from which to assess Chinese policy during the World War II era. Despite the corruption and frequent ineptitude of the Nationalist regime, its contribution to the Allied victory during the Second World War should not be diminished. Their Jewish policy, though ill-fated, demonstrates that the Chinese Nationalists were determined not only to fight the war, but to use every possible tool, domestic and international, to win.

Documents from the Diplomatic Record Office of the Ministry of Foreign Affairs of Japan and the Ministries of the Army and Navy detail the plans of these military "Jewish experts" to make use of the Jews. The records of the "experts'" speeches and reports to the central government clearly indicate that Yasue and Inuzuka never cared about the fate of the Jews. In order to obtain the cooperation of the East Asian Jews, they simply needed to threaten that Japan would not provide Jews protection. In addition, they always made it clear that the Jews were entirely dependent on the Japanese for their survival. These documents further confirm that Japan's policy was never "pro-Jewish."

The Japanese Foreign Ministry's documents are also important sources, which clarify the evolution of German-Japanese relations from the late 1930s to the early 1940s. Kranzler, Sakamoto, and Ristaino all emphasize that Japan adopted a different Jewish policy from that of their allies, Germany and Italy. Still, these scholars neglect Germany's influence over Japan's Jewish policy making at the time the two nations concluded the Tripartite Pact in September 1940. The Foreign Ministry's documents demonstrate that around September 1940, pro-German factions in both the military and the government came to power because of Japan's ongoing negotiation of a military alliance with Germany. The "Jewish experts," Colonel Yasue and Captain Inuzuka, were soon removed from their positions in China, and the Japanese government decided to change its policy toward the Shanghai Jews. Kranzler, Sakamoto, and Ristaino all argue that after Pearl Harbor the Japanese realized that the Jews were useless to them and decided to relegate them to a ghetto in Shanghai. However, Pearl Harbor was not the cause; what befell the Jewish refugees following Pearl Harbor resulted, ultimately, from the conclusion of the Tripartite Pact.

This study also for the first time uses the research reports of the South Manchurian Railway Company concerning Jewish matters. The SMR's research reports provided the "Jewish experts," Colonel Yasue in particular, with significant "evidence" to establish their Jewish policies. The SMR's research reports thoroughly convinced the "Jewish experts" that world

Jewry was financially and politically powerful. Although these reports exaggerated "Jewish power," they indirectly saved the lives of tens of thousands of Jews in East Asia.

In sum, this book is a work of East Asian history, but it is also an *international* history. It reveals that both the Chinese Nationalist government and the Japanese occupation authorities thought very carefully about the Shanghai Jews and how they could be used to win international financial and political support in their war against one another. Nevertheless, there was striking difference between their policies. The Chinese never threatened to harm the refugees if they refused to cooperate. On the other hand, the Japanese made it clear that the survival of the refugees depended on their contribution to the plan. This study further emphasizes that the Holocaust had complicated repercussions that extended far beyond Europe. The diaspora of Jews to East Asia in the era of the Second World War emerges as a rich and complex story, equally deserving of attention because it illuminates more fully the intricacies of wartime diplomacy and tragic human consequences of the global conflict.

CHAPTER 1

Chinese and Japanese
Perceptions of the Jews

Jews first came to China as early as the tenth century, and they later established a community in the city of Kaifeng. The Kaifeng Jews remained in China and became fully integrated into Chinese society and culture. Japan, on the other hand, was never home, historically, to a Jewish community. Yet, by the late 1930s the country witnessed the emergence of anti-Semitism in spite of the fact that very few Japanese had direct knowledge of Jews and Jewish culture. Pan Guang, China's leading scholar in Jewish studies, points out that the Chinese never harbored the same type of religious prejudice and racial discrimination that gave birth to Europe's virulent anti-Semitism.[1] Pan's argument is important for understanding the historical context in which the Chinese attitudes toward Jewish refugees in the late 1930s were shaped.

In the early twentieth century, the Chinese successfully overthrew alien Manchu rule and sought to restore and rescue the Chinese nation. Many Chinese nationalists and intellectuals embraced the Zionist movement, the "Jewish nationalist movement," as it was termed in China, to inspire their fellow countrymen. In the late 1930s, when China faced the challenge of the Japanese invasion, a number of intellectuals used the example of the Jews, a people without a homeland, to caution other Chinese about the danger of losing their own country and to call for Chinese resistance against Japan.[2]

Meanwhile, Japan's Siberian Expedition, from the late 1910s to the early 1920s, exposed Japanese military officers to the "Jewish problem" for the first time. As a result, Army Colonel Yasue Norihiro and Navy Captain Inuzuka Koreshige developed a powerful interest in Jewish affairs. These "Jewish problem experts," as they later became known, not only studied Jews in Europe, but also conducted comprehensive research on Jewish-related matters in Manchuria, Tokyo, and Shanghai with the help of military intelligence agencies. In the late 1930s, this Jewish research greatly contributed to the formation of Yasue and Inuzuka's unique anti-Semitism, which led them to urge their government to exploit alleged Jewish political and financial power to help achieve Japan's goals in its war in East Asia.

Therefore, at the time Jewish refugees were fleeing Nazi-controlled Europe for the safety of Japanese-occupied Shanghai, in a general sense, Jews were considered symbols of national independence and salvation in China and of wealth and power in Japan. These dissimilar perceptions of the Jews determined the strikingly different policies of China and Japan toward the Shanghai Jewish refugees between the late 1930s and early 1940s.

The Chinese Perception of the Jews

Scholars believe that the first Jewish merchants came to the capital of China's Tang Dynasty, Chang'an (today's Xi'an), the eastern terminus of the Silk Road, around 900 A.D.[3] However, Jews did not establish a permanent settlement in China until some two hundred years later. By about 1120, Jewish merchants began settling in Kaifeng, the capital of the Northern Song Dynasty. Kaifeng was also the center of trade, communication, and transportation that greatly stimulated imports and exports between the capital, with a population of more than one million, and the southern coastal cities. The Jewish community built a synagogue there in 1163. In the following centuries, the Kaifeng Jews adopted Chinese customs and integrated into the dominant Chinese society. After the death of their last religious leader in the early nineteenth century, no surviving members had knowledge of Hebrew. Their synagogue was eventually razed in the middle of the century, and the Jewish community gradually lost touch with most aspects of its faith.[4]

A consensus among Chinese scholars is that in spite of the presence of the Jewish community in Kaifeng, most Chinese remained unaware of the Jews and Judaism until the middle of the nineteenth century. The Chinese simply considered the Kaifeng Jews either Muslims or, as political scientist Xiao Xian contends, "a small, mysterious and peculiar religious sect that survived from ancient times."[5] After the middle of the nineteenth century, information about Jews and the "Jewish Question" in Europe became more widespread in China via missionaries, businessmen, and Jewish immigrants to Shanghai. Later in the century, China began to dispatch its own students and diplomats overseas. These elite Chinese acquired direct knowledge of Europe's "Jewish Question" and experienced European anti-Semitism.[6]

At the beginning of the twentieth century, Chinese intellectuals began introducing Jewish-related topics in *Dongfang zazhi* (Eastern Miscellany), a journal based in Shanghai that began publication as a monthly and later changed to a biweekly. *Dongfang zazhi* was published from March 1904 to December 1948 and was intended to reflect the atmosphere and "mores" of the country. Its 808 issues contain 53 articles related to Jews or Jewish matters.[7]

Dongfang zazhi covered topics such as the history of the Jews and especially "the intelligence and talent of Jewish people, their sufferings in Europe, and their economic power."[8] Many of the early articles were translated from journals published in Japan and the United States. In these articles, Jews were characterized as "a people of genius" who made great achievements in financial and academic endeavors.[9] Also, according to these articles, economic reasons were often the causes of anti-Semitism and the persecution of Jews in Europe.[10] Chinese historian Xiao Xian points out that in early introductions "the image of Jews was a mixture more negative than positive." Nevertheless, since China itself suffered war, revolution, and natural disasters at the beginning of the twentieth century, matters pertaining to Jews were "only considered by a small group of intellectuals....Ordinary people had neither the opportunity nor the interest to learn the story of a seemingly remote people with whom they had little contact."[11]

From the early 1920s, a group of Chinese nationalists, represented by Sun Yat-sen, attempted to equate Zionism with Chinese nationalism. Zhou Xun observes that "Zionism, which was perceived as the 'Jewish nationalism,' was considered to be the sole solution for the survival of the 'great Jewish people.'...Such a perception was appropriated by Sun Yatsen, and some other Chinese nationalists of his time."[12] The 1911 Revolution destroyed the Qing Dynasty, an alien regime established by the Manchus who had conquered and ruled China for more than two and a half centuries. Many Chinese nationalists considered Zionism "an inspiration for promoting their own...nationalism" and for the survival of the Chinese race.[13]

The Republic of China, after November 1917, was a great supporter of the Zionist movement.[14] Zionism first reached China in 1903 when Nissim Ezra Benjamin Ezra, a Jewish merchant of Sephardic ancestry, established the Shanghai Zionist Association (SZA). Ezra also founded *Israel's Messenger*, the official monthly organ of the SZA, in 1904 to promote the goals of Zionism.[15] Historian Jonathan Goldstein notes that the "first major international challenge" that the Zionists in China faced was to obtain the Chinese government's support for the so-called Balfour Declaration. Articulated on November 2, 1917, by the British foreign secretary, Arthur James Balfour, the declaration expressed London's qualified support for the establishment of a Jewish homeland in Palestine.[16]

In late 1918, Chen Lu, vice minister of foreign affairs of the Chinese government in Beijing at that time, expressed his "personal sympathy" for Zionism. He wrote the SZA chairman, Elly S. Kadoorie, on December 14, 1918, informing him that "the Chinese government had adopted the same attitude toward the Zionist aspirations as the British Government."[17] The Chinese government's support for the Balfour Declaration was emblematic of the friendly approach on the part of China's political elites toward Jews and the Jewish national movement.

Support from the Chinese government greatly encouraged Zionists both inside and outside China. On February 23, 1919, Charles A. Cowen, acting executive secretary of the Zionist Organization of America, sent a letter to the vice minister of foreign affairs and expressed the gratitude of the organization to the Chinese government. Cowen also emphasized that the organization "look[ed] forward with confidence to the establishment and maintenance of the closest and most friendly relations between the Jewish Commonwealth, to be established in Palestine, and the great Chinese Republic."[18]

Sun Yat-sen was then in Shanghai, and he also wrote N. E. B. Ezra on April 24, 1920, to express his sympathy for the Zionist movement. He reassured Ezra that "all lovers of Democracy cannot help but support wholeheartedly and welcome with enthusiasm the movement to restore your wonderful and historic nation, which has contributed so much to the civilization of the world and which rightfully deserves an honorable place in the family of nations."[19] Sun Yat-sen's appraisal of Zionism appears to have been based on his genuine admiration for the movement but also by an appreciation that Zionism's vocabulary and fervor could be adapted by the Chinese nationalist movement.

Meanwhile, after the May Fourth Movement, nationalism in China continued to mount in the early 1920s, and Sun Yat-sen worked to ensure that China would be reunified, reconstructed, and modernized. At the beginning of 1924, Sun Yat-sen fully developed his "Three Principles of the People"—nationalism, democracy, and people's livelihood—and made them the official ideology of the Chinese Nationalist Party. At the same time, he started delivering lectures about the Three Principles to a broader audience including soldiers, students, merchants and laborers.[20]

Sun Yat-sen positioned nationalism first among the three principles. In his lectures about nationalism in early 1924, Sun emphasized that "if we want to save China and to preserve the Chinese race, we must certainly promote Nationalism."[21] "Nationalism," he argued, was "the precious possession which enables a state to aspire to progress and a nation to perpetuate its experience. China today has lost that precious possession."[22] Sun Yat-sen pointed out that Chinese nationalism vanished when the country had been conquered by the alien Manchus. Nevertheless, the Chinese were not the only race in the world that had lost their country. "Jews also lost their country. . . . Although their state was destroyed, the Jewish race itself has survived . . . and so has its national spirit. The Chinese, [on the other hand], once China was conquered forcefully by aliens, lost their national spirit as well."[23]

Historian Audrey Wells observes that "to Sun nationalism held a nation together and enabled it to survive. He believed that this is what had enabled the Jews to continue as a stateless people for nearly two thousand years."[24] Sun Yat-sen used the experience and spirit of the Jews to warn and inspire his fellow countrymen in their battle to save China and restore Chinese nationalism. In this sense, Jews were role models for the Chinese and their nationalist movement.

After Sun Yat-sen's death in 1925, the leaders of the Nationalist Party inherited and reconfirmed his attitude toward the Jews and the Zionist movement. On the tenth anniversary of the Balfour Declaration in November 1927, the Chinese Foreign Ministry sent a letter of goodwill to the Shanghai Zionist Association. The message once again confirmed that "the Chinese government is quite in sympathy with the Zionist aspiration for the establishment in Palestine of a National Home for the Jewish people." The Zionists in Shanghai considered this message "another indication of her [China's] desire to associate herself in the universal joy of New Judea's awakening."[25]

Furthermore, in March 1928, *Israel's Messenger* published a speech by Guo Taiqi (Quo Tai-chi), commissioner of the Bureau for Foreign Affairs for Jiangsu and later vice-minister of foreign affairs in the Nationalist government, expressing his "faith in Jewish nationalism" and "harmony and goodwill between Jews and China." He called for further cooperation between Chinese and Zionists:

I hope that before very long a new rejuvenated China would come into being which would then work for Chinese salvation. China had the greatest regard for the Jews and sympathized with their aims and aspirations. Zionism aims to emancipate your oppressed and weak nation which had struggled for two millennia for independence. I hope that the Jewish national status would be a recognized fact in the not distant future, and I want to assure you that China would readily join hands and create a Sino-Judean *entente cordiale*. With the success of your Homeland there should be close co-operation with Chinese nationalists who are equally struggling to win independence and recognition for their modern national aspirations.[26]

Thus, Guo Taiqi underscored the Nationalist leaders' continued admiration for the Zionist movement. They regarded it as inspiration for China's own national regeneration, and they intended to reassure the Jewish people that the Chinese government was committed to cooperating with them. The commissioner also mentioned the Jews of Kaifeng and assured his audience that Jews "are always welcome to our shores."[27]

In 1929, when Sun Yat-sen's remains were reinterred to the mausoleum dedicated to him in Nanjing, the Chinese government officially invited Ezra and R. E. Toeg, the previous and sitting presidents of the Shanghai Zionist Association, to attend the ceremony, thus affirming the influence and status of the Zionist movement in China.[28]

Sun Yat-sen's widow, Song Qingling (Soong Ching-ling), continued to espouse his views concerning the Jews. In 1932 Song Qingling worked with a group of prominent Chinese intellectuals to establish the China League for Civil Rights. Other members included Lu Xun, one of the greatest modern Chinese writers, and Cai Yuanpei, a renowned educator and a former education minister in the Nationalist government.[29] In the spring of 1933, Song and the members of the China League for Civil Rights lodged a protest against Nazi persecution of Jews with the German Consulate in Shanghai. They also issued a formal "Denunciation of the Persecution of German Progressives and Jewish People."[30]

Meanwhile, a group of Chinese intellectuals in the 1920s, represented by the publishers of *Dongfang zazhi*, also began to examine issues such as anti-Semitism and the continuing Zionist movement.[31] Jewish nationalism equally motivated intellectuals in China, and they hoped that the Chinese could learn from the Jewish experience and build China into a strong country. During the New Culture Movement, many Chinese intellectuals, such as You Xiong and the German-educated Yu Songhua, were attracted to "elements of the cultural Zionism."[32] These intellectuals interpreted Zionism as "an international movement of restoring the Jewish cultural heritage in order to save the Jewish race" and were drawn to the "ideal of renaissance within Zionism." They held that China was also in need of a "cultural renaissance, or intellectual renewal...[to ensure] the future survival of the 'Chinese nation/race.'"[33]

Yu Songhua, in his article "The Jews and the Jewish Zionist Movement" in 1927, used the Zionist movement to encourage his fellow Chinese to increase China's national prestige and build the country's national strength. Yu Songhua argued that the Chinese could learn much from the stateless Jews. He emphasized that although the Jews did not have their own nation and were discriminated against by other peoples, they struggled heroically to restore their homeland, and they never lost hope. The Chinese, he continued, like others who had their own countries, should make greater efforts to strengthen their nations. Yu Songhua concluded that if his fellow countrymen had "the same enthusiasm and persistence as that of the Jews toward the Zionist movement," China would no doubt achieve more than that of the Jewish national movement.[34]

When European Jewish refugees began fleeing Nazi-controlled territories for Shanghai in the summer of 1938, the Chinese were at a crucial moment in their struggle against the invading Japanese. Chinese intellectuals once again linked the fate of the Jews to the fate of their own people. They realized that the Jewish and Chinese peoples were facing the same challenge from fascist enemies. While they harshly criticized Nazi persecution of Jews, the intellectuals implored their fellow Chinese to fight against the Japanese. At the same time, they called on the Chinese people to sympathize with the Jewish refugees.

Shenbao, the Shanghai News, reported almost every day at the end of 1938 on Germany's persecution of the Jews and the world's reaction to it. In one editorial, "The Sufferings of the Jews," on November 15, 1938, the paper pointed out that the sufferings of the Jews raised an important issue: no matter how wealthy the Jews became, "they are unable to protect their lives and freedom...since they don't have their own country." The stateless Jews were tragic examples for the Chinese. The editorial continued, "China is currently in the middle of a struggle for survival, if the Chinese people want to avoid the same sufferings that the Jewish people are experiencing, they must save their precious homeland...so that the Chinese would not become the second Jews."[35]

Yi Bao Zhou Kan, or Yibao Weekly Edition, was published in Shanghai from October 1938 to June 1939. The editors of the weekly regularly called for Chinese resistance to the Japanese invasion and opposed appeasing and capitulating to the Japanese. In his article "About Anti-Semitism," published in December 1938, Li Zheng concluded by saying, "I always hear people say that Jews are using their blood, tears and death to inspire us to rise and fight against the fascists. [We] can not let our country be conquered! We believe that China will never perish! The Chinese nation will survive for ever!"[36]

Chinese intellectuals in Shanghai also played a significant role in appealing to the locals to support the Jewish refugees. In June 1939, He Yiwen published "The Jewish National Problem" in *Dongfan zazhi* and pled for public assistance for the refugees in Shanghai. According to He Yiwen, although the five to six thousand Jews caused a serious social problem for the city, "we should 'treat other people as you would want them to treat you' and be sympathetic to Jewish refugees." He also emphasized that it was difficult already for the Chinese to assist one hundred thousand of their own refugees there; however, "we still should do everything we could to help the Jewish refugees... [and to] unite and stand" with them to fight against the fascist powers.[37]

From the early twentieth century to the late 1930s, when European Jewish refugees began arriving in China, the Jews and their national movement made an extraordinary impression on the Chinese, especially the intellectuals and nationalists. Clearly China was not afflicted with anti-Semitism in the same way that many Western countries were. In fact, many Chinese and Western scholars argue that in China's past anti-Semitism never took root. Xiao Xian notes that particularly in the case of the Kaifeng Jews, "in Chinese historical literature, there is no record of Chinese discrimination or persecution of any kind";[38] Irene Eber concludes that "neither in these [the seventeenth and eighteenth] nor in later centuries is there evidence of discrimination against the Jews."[39]

This is certainly true in the case of the Kaifeng Jews. However, the Chinese perception of Germany's anti-Semitism during the late 1920s and 1930s, when China and Germany maintained a cooperative relationship, was a more complicated case. Although the majority of people in China at the time were actually sympathetic to the Jews and did not accept Germany's anti-Semitism, Nazi policies affected different Chinese in different ways. Regarding Chinese views of German racial policy, historian William Kirby argues that "German anti-Semitism received relatively little notice [from the Chinese]," and that the Chinese interpreted racism in a different way than the Germans did.[40]

Unlike Germany and other European countries with long experience of Jews and the "Jewish Problem," Max Bauer, Chiang Kai-shek's first German adviser, complained that "there were no Jews in China, and that there was 'not the slightest understanding of [Germany's] racial question.'"[41] With little knowledge of the "racial" reality in Germany, some Chinese leaders actually admired and tried to mimic Nazi racism. These Chinese found "the Nazi concern for a healthy, vibrant race something positive and necessary for national revival," and attempted to advocate a national program for "the future of the Chinese race." However, Kirby points out that while the term *race* in Chinese signifies both "nation" and "race," in German it is biological and constituted "the main source of unity of the *Volk*."[42]

Rather than anti-Semitism, the Chinese at the time were more concerned about, and felt offended by, being considered a "lesser" race by the Germans. However, there were groups in China, such as the Blue Shirts, who published articles sympathizing with German anti-Semitism.[43] In the 1930s an elitist faction of Chiang Kai-shek's followers within the Nationalist government established the Blue Shirts, an organization they hoped would harness the energy of fascism to promote China's rapid economic and political modernization.[44] Further, in 1935, the organization called for "direct Chinese emulation of Nazi racial and exclusionary policies" to "recognize the lofty and superior position of the race, restore the race to its old glory, and discriminate against aberrant strains which disrupt the race."[45] Although the Blue Shirts was a fascist organization, historian Lloyd Eastman contends that it was distinctly different from its European counterparts. In many respects, in fact, the group shared similar goals and policies with the Chinese Communists, including an emphasis on nationalism, glorification of a strong leader, and the establishment of totalitarian institutions.[46]

Kirby concludes that "there is no evidence that Chinese shared the revulsion of much of the international community against the NS [National Socialist] racial policies or doctrine" during the 1930s. However, the Chinese "interpreted it in the light of their own (much less virulent) culturalism and racial prejudices and in terms of their own desire for recovery [of their own "nation"]."[47] Kirby's views accurately reflect both the basic tendency and complex reality of the Chinese attitudes toward Germany's racial policies in the 1930s.

The Japanese Perception of the Jews

In February 1935, thirty years after the Russo-Japanese War, when the representatives of the local Jewish community in the Manchurian city of Harbin visited Japanese consul general Morishima Morito, the consul general told his visitors that the Japanese "appreciated the kind help and good will expressed by the Jewish people at the time of the Russo-Japanese War."[48] Morishima was referring to banker Jacob Schiff's loan to the Japanese at a crucial moment in that conflict, which guaranteed Japan's victory. The Japanese never forgot his role in their success.

Although Japanese historians argue that there was no historical contact between Jews and Japanese in the past, Jacob Schiff was, according to historians David Goodman and Miyazawa Masanori, one of "a handful" of prominent Jews who had "direct influence on Japanese attitudes."[49] Schiff, an American Jewish financier, was outraged by the persecution of Jews under the Czarist regime and helped to raise a $200 million loan for Japan in its battle with the Russians. Schiff was the first foreigner to receive the Order of the Rising Sun, the second most prestigious Japanese decoration, from the emperor. He soon became famous in Japan as a wealthy American Jew. At the same time, as Goodman and Miyazawa argue, Schiff's "fame lent a degree of credibility to the myth of Jewish control over the world economy."[50]

In addition to the early knowledge of "Jewish financial power" from Jacob Schiff, the Japanese learned more about Jews and anti-Semitism from the White Russians during the Siberian Expedition. Japan sent troops to intervene in the Russian Revolution in 1918 along with other foreign powers, and their forces remained in Siberia until 1922, longer than those of the other nations.[51]

In Siberia, the Japanese for the first time had an opportunity to encounter directly Western anti-Semitism. Since Czarist Russia was very anti-Semitic, huge numbers of anti-Jewish works were published there. These tracts were later exported to other countries. Contemporaries, their relatives, and later historians often claimed that at the time of the expedition, one copy of *The Protocols of the Elders of Zion* was given to every White Russian soldier.[52] Because of the easy accessibility of anti-Semitic works during the Siberian Expedition, many Japanese military officers, as well as civilians, developed an interest in Jewish affairs. The later "Jewish Problem experts," Colonel Yasue Norihiro from the army and Captain Inuzuka Koreshige from the navy, who initiated and greatly influenced Japan's Jewish policy in the late 1930s, were among these.[53]

In his own son's estimation, one cannot speak of "Japan's Jewish issue before and during the war without mentioning Yasue."[54] Yasue Norihiro was born in 1888 and graduated from the army academy at age twenty-one. He began learning Russian at the preparatory school of the army academy and continued his study of the language afterward on his own. The Russian Department at the Tokyo School of Foreign Languages (now the Tokyo University of Foreign Studies) recruited Yasue when he was twenty-eight years old. After completing his training there, Yasue joined the Japanese forces in Siberia in 1918.[55]

The Siberian Expedition marked the start of Yasue's research on Jewish affairs. After returning to Japan, Yasue began his research on the Jews by delving into the anti-Semitic materials he brought back from Siberia.[56] In 1924, he published *Sekai kakumei no rimen* [Behind the World Revolution] under the pseudonym Hō Kōshi and translated and introduced *The Protocols of the Elders of Zion* to Japanese readers.[57]

Yasue continued his research and eventually submitted a report on the Jews to the Army's top officials. His work soon won recognition from the minister of the army, and in 1927, the ministry decided to dispatch him to Europe for field research.[58] Yasue observed Jews in a number of European countries, including Britain, Germany, Austria, Poland, Belgium, and Russia, and studied their interactions with their non-Jewish compatriots. During his travels, Yasue also had the opportunity to meet and talk to some Zionist leaders in Palestine.[59] In the late 1930s, he was serving as an intelligence officer in Manchuria.

Inuzuka Koreshige was born in 1890 and entered the Naval Academy in 1909. In April 1918, while enrolled at the Naval College, he was sent to study French at the Tokyo School of Foreign Languages. After his graduation in 1920, Inuzuka, like Yasue, joined the Siberian Expedition and became interested in Jewish studies. His research soon drew attention from the navy, and when Inuzuka was appointed naval attaché to the Japanese embassy in Paris in 1928, the naval leadership secretly ordered him to observe the "Jewish problem" in Europe.[60]

In order to become more knowledgeable about Jewish affairs, Inuzuka took every opportunity he had in Paris to study them. He stayed with a Jewish family and patronized Jewish-owned stores. France was the first European country that accorded Jews equal rights as citizens, after the French Revolution. Nevertheless, although there were a great number of Jewish politicians at the time, the majority of French people were Catholic, and anti-Semitism ran deep in the country. Since many French believed that most of the Bolshevik leaders were Jews, and that a German Jew had drafted the Weimar Constitution, the fear of the "Jewish Peril" was spreading to France. Under such circumstances, anti-Semitic publications flooded the streets. Inuzuka was therefore able to collect books about Jews that were inaccessible in Japan. After his return to Tokyo, Inuzuka was promoted to captain and began working at the Third Department, the intelligence branch of the Naval General Staff, in 1934. In the General Staff, Inuzuka took charge of propaganda, counterespionage, and Jewish research.[61]

Yasue Norihiro and Inuzuka Koreshige authored many anti-Semitic tracts in the 1920s and 1930s. For instance, in addition to *Behind the World Revolution* in 1924, Yasue published *Yudaya minzoku no sekai shihai?* [The Jewish Control of the World?] under his real name in 1933.[62] Inuzuka published *Yudayajin no inbō to kokusai supai* [The Plot of the Jews and International Spies] in 1938 and *Yudaya mondai to Nihon* [The Jewish Problem and Japan] in 1939 under the pseudonym Utsunomiya Kiyō.[63]

Captain Inuzuka also spoke widely about Jews and European anti-Semitism. In a 1933 speech to the Naval Paymasters Academy, Inuzuka emphasized that the "Jewish problem" was considered the "cancer of the West" in Western countries. According to him, the "Jewish problem" had already penetrated into religious, social, political, and educational fields, and non-Jewish peoples were seriously suffering from it. The captain also defended Nazi Germany's anti-Semitic movement and explained that it was inaccurately reported in Japan, since Jews controlled the world's media. He stated that it was the Germans, in fact, who had no choice but to overthrow the oppression of the Jews.[64]

In the 1930s, Colonel Yasue and Captain Inuzuka also conducted comprehensive research on Jewish-related matters with the assistance of the Research Department of the South Manchurian Railway Company and the Third Department of the Naval General Staff. The result of Yasue's and Inuzuka's research helped them confirm their belief that Jews, American Jews in particular, were financially and politically powerful in the Western world. This belief eventually shaped the "Jewish experts'" unique policy toward the Jewish refugees who fled to Japanese-occupied Shanghai from the summer of 1938. Instead of adopting Nazi Germany's Jewish policy of exterminating the Jews, the Japanese "experts" attempted to exploit the Jews' purported financial and political power in the service of Japan's war in East Asia.

After Japan's victory in the Russo-Japanese War of 1904–1905, it assumed all of Russia's rights and concessions in Northeast China, or Manchuria. The Russians also transferred their control of the southern branch of the Chinese Eastern Railway to Japan. In November 1906, the Japanese government established the South Manchurian Railway Company (SMR) to manage the railway transportation system in Manchuria. But the SMR also played a central role in the economic life of the region through its dominance of activities such as coal mining and industrial management.[65]

The SMR was not simply a railway company. It was also Japan's biggest and most comprehensive wartime research institute in and about China. Gotō Shimpei, the former civilian administrator of Taiwan and first president of the SMR, established a research department within the company in December 1906.[66] Based on his own experience of governing Taiwan, Gotō explained, "Only after we have completed research in our hands can we undertake specific policies."[67]

Itō Takeo, a former researcher in the SMR, recalls in his memoirs, "My life with the SMR…was spent without knowing a thing about the railroad business. I spent my entire tenure there with the research division."[68] The SMR's research department gathered experts from Japan and conducted research on economic, social, cultural, and political issues.[69] In early 1932, before the Kwantung Army established its puppet regime of Manchukuo, the SMR organized the Economic Research Association at the request of its chief of staff. The establishment of a "new state" made the chief of staff "keenly feel that we must offer careful guidance concerning political, diplomatic, economic, and cultural issues if we expect a healthy development."[70] The creation of the Economic Research Association was a major turning point in the relationship between the SMR and the army. This relationship further improved after the outbreak of the Second Sino-Japanese War in 1937. As scholar John Young observes, "the deeper the Japanese Army became involved in war on the continent, the more it required solidly based studies which produced reliable data and indications of future economic, political and social trends."[71]

SMR researcher Itō remembers that because of the "inseparable relationship between the capacity to transport and intelligence activities," the ties between the SMR and the army "Special Service Agency" [the army intelligence agency] became closer, and eventually "moved to a relationship of mutual assistance and sharing."[72] In June 1938, the chief of staff of the Kwantung Army contacted the vice president of the SMR and asked that SMR do research to "reveal the truth about Jews, and to predict their future moves." The chief of staff believed that such research was "vital to both Japan and Manchukuo." He also wanted the SMR to assign staff especially to this research and to put them under the leadership of Colonel Yasue, at the time the head of the Dalian Special Service Agency.[73] In response to the Kwantung Army's request, the SMR established the Section of Foreign Economic Research to investigate Jewish-related matters. The section was later renamed the Special Research Team.[74]

Ishidō Kiyotomo, a former researcher on the Special Research Team, later confirmed in a collection of reminiscences that "the establishment of the Section of Foreign Economic Research was, in fact, Colonel Yasue's idea."[75] He also noted that at the time, the leaders of the Kwantung Army realized that Manchuria had not received as much investment as expected from the Japanese homeland for its economic development. This financial predicament made them worry about Japan's, especially the army's, ability to defend Manchuria, and even the Japanese homeland.[76] Yet there was little possibility of introducing foreign capital to the area. The only course Yasue believed that they were able to pursue was to "mobilize Jewish capital in the United States."[77] Yasue attempted to use the Jewish community in Manchuria and their close relations with Jews in Shanghai and the United States to attract Jewish investment.

Although the Special Research Team was ostensibly managed by the SMR, the Kwantung Army actually exercised direct control of the team. Ishidō believed that because of the army's influence, this new research team received a huge budget and was therefore able to afford "quite a collection of Jewish related materials."[78] Under Colonel Yasue's leadership, the Special Research Team published nearly fifty reports and issued a periodical on Jewish related matters from 1938 to 1943.[79] The team conducted research on topics such as the social, political, and economic influence of Jews in European countries and the United States, anti-Semitism in Europe, Germany's and Italy's racial policy, Jewish communities in the Soviet Union and Manchuria, and Jewish refugees in Shanghai.

From summer 1938 to December 1941, the research topics of the Special Research Team focused on "Jewish power" in various fields in the United States and major European countries such as Britain and France. Most of the reports, however, exaggerated or fundamentally misunderstood the role that Jews played in those countries. Perhaps this reflected the scant knowledge that the Japanese had of the Jews at the time, despite their attempt at research. Perhaps they simply believed the anti-Semitic propaganda of their Nazi allies. Perhaps most important, as Ishidō Kiyotomo contends, he and his colleagues were "ordered" to compose reports that would "suit Colonel Yasue's taste."[80]

For instance, in Ishidō's 1938 report to the research department on "Jewish influence in the British political world," he translated an article by Arnold Spencer Leese, an extreme anti-Semite and the founder of Britain's Imperial Fascist League, which claimed that every member of the cabinet had either family members or relatives who were Jewish. Ishidō, however, did not mention, or perhaps was unaware of, Leese's anti-Semitic pedigree, although his report explained that the reason he translated Leese's article was because he was still in the process of doing research and could not find any other "reliable" sources.[81]

Narahashi Wataru, a legal adviser to the Japanese embassy in France and the SMR's European office, was involved with a public bond issue with France at the time. During a visit to Manchuria in late 1938, Narahashi delivered a lecture to the SMR staff. His experience with Jews in France became an important firsthand source to the Special Research Team and was recorded as a "Jewish problem" report. According to Narahashi, in France "the former prime minister, who is the current leader of the Socialist Party, and the leader of the Independent Party, who is the current Minister of Colonial Affairs, are both Jewish. I visited and went to court for the public bond problem in dozens of cities in almost all French provinces, it is not too much to say that all the lawyers I worked with and against were Jewish."[82] After reconfirming Jewish social and political power in France, Narahashi brought news to the SMR that was sure to delight the leaders of the Kwantung Army. In Paris at the end of 1938, he made the acquaintance of a member of the Rothschild family, the prominent Anglo-French Jewish bankers. Narahashi told the SMR staff that Rothschild was deeply moved by the news that the Far Eastern Jewish Conference, supported by the Kwantung Army, had been held in Manchuria. In return for Japan's hospitality, "Mr. Rothschild said that they would take the foreign loan, which was what Japan most wanted, into special consideration in the future."[83]

In 1939, the Special Research Team translated *Jewish Community and Organization in the United States: An Outline of Types of Organizations, Activities, and Problems* by Maurice J. Karpf, himself a Jewish scholar, into Japanese. Karpf's work of 234 pages drew a comprehensive picture of organized Jewish life in the United States. He covered topics such as the Jewish population and its distribution in the country, its economic and professional distribution, and the relationships between Jews and non-Jews in America. Since this work was originally prepared for the Second International Conference on Jewish Social Work in London in 1936, it explained to readers, especially foreign readers, the achievements of the American Jews in various fields.[84]

The Special Research Team's investigation of Jewish "power" in Europe and the United States only deepened Colonel Yasue's belief in Jewish influence throughout the world and further confirmed his plan to take advantage of Jews in East Asia. Yasue treated the research reports as solid evidence that proved every rumor the Japanese had embraced about "Jewish power."

Nevertheless, the number of the research reports dramatically diminished after Japan signed the Tripartite Pact with Germany and Italy in September 1940, and were further curtailed after Japan's Pearl Harbor attack on December 7, 1941. No further records on Jewish research published after 1943, when the Japanese occupation authorities in Shanghai forced the Jewish refugees into a ghetto, have yet been discovered. After the conclusion of the Tripartite Pact, Japan's pro-German groups in both the military and the government came to power and removed Yasue Norihiro from his position at the end of 1940. The pro-German groups did not want to contradict Germany's Jewish policy and opposed Yasue and Inuzuka's theory of taking advantage of Jewish refugees in China. Seven months after Colonel Yasue left his position, the Ministry of Army ordered the Kwantung Army to dismiss the Special Research Team and to reduce the numbers of researchers on Jewish affairs from ten to four.[85] The army completely lost its interests in Jews after the outbreak of the Pacific War.

On the other hand, Captain Inuzuka Koreshige of the navy led his own systematic research on Jewish affairs in Tokyo. First of all, Inuzuka was a major contributor to the journal *Kokusai Himitsuryoku no Kenkyū* [Studies on International Secret Power]. The journal was first published in 1936 by *Kokusai Seikei Gakkai*, the Society of International Political and Economic Studies. *Kokusai Seikei Gakkai* was associated with the Ministry of Foreign Affairs and aimed to "provide the government with reliable information about the Jews."[86] Inuzuka wrote the introduction and six articles for the inaugural issue of *Kokusai Himitsuryoku no Kenkyū* and remained a valuable "expert" writer for the journal along with Colonel Yasue.

At the Third Department of the Naval General Staff, the captain was in charge of three different newsletters on Jewish issues that were issued around 1938: *Jewish Information*, *Secret Jewish Information*, and *Top Secret Jewish Information*. From early 1938 to late 1939, the Third Department published nearly one hundred issues of these newsletters. The researchers at the Naval General Stuff translated Jewish-themed articles that had originally been published in Jewish or non-Jewish journals, mostly in Britain, France, and the United States.

The *Jewish Information* series focused on two major issues: Jewish political and financial power in the United States, and the European Jewish refugees in Shanghai. Since the Jewish refugees in Japanese-occupied areas in Shanghai were under the control of the Naval Landing Party, Captain Inuzuka was in a convenient position to carry out his Jewish policy. The captain attempted to use the Shanghai Jews and their connections with the "powerful" American Jews to serve Japan's war plan in East Asia. After the number of Jewish refugees in the city increased dramatically from late 1938, Inuzuka began traveling frequently between Tokyo and Shanghai and became fully involved in the management of the refugee problem.[87]

The naval reports on Jewish research, like those of the SMR's Special Research Team for Colonel Yasue, provided Captain Inuzuka "evidence" to underscore his Jewish policy. For instance, one report was a translation of a story from "the leading American Jewish journal in New York," the *American Hebrew*, about the news that President Franklin D. Roosevelt appointed Jewish judge Felix Frankfurter to the U.S. Supreme Court to succeed Benjamin Cardozo, a Jew and a friend of President Roosevelt. The most interesting part of this report was the subtitle to the story, presumably added by the researchers at the Third Department, "Proof of the Close Relationships between Frankfurter, Henry Stimson [the secretary of state] and President Roosevelt."[88]

The naval research also emphasized the importance of the Jewish refugee issue in Shanghai. One report stated that it was an inevitable consequence of the internationally intensified "Jewish problem." Since Shanghai was a long time "strategic base" of Jewish influence in East Asia, the report continued, the refugee issue in this city would have a huge impact on different aspects then and in the near future.[89]

The researchers at the Naval General Staff were optimistic about the attitude of the Shanghai Jews toward Japan. They briefly divided the Shanghai Jews into two categories. The first group was wealthy Jews of "Arabic" (presumably Middle Eastern) origins, who took a leading part in the Zionist movement. They were also closely associated with the British authorities in Shanghai. The second group consisted of professionals, such as doctors and lawyers, and merchants. The majority of the European Jewish refugees from Germany and Austria belonged to this group and had to depend on the Japanese authorities to make a living. The naval researchers observed that although these refugees originally had tended to be anti-Japanese as a result of Soviet propaganda, some of them were subsequently influenced by the pro-Japanese policy adopted at the Far Eastern Jewish Conference in Manchuria in late 1938.[90]

Although Russian Jews were also cited in this report, it doesn't appear that the Japanese researchers were fully aware of the important difference between the two Jewish communities in Shanghai: the Baghdadi and Ashkenazi Jews. The previously mentioned Sassoons, Hardoons, and Kadoories were Baghdadi Jews, and Jewish immigrants from Russia after the early twentieth century belonged to the Ashkenazi community.

While the military "experts" were devoting themselves to Jewish research, Japanese intellectuals in the 1930s were also fascinated by German anti-Semitism. Japanese historian Miyazawa Masanori notes that "the Japanese do not have a history of living with Jews, and so do not like or dislike the Jews as a result of contact.... However, Anti-Semitism can also exist without Jews altogether."[91] He points out that after Japan withdrew from the League of Nations in 1933, the country became internationally isolated. Japan subsequently drew closer to Germany, which also left the league the same year. While "the psychological dependence of isolated Japan on Germany increased, the voices praising Hitler dominated the domestic scene." Although in the beginning there was still criticism of the Nazis' racial policy, after 1935 the general attitude toward Hitler and Nazism became sympathetic. As a result, the

Japanese did not "interpret the persecution of Jews in Germany as barbaric; on the contrary, they regarded it as proof that Jews are evil."[92]

During the time that Japan was pursuing a military alliance with the Axis powers in the late 1930s and early 1940s, admiration of Hitler's Germany "came to dominate Japanese intellectual life."[93] By the late 1930s, Nazi literature began pouring into Japan, and the German government also supported and helped to develop anti-Semitic "research" in Japan. Consequently, Nazi propaganda successfully influenced and captured Japanese intellectuals, even those without an anti-Semitic background.[94]

Nunokawa Magoichi taught at the prestigious Meiji Gakuin University and also served as an adviser to the Ministry of Agriculture and Commerce. Nunokawa, like the military "Jewish experts," had firsthand experience of Jews in European countries. When he wrote sympathetically about Jews in 1926, he tried to explain that "Jewish character" was a "product of the Jews' struggle for survival." He remarked that "many peoples have been perse-cuted and abused throughout history, but the Jews are a rare example of a people [that] has persevered, learned from their experience, and used it to survive."[95]

Nunokawa, on the other hand, was a friend of Wakamiya Unosuke, who was a professor at equally prestigious Keio University and who had promoted anti-Semitism in Japan since the 1920s. When Nunokawa eulogized Wakamiya following the latter's death in 1938, he claimed, "After twenty years, I have finally awakened to the correctness of Wakamiya's views. How foolish are those, if such there be, who even now refuse to acknowledge his foresight. All those who mourn his passing should carry on his pioneering work and deepen their appreciation as a tribute to his memory."[96] Nunokawa was actively involved with the Society of International Political and Economic Studies, and eventually became editor of *Yudaya Kenkyū* [Jewish Studies], the successor and replacement of *Kokusai Himitsuryoku no Kenkyū*, in 1941.[97]

Kuroda Reiji was a Tokyo University graduate and a correspondent for *Asahi Shimbun* in the 1930s. Kuroda was a radical leftist in the 1920s and embraced Marxism after the Bolshevik Revolution. However, he became a follower of Hitler and a defender of the Nazi racial policy after he had per-sonally interviewed and been impressed by Hitler in 1931.[98] After Japan signed the Anti-Comintern Pact with Germany in 1936, Kuroda published an article in *Kokusai Himitsuryoku no Kenkyū* in which he argued that Japan had become a friend of Germany, "a nation of anti-Semites, and so it is only natural that we must also study the Jewish problem. Since in my view this agreement has no meaning unless people understand the true nature of the Jews, I regard this as an ideal opportunity to inform the general public that the Anti-Comintern Pact is of necessity a matter of antisemitism."[99]

Miyazawa concludes that the transformation of Nunokawa Magoichi's and Kuroda Reiji's views toward Jews and anti-Semitism did not simply indicate the change of heart of two prominent individuals. On the contrary, it "represents a process that many Japanese intellectuals went through in the 1920s and 1930s."[100] Eventually, a susceptibility to Nazi propaganda and a growing admiration of Hitler's Germany helped win the hearts and minds of many Japanese opinion leaders, even those who had never previously espoused anti-Semitic views.

Conclusion

In early 1939, Sun Ke, president of the Legislative Yuan, formulated a plan to settle European Jewish refugees in Southwest China. Simultaneously, the Japanese military "Jewish experts," Colonel Yasue and Captain Inuzuka, initiated Japan's first Jewish policy in late 1938. They insisted that Japan should not follow Nazi Germany's policy of exterminating the Jews. In the summer of 1939, the two "experts" also proposed and investigated a scheme to establish a Jewish settlement for the refugees in Japanese-occupied China.

China and Japan were then at war, and they both attempted to use their settlement plans to impress and attract capital from world Jewry, American Jews in particular, in order to support their war efforts. However, in this war, China was a victim and Japan was the aggressor. This significant difference legitimized China's need for financial support. Japan, on the other hand, wanted the Jewish investment to subsidize its conquest of East Asian territories.

The Chinese had traditionally embraced Jews, and there was no record of persecution or discrimination against Jews in Chinese history. China's policy toward the Jewish refugees in Shanghai from the late 1930s to the early 1940s was rooted in a historical tradition and a cultural environment that were in essence not compatible with the European brand of anti-Semitism. Meanwhile, although scholars recognize that violent anti-Semitism never existed in China, the stereotype held by many Chinese of all Jews as wealthy people was a sort of soft anti-Semitism. Like the Japanese, the Chinese at the time also believed that Jews were financially and politically powerful. However, from the late 1930s to the early 1940s, China was essentially fighting alone against Japan's invasion and desperately needed financial support in any form. The Chinese did not have many options and could not afford to miss any possible source of funds. Although the Nationalist government's plan to introduce Jewish capital through its settlement scheme was grounded in stereotypes of Jews as financially powerful, China's plan, unlike Japan's, did not aim to use this soft anti-Semitism in the service of a cause which would inevitably and logically bring harm to the refugees.

On the other hand, the SMR's research reports and the Navy Third Department's Jewish information newsletters demonstrate that the Japanese military "Jewish experts" in Manchuria and Shanghai had a well-prepared and well-researched long-term plan for harnessing the European Jewish refugees' financial and political "power" to Japan's ongoing war in East Asia. Japan did not save the Jews for humanitarian or ethical reasons, as some Japanese authors argue.[101] Such a decision would not require spending multiple years and enormous sums of money researching the "Jewish problem."

Through their research, the SMR's Special Research Team and the Third Department of the Navy General Staff provided the "experts" with enough supposed evidence to establish Japan's Jewish policy in the late 1930s. Ironically, even though most of the military research reports exaggerated "Jewish power," they helped save the lives of Jewish refugees in China.

Although the Chinese and Japanese governments both attempted to attract capital through the Jewish refugees in Shanghai during the Second World War, their policies sprang from different historical backgrounds, considerations, and contemporary circumstances. The different perceptions that the Chinese and Japanese held of the Jews help to explain the important differences between China's and Japan's Jewish policies from the late 1930s to the early 1940s.

CHAPTER 2

The Chinese Nationalist Government and the Shanghai Jewish Refugees

W hen European Jewish refugees began fleeing Nazi persecution to Shanghai in the summer of 1938, China was at a critical moment in its war against the invading Japanese. On July 7, 1937, the Japanese army contrived the "Marco Polo Bridge Incident," which marked the beginning of the Second Sino-Japanese War. In October 1937, the Chinese Nationalist government retreated from Shanghai, and the treaty port fell to the Japanese.

The Chinese authorities' absence in Shanghai has led former refugees as well as scholars to believe, mistakenly, that the Chinese government had nothing to do with the Jewish refugee issue. In fact, the Nationalist government in Chongqing at the time not only had a carefully considered Jewish policy, but was also deeply involved with the European Jewish refugees. At the same time, the Jewish refugee issue in Shanghai directly and indirectly complicated China's relationship with Germany, Japan, and the United States from the late 1930s to the early 1940s.

The story of the European Jewish refugees in Shanghai during World War II provides insights not only into the history of modern China, but also into the international history of the era. Although China enjoyed a de facto alliance relationship with Germany from the late 1920s to 1937, it lost this important strategic partner to Japan after Germany concluded that the Japanese would provide a more effective check to the Soviet army in East Asia. China was now fighting the Japanese alone and was forced to look elsewhere for both military and financial support. Both China and

Japan attempted to wring money from European and American Jewish communities, which supported the Shanghai Jews, in order to fund their war against one another. The Nationalist government was especially interested in the potential support from the United States promised by American Jewish leaders.

As the Chinese government pursued international aid, several private individuals came to play important roles. A German Jewish businessman, Jakob Berglas, and a politically active American Jewish dentist, Maurice William, presented plans to both the Nationalist and American governments to transplant oppressed European Jews, German Jews in particular, to China. Their stories underscore the efforts by private citizens to shape the official policies of these nations. The work of Berglas and William bore fruit in China, but they failed to persuade Franklin Roosevelt's administration in Washington to support their plans.

Chinese diplomats in Europe were also deeply involved in the Shanghai Jewish refugee issue, although their role has been widely misunderstood. In 2000, Yad Vashem, Israel's Holocaust Martyrs' and Heroes' Remembrance Authority, honored He Fengshan (Ho Fengshan), the former Chinese consul general in Vienna, as one of the "Righteous among the Nations." Although the Jewish refugees did not need visas to enter Shanghai at the time, officials at Yad Vashem explained that He Fengshan disobeyed the orders of his superior, the Chinese ambassador to Germany, in order to issue visas to escaping Austrian Jews.[1] Shanghai survivors' visas reveal that other Chinese consuls in multiple European cities also granted Jews travel documents. If He Fengshan issued visas to Austrian Jews for humanitarian reasons, why and how did these other diplomats do the same? Were they similarly motivated? Documents from the Chinese Nationalist government's archives suggest that these consuls were simply following orders from the Ministry of Foreign Affairs. Chiang Kai-shek's regime had instituted a "liberal visa policy" governing the entry of European Jews to China.

The Sun Ke Plan

On February 17, 1939, Sun Ke, president of the Legislative Yuan and Sun Yat-sen's only son, proposed a plan at the first meeting of the Highest National Defense Council (*Guofang zuigao weiyuanhui*) to settle "destitute and homeless" European Jewish refugees in southwestern China. He explained the plight of European Jews and criticized Nazi Germany's persecution of the Jews. Furthermore, he said that the entrance of Jewish refugees into Shanghai was about to be restricted by the Japanese and the

Municipal Council. Sun Ke suggested that the Chinese government set up a Jewish settlement near the country's southwestern border area to accommodate the refugees.[2]

Sun Ke emphasized four reasons for presenting this plan. First, it was consistent with Sun Yat-sen's teachings that China should help and ally with minor powers and peoples. Second, helping the Jews might increase British sympathy for China. Sun Ke believed that powerful business and banking interests controlled Britain's East Asian policy. These interests, he believed, had initially obstructed, but were now encouraging, the British government to aid the Chinese financially. Since he further believed the majority of British business and banking interests operating in East Asia were Jewish-controlled, this settlement plan might favorably affect the relationship between China and Britain. Third, this plan might also favorably impress the American public. Since he believed the Americans were aiding Jews, Sun Ke hoped that this plan could also help to shift the American people's attention from the Jews to the Chinese and China's resistance against Japan. Finally and most important, Sun Ke argued that "Jews were wealthy and talented, if we could make a favorable impression on them and obtain their support, it would be a great help to us [to achieve victory over Japan]." Chiang Kai-shek adopted Sun Ke's proposal two weeks later and ordered the Executive Yuan to consider it further.[3]

After his father's death in 1925, Sun Ke, as well as many other Nationalist leaders, had strived to counter Chiang Kai-shek's attempt to control of the Guomindang (or Nationalist Party) and the government. Eventually, however, Chiang prevailed and was able to strengthen his authority and power by the mid-1930s.[4] It is possible that Sun Ke also tried to use his Jewish settlement plan to improve his reputation and visibility within the Nationalist government. Whatever the motives, Chinese officials took the plan seriously.

In the following month, the Ministries of Interior, Foreign Affairs, Military Affairs, Finance, and Transportation of the Executive Yuan studied the settlement plan and established specific regulations for the entry of Jewish refugees into China. During the discussions, almost all the ministries concluded that the nationality of the Jewish refugees was an important factor that would affect China's future control over them. For example, if the refugees were from a country that exercised consular jurisdiction in China, they were not subject to Chinese law. Therefore, the final draft of the settlement plan presented to the Highest National Defense Council contained specific articles pertaining to the entry of "Jews with nationality" and "Jews without nationality." According to these articles, the Chinese government would use the same rules to handle the entry and residence of Jewish refugees with nationality as all other foreigners. At the time, foreigners were permitted to reside only in treaty ports and not in the interior with the native Chinese. In the case of refugees without nationality, or stateless Jews, the Chinese government would order its diplomats abroad to grant special passports or visas to assist them in entering China. In addition, stateless refugees were required to stay temporarily in port cities after their arrival. There were also specific articles aimed at helping stateless refugees obtain Chinese citizenship, if they wished, and to find jobs in China.[5]

Chinese Nationalist officials understood that although Italian and German Jews left their countries because of their governments' persecution, the vast majority of them maintained their original nationalities. Russian Jews, in contrast, were stateless at the time.[6] The Chinese government was deeply concerned that if a great number of Jews, such as Italian Jews, whose government exercised consular jurisdiction in China, lived in the interior and out of the reach of Chinese law, this would present difficulties for the Chinese government. On the other hand, although Germany did not enjoy consular jurisdiction in China, Chinese officials worried that if they allowed German Jews to stay in the interior, Germany would invoke its right to protect its own citizens diplomatically to interfere in China's internal affairs.[7]

Although on March 22, 1939, the Secretariat of the Executive Yuan expressed concerns about the potential economic difficulties associated with the settlement plan, these comments were omitted from the final draft. The secretariat believed that the Chinese government should not reject Jews who had skills that would be useful to the state as China attempted to develop its economy.[8] However, Sun Ke's plan actually targeted "destitute and homeless" Jews, who may in fact have comprised the majority of the immigrants. The secretariat worried that if the Chinese government allowed these people to settle in China, they "would not benefit us but might increase burdens on our country and society." The secretariat further reasoned that "at the moment when we are fighting a full-scale anti-Japanese war, we already have difficulties supporting and taking care of [our own] refugees. It might be even harder for us if we have to accommodate Jewish refugees as well." The Executive Yuan likely withdrew these comments later because of concerns about the wording of propaganda when advertising the settlement plan. In the same document of March 22, the secretariat suggested that in order to make its international propaganda appear more legitimate, the Chinese government should emphasize the plan's humanitarian aspects.[9]

Nevertheless, the Nationalist government's settlement plan, in its early stages, clearly favored stateless Jews. In addition to being concerned about refugee control, the Chinese government did not want to offend Germany since China and Germany were still allies in name. In fact, the Germans had already expressed their disapproval of the Chinese government's Jewish settlement plan. In mid-March 1939, when the ministries of the Executive Yuan were examining the Sun Ke plan, a secretary from the German embassy visited the Ministry of Foreign Affairs. Although the German secretary did not lodge a formal protest with the Chinese government, he let it be known in no uncertain terms that his government was very concerned about this plan. The secretary also hinted that the Chinese government should consider this plan carefully since "Jews always hated Germany." Officials of the Foreign Ministry commented shortly thereafter in a memorandum that "under the current situation, we cannot neglect Germany's policy toward Jews. If we suddenly allow Jews to settle down in China now, it might increase Germany's animosity against us."[10] The most important purpose of the settlement plan was to help China win the war against Japan by enlisting the aid of the foreign powers. The Nationalist government did not want, and could not afford, to make Germany another enemy.

In May 1921, China and Germany had signed an agreement to reestablish diplomatic relations in the wake of World War I. Germany needed China's market and strategic raw materials for its recovery from the war. China, for its part, required German aid for its military modernization and economic development. Beginning in 1921, Sun Yat-sen planned to invite political, economic and military advisers from Germany. He hoped that Germany could serve as the model for his country in order to strengthen China in the shortest time possible.[11]

When the Nationalist government was established in 1928, many of its influential members, including Chiang Kai-shek, shared Sun's pro-German sentiment. Chiang Kai-shek even sent his own son to Germany for military training. Chinese government officials worked closely with their German counterparts in both economic and military matters from the late 1920s until the late 1930s, especially during the first half of the Sino-Japanese war. As William Kirby points out, "the Nanking decade of Kuomintang rule in China from 1928 to 1938...was a decade of German influence in China."[12]

In the beginning, China and Germany dealt with each other as equals. Unlike other Western powers, Germany, after its defeat in the First World War, pursued only its economic interests in East Asia, as it had no special political rights or territorial dependencies in the region.[13] Therefore, Germany kept neutral in the early stage of the Sino-Japanese conflict. The conclusion of the Anti-Comintern Pact between Germany and Japan in November 1936 and the start of Japan's full-scale invasion of China in

July 1937 changed the situation. Japan began pressuring Germany to stop exporting military equipment to the Nationalist government and withdraw German advisers from China.[14]

Concerned that the war with Japan would eventually drive China into the arms of the Soviets, Germany attempted to mediate between China and Japan beginning in late 1937. The mediation failed, though, and Germany reversed its East Asian policy thereafter.[15] Obviously, Japan was of greater use to Germany than China in tying down the Soviet military in East Asia. On February 20, 1938, Hitler unexpectedly declared that Germany would grant diplomatic recognition to the Japanese puppet regime of Manchukuo. In the following months, the German government asked the Nationalist government to withdraw Chinese military trainees from Germany and pulled its own advisers out of China. At the same time, Hitler imposed an arms embargo on the Nationalist government. The German government also recalled its ambassador to China in June 1938.[16]

William Kirby argues that since the relationship between China and Germany was based "to a large degree on respective military needs, the fortunes of war [helped] to decide its fate."[17] As Germany's ambition and desire in Europe grew and its interest in East Asia changed from an economic one to a strategic one, China lost its "partner" to Japan. But the Nationalist government did not give up completely. In November 1938, China dispatched its vice foreign minister, Chen Jie, to Berlin as the new ambassador in an attempt to improve Sino-German relations. Not surprisingly, the German government ignored diplomatic protocol and repeatedly delayed Ambassador Chen's presentation of his credentials.[18] The Germans' behavior outraged and embarrassed the Chinese, and the Sino-German relationship entered a tumultuous era.

Meanwhile, although the military reorganization and modernization fostered by Germany before July 1937 "led to a growing confidence in Nanking in China's ability to resist Japan," the Japanese inflicted disastrous defeats on Chiang's armies in the summer and autumn of 1937. By the middle of December, "at least one-third of the 300,000-strong central force was lost, with some estimates ranging as high as 60 percent. The elite divisions suffered the most, as 10,000 junior officers were lost.... In a matter of months, the work of ten years and five German Advisers-General was undone."[19] The deterioration of Sino-German relations in late 1938 made China's confrontation with Japan desperate. Germany's withdrawal from China cleared the way for further Japanese action there. Chiang Kai-shek and his government were forced to search elsewhere for financial and military support.

The Jakob Berglas Plan

The Jewish settlement plan of early 1939 brought the Nationalist government new hope for defeating the Japanese. Even as the Chinese officials examined the Sun Ke plan, a German Jewish businessman in Shanghai, Jakob Berglas, also submitted in May a "Plan for the Immigration of Central European Immigrants into China" to the Central Executive Committee of the Chinese Nationalist Party through the Chinese League of Nations Union.[20]

Although Jakob Berglas's settlement plan was widely reported in Shanghai at the time, very little about the Jewish businessman himself is known. A contemporary newspaper article forwarded to the U.S. Department of State described him as "the head of the banking and woolen concern of Berglas Brothers of England and Germany."[21] He had previously made several trips to East Asia on business, and "taken a keen interest in the problem of the Jewish refugees" there.[22] Berglas ran the prominent Berglas Bank in Berlin until 1938 when he came to Shanghai to escape Hitler's persecution of Jews in Germany.[23]

Jakob Berglas proposed to let one hundred thousand Jewish emigrants settle in the interior of China. He also requested that the Chinese government provide protection for the Jews, treat them as equals with Chinese citizens, and offer them employment opportunities. Most important, Berglas emphasized that "each immigrant shall before his arrival in China pay a sum of £50: either himself or by another person or organization for him in favor of a committee, which will be formed for the express purpose of carrying out the present plan." Therefore, as soon as the plan would be carried out, "a sum of £5,000,000 . . . will be brought into the country." Berglas believed that the Jewish immigrants would constitute "a valuable asset for the reconstruction and industrial development of China."[24]

Berglas made a trip to the interior of China himself after submitting his plan. In a letter to Kong Xiangxi (H. H. Kung), president of the Executive Yuan, on June 6, 1939, Berglas wrote that as a result of his trip he believed that Kunming, the capital city of Yunnan Province, might serve as an appropriate place for settling Jewish immigrants. Berglas also pointed out to Kong that transportation to China's interior was a major problem, and it would make the plan "impractical" if it took too long to transport Jews to Yunnan. He thereafter suggested that the Nationalist government should use the money, which would be available through the immigration payments, to buy trucks and buses and establish a transportation company. After using these vehicles to transfer Jews to Yunnan, the transportation company could function as a regular business.[25]

The Chinese League of Nations Union showed great interest in the Berglas plan. The union had become concerned about the Jewish refugee issue over the previous six months and even sent staff to Shanghai to investigate the refugees there. It concluded that since more than ten thousand Jewish refugees were already in Shanghai and as "too little porridge cannot feed too many monks," the situation would only get worse with time. In its letter introducing the Berglas plan to the Central Executive Committee of the Nationalist Party, the Chinese League of Nations Union listed three reasons for its concerns about the Jewish refugee issue. In addition to following Sun Yat-sen's principles of helping small nations, the Union believed that since Jews were scattered throughout the world and many of them were wealthy and politically influential, if the Chinese government assisted Jewish refugees through this immigration plan, "China would win sympathy directly from Jews all over the world. It would also help China win sympathy indirectly from all peoples and countries that could morally and materially contribute to our war against Japan." The union emphasized that if the government "could appropriately allow Jewish immigration, their capital could also be gradually introduced to China and their technicians could be used by us. We believe it would be beneficial to China at present and especially in the future."[26]

After approving the immigration plan, the Chinese League of Nations Union proposed four conditions to Jakob Berglas for carrying out the plan:

> First, [Jews should] let the Chinese government organize the committee for Jewish immigration although Jewish representatives would be invited; second, after Jews came to China, they should unconditionally obtain Chinese nationality; third, [the Chinese government] would establish the settlement in the interior of China (such as Xichang [in Sichuan] or Yunnan) so that the immigrants could live and do business there; finally, each immigrant, before his or her arrival, should deposit £100 [to a designated bank in China].

Although Berglas completely agreed with the first three points, he considered the increase in payment from £50 to £100 problematic. Nevertheless, he promised to go back to Shanghai and discuss the matter with other Jewish leaders there.[27]

On June 17, Long Yun, governor and warlord of Yunnan Province, also contacted the secretary general of the Highest National Defense Council and asked the central government's permission to use the Jewish refugees for cultivating Yunnan. Although it is unclear whether or not Long Yun met with Jakob Berglas during the German businessman's trip to the interior, he clearly had already learned that the central government was considering a plan to settle European Jewish refugees in southwestern China. Long Yun contended that although Yunnan had plenty of fertile land, it was a sparsely populated region and could not afford to import immigrants there to help cultivate the province. Since he recently discovered that many stateless Jews had come to Shanghai, and they were "more talented and wealthy than ordinary people," Long Yun argued that "it could kill two birds with one stone" if he would "be able to relocate those homeless people to Yunnan and use them to farm the land."[28]

On one hand, these two Jewish settlement plans seemed to meet the Nationalist government's financial needs at a crucial moment in its war against Japan. On the other hand, the prospect of a massive immigration of European Jews to China made the Nationalist leaders anxious about their already deteriorating relationship with Germany. In fact, although Germany was persecuting Jews at the time, most German Jews still retained their German nationality. As the secretary general of the Central Political Council, Zhu Jiahua, commented, "if we require Jews to change to [Chinese] nationality, they must abandon their German nationality first. Germany might not be willing to allow 100,000 Jews to give up their German nationality in order to emigrate to China." Also, Zhu Jiahua questioned the practicality of Long Yun's plan. He believed that Jews were not suited to develop Chinese agriculture since a survey of Jewish occupations indicated that only 1.74 percent of them were engaging in farming and forestry.[29]

After the Nationalist government's careful consideration Wei Daoming (Wei Tao-ming), secretary general of the Executive Yuan, officially informed Jakob Berglas on July 26, 1939, that in accordance with the orders of Kong Xiangxi, "The Chinese Government is prepared under certain conditions to be announced later to admit Jews without nationality into the treaty ports of China and afford them protection and right of residence and work, provided that they do not engage in political activities and propaganda and that their occupations conform to the economic requirements of the country." In his letter, Wei Daoming specially pointed out that the Chinese government at the time would not be able to allow the number of Jews that Berglas detailed in his plan to enter China. Rather, the Chinese officials believed that the number should be decided later when they "can see more clearly how the scheme works." Wei Daoming also attached a copy of an English version of "General Principles Governing the Working of the Plan for the Immigration of Jews into China" that was adopted by the Executive Yuan on July 25. The General Principles clarified that "Jews with foreign nationality will be treated exactly as all other foreigners are treated in this country. Only Jews without nationality are privileged to have the special treatment mentioned in the proposed plan."[30]

The Maurice William Plan

While the Nationalists struggled to muster the financial resources to wage war with Japan and grew increasingly anxious about their worsening relationship with Germany as a result of the Jewish settlement plans, the American Jewish leader Maurice William proposed a third plan to Chinese officials to transplant German Jews to China. William approached the Chinese from a different angle, and his plan clearly received greater attention from the Nationalist government than the other two.

Maurice William was a familiar name in China. He was a Russian-born Jewish dentist in New York who was active in socialist political circles. It is believed that Sun Yat-sen was influenced by William's work and adopted many of his social and economic theories from William's 1921 book *The Social Interpretation of History: A Refutation of the Marxian Economic Interpretation of History*.[31] Maurice Zolotow, author of *Maurice William and Sun Yat-sen*, goes so far as to argue that one cannot understand the Three Principles of the People—nationalism, democracy, and peoples' livelihood—without understanding *The Social Interpretation of History*.[32] James Shotwell also observes that William's ideas concerning socialism, in particular, informed Sun Yat-sen's concept of "peoples' livelihood."[33] William himself noted in his letter to President Herbert Hoover that Sun Yat-sen's principle of peoples' livelihood "followed a study of my work."[34]

Maurice William, realizing the great impact his book had on Sun Yat-sen, came to the conclusion that it was his responsibility to help establish a close bond between China and the United States. William had argued that the United States should export a greater volume of American products to the Chinese market in order to avoid a post–World War I depression. He had also believed that the United States "must, by means of the same sort of loans which English capital made to this country during the nineteenth century, help to develop the huge potentialities of China. In this way, we will not only help the Chinese, we will enrich ourselves."[35] William's later plan to relocate German Jews in China was also based on his analysis of China and its economic development.

In 1936, Maurice William joined the Chinese Nationalist Party and became its only non-Chinese member in the United States.[36] During the Sino-Japanese War, he served as secretary of the American Bureau of Medical Aid to China and was an important member of the United Council for Civilian Relief in China, along with Albert Einstein and former president Herbert Hoover.

In the early 1930s, Maurice William established a close relationship with certain prominent figures within the Chinese government, Sun Ke in particular. In 1932, William published *Sun Yat-sen versus Communism: New Evidence Establishing China's Right to the Support of Democratic Nations.*[37] It appears that he also extended his sympathies to Sun Ke during the power struggle within the Nationalist regime at the time. In a letter to Sun Ke, William noted that he hoped "my new volume might prove helpful in two directions: (1) promote a better understanding between China and America; (2) throw some light upon the possible cause of the conflict between Dr. Sun's loyal followers and suggest a cure."[38] Sun Ke expressed his appreciation and made it clear that he recognized William's "intellectual relationship to his father" and that he believed "Dr. Sun's disciples have failed to understand and correctly interpret Sun Yat-sen's teachings." Sun Ke also welcomed William's "aid in promoting a better understanding and interpretation of his father's teaching."[39]

As early as 1934, William and Albert Einstein formulated the idea of "finding a new home in China for German Jews." The two corresponded between 1934 and 1935 concerning this Jewish resettlement plan. In his response to Einstein's request on January 30, 1934, for information about this plan, William told Einstein that he had "made a special study of this important problem" and had "discussed it in great detail with the Chinese Minister at Washington." According to William, "the Chinese Minister" [Shi Zhaoqi, also known as Sao-ke Alfred Sze, later the first Chinese ambassador to the United States] agreed that Hitler's persecution of Jews "made it possible for China to obtain the services of trained men and women who under normal conditions would not be willing to leave Germany." William thereafter discussed this idea further with U.S. Supreme Court justice Louis Brandeis, James T. Shotwell, professor of history at Columbia University and founder of the International Labor Organization, and philosopher John Dewey, and reached the conclusion that China was "the one great hope for Hitler's victims." William was well aware that his reputation in China had won him the respect of the people there, and he was willing to use his connections to serve his coreligionists in Germany.[40]

Einstein was deeply impressed by William. In his letter of February 1934, Einstein praised William's plan as "very hopeful and rational and its realization must be pursued energetically." Meanwhile, Einstein raised the issue of employment opportunities. He pointed out that "the most difficult part would seem to be to ascertain just what possibilities China offers for finding employment for German Jews." Einstein also suggested that American Jewish leaders who would take charge of collecting funds for this plan should go to China to investigate the opportunities for Jewish immigrants there.[41] Many Jewish leaders insisted that it would bring the most salutary results if

William traveled to China himself because of "the good-will of the Chinese people and the Chinese Government" toward him.[42]

Although questions about the William-Einstein plan remain, there is no record that demonstrates whether William ever discussed this plan with the Chinese government, or if so, how the Chinese government reacted. Only one letter from William to Einstein in February 1935, a year after they originally proposed the plan, suggests that the Chinese government might not have accepted the plan at the time. William's letter to Einstein ended, "I trust some day in the near future, I may be privileged to discuss with you the details of our plan. Those who have studied the problem seem convinced that China offers unusual possibilities for German Jews."[43]

Although there is no direct evidence affirming that the Chinese government rejected the William-Einstein plan to transplant German Jews to China, it is reasonable to conclude that the Chinese were unlikely to have done anything to upset the Germans, since Sino-German relations were still in their "honeymoon" period. Furthermore, in early 1938, the Nationalist government rejected a proposal from Wang Zhengting (Chengting Thomas Wang), Chinese ambassador to the United States from 1936 to 1938, to aid German Jews. Wang recalled in the summer of 1939 that he had earlier broached the issue of assisting Jewish victims of Germany to his government. However, he wrote, "The government felt at the time that we did not want to offend Germany, so I did not press it any further."[44] Since Maurice William discussed with Wang Zhengting's predecessor, Shi Zhaoqi, the plan to find a new home in China for German Jews in 1934, it might well have been William who had appealed to Wang Zhengting for support. Wang had sponsored William's membership in the Chinese Nationalist Party, and he thus had strong personal ties to William.[45]

Nonetheless, his previous failures did not discourage Maurice William. In early 1939, he learned that the Nationalist government itself was planning to settle Jewish refugees in southwestern China. The Chinese government insisted that it would assist Jews in finding jobs in China. This announcement solved the issue of employment that had concerned Einstein in 1934.

In fact, the Chinese officials themselves actively publicized the Jewish settlement plan, to the United States in particular, right after they had received Sun Ke's proposal. Dong Xianguang (Hollington K. Tong), vice minister of propaganda, wrote the following in a telegram to Michel Speelman, chairman of the Committee for the Assistance of European Jewish Refugees in Shanghai (CAEJR),[46] at the beginning of March 1939:

I learn that Jews will be denied entrance to Shanghai. The Chinese people, despite undergoing unprecedented suffering, are deeply sympathetic with the predicament of the Jewish people. What would be your reaction to try to persuade the Chinese Government to set aside in China's southwest or northwest areas for their temporary or permanent residence and create a semi-official employment agency to find work for Jewish technicians. Please discuss this matter with your colleagues and reply by same means.[47]

Speelman replied that he was "very much interested" in the plan and was "studying [the] question from all angles." As Nationalist officials almost certainly expected, Speelman forwarded Dong's telegram and his reply to the American consul general in Shanghai. One week later, on March 8, 1939, the same telegram reached the U.S. Department of State in Washington.[48]

At the same time, Dong Xianguang made a proposal to the American Red Cross in the name of the Chinese Aid to Jewish Refugees Committee regarding the establishment of a Jewish settlement in China.[49] This information also made its way to the *New York Tribune*, one of the leading newspapers in the United States.[50] The Chinese government's propaganda strategy turned out to be successful. Maurice William promptly received the news and immediately made contact with Hu Shi (Hu Shih), the Chinese ambassador to the United States. Hu Shi wrote the following telegram to Dong Xianguang, in English (original wording retained): "Your suggestion interest quite a few Jewish leaders here who wish know details especially employment of Jewish technical experts including doctors engineers. Dr. Maurice William whose book was quoted by Dr. Sun Yetsen even volunteer visit China investigate possibilities."[51]

William's plan received the full support of Ambassador Hu, one of the leaders of the New Culture Movement and a former student of John Dewey at Columbia University. Hu Shi recalled in his autobiography, "I had very good relationships with some Jews. [My] Jewish friends included professors and students, first at Cornell, then in Columbia."[52] Obviously, Ambassador Hu's firsthand experience and friendship with Jews in the United States influenced him deeply and predisposed him to be sympathetic to the William Plan.

On May 18, 1939, Hu Shi forwarded the English translation of "Text of a Telegraphic Message from the Ministry of Foreign Affairs" to William. The Foreign Ministry informed William of China's difficulty in executing the plan to settle Jewish refugees in the southwest. The main problem was that "the Jewish refugees with the exception of a few who have no nationality, have all maintained their original nationality. Some of the nations to which they belong still enjoy consular jurisdiction in China. Should they be permitted to reside in the interior, there would be difficulty in exercising administrative jurisdiction over them." Although "the Highest National Defense Council to which the matter has been submitted for final approval has yet taken no action," the Foreign Ministry clarified that the Executive Yuan had now decided to offer "sympathetic assistance" to stateless Jews upon their entry, and even employment "on humanitarian ground[s]."[53]

Although the Chinese government at the time obviously aimed to help stateless Jews, William did not give up his idea of transplanting German Jews to China. He believed that his plan differed significantly from that of Berglas and thus would be more likely to succeed. According to William, the basic weakness of Berglas's plan was that it was "one-sided" and that Berglas "asked China to help solve the German Jewish problem." The Maurice William plan, in contrast, was intended to assist China since "[being l]ocked in a life and death struggle, China cannot and should not be expected to assume additional burdens." William emphasized that his project was based on "a diametrically opposite principle; instead of asking China for help, I propose that we concentrate on China's problem and use the help of German Jews to solve those problems. A home and employment in China awaits German Jews only as a by-product of their services in promoting China's welfare."[54]

After being advised by Hu Shi, on May 31, 1939, Maurice William responded in a lengthy letter to the message he had received from the Foreign Ministry.[55] William's letter had three main points. First, Chinese and Jews were both victims of aggressive wars and should cooperate and provide one another with aid. German Jews could offer China "technical and scientific training; industrial, commercial and financial experience; skill and capital." In raising this issue, William especially emphasized that German Jews were not alone; they were supported by world Jewry and American Jews, and would "carry with them the good-will of the Jews of every nation [to China]."[56]

Second, American Jews were capable of providing China help in its war with Japan. William used the case of the recent $25 million American loan to China to demonstrate the "whole-hearted cooperation" of U.S. treasury secretary Henry Morgenthau, himself a Jew. Quoting the Chinese foreign minister's complaint that U.S. neutrality legislation benefited the aggressors, William asserted that "these statements seem to establish that Chinese leaders have reached the conclusion that China's future will be largely determined not by what her heroic defenders do in China but by what we do here in America." Although "an overwhelming majority" of American people, as well as their president and government, were nominally supportive of China and in opposition to Japan, William claimed that "America is actually helping Japan to destroy China" since "China is opposed by the combined military resources of America and Japan."[57]

Nevertheless, William was confident that American Jews could raise a powerful voice to "help swing American support away from Japan and toward China." In return, he hoped that the Chinese government could invite American Jewish representatives to China to investigate the possibility of establishing the Jewish settlement. William also promised that "the American Jewish people and others interested in the refugee problem will raise significant sums of money to finance the program."[58]

Third, William argued that the United States had the largest Jewish population in the world and that they contributed the largest amount of money for overseas relief. However, "the funds for relief are only palliative; they do not solve the refugee problem." William concluded that only the Chinese settlement plan could offer a "constructive solution." If the plan were successful, it would have a stimulating impact on the American public. William predicted that public opinion could eventually help "convert American aid to Japan into American aid for China."[59]

In order to make the Chinese consider his proposal more seriously, William also wrote governmental officials Kong Xiangxi, Wang Zhengting [the foreign minister], and Sun Ke, respectively, in June and July 1939. William informed the Chinese leaders that as the chairman of the Campaign Committee of the United Council he had successfully collected $15,000 for the project.[60] Wang Zhengting immediately expressed his support for the Maurice William plan, stating that he was "strongly convinced," as he had been in early 1938, that William's plan "will be beneficial to us." But, he added, "of course it is most beneficial to the poor victims themselves." Wang Zhengting, a Yale graduate and former ambassador to the United States, believed that through this plan China "will win support from the Jews all over the world, particularly from those in America and England where the Jews exercise great influence not only in the financial field but also in the political field." He also insisted that "among the government leaders in these two countries, the Jews have been most staunch friends of ours."[61]

Sun Ke's reply was even more encouraging. He "heartily" supported William's plan and was "more confident of our ultimate victory [over Japan] today than at any other time." Sun Ke explained that since "from the military point of view we have created a stalemate," the emphasis of the war would "probably become economic and financial." He also emphasized to William that he "always felt that the power and influence of world Jewry especially in financial and governmental circles should be enlisted to support our cause."[62]

On August 9, 1939, Wei Daoming informed Maurice William on behalf of Kong Xiangxi that "the Chinese government welcomes any Jewish representatives from America to come to this country at their own expense for the purpose of making investigations about the possibility of settling in China those Jews now being expelled from Germany." Wei Daoming also attached, for reference, a copy of the "General Principles Governing the Working of the Plan for the Immigration of Jews into China," the governing principles of the Berglas plan.[63]

The Chinese government's message was, in fact, confusing and contradictory. In Wei Daoming's letter, he clearly stated that the settlement plan was for "Jews now being expelled from Germany." The letter therefore demonstrated that the Chinese government was considering the acceptance of German Jews. However, the attached "General Principles" dealt almost exclusively with "Jews without nationality." The document stipulated explicitly, "Only Jews without nationality are privileged to have the special treatment mentioned in the proposed plan" and "Jews without nationality will be admitted only to the treaty ports and are not allowed to settle in the interior."[64]

Why did the Chinese government send such an ambiguous message to William? It is unlikely that Wei Daoming mistakenly attached the wrong document, since it was he who informed Jakob Berglas of the General Principles, and he must have been well aware of its content. Rather, it is more likely that the Chinese were eager to negotiate with the American Jewish leaders in order to obtain American support. Nevertheless, they did not want to antagonize the Germans. Since the attached General Principles were provided merely for his personal information, William had every reason to believe that the Chinese officials would no longer limit immigration to China to those Jews without nationality. In his letter acknowledging Wei Daoming's message, William clearly demonstrated that he understood that the invitation was for "the purpose of investigating the possibility of settling German-Jewish refugees in China."[65] Although William accepted the invitation, there is no record demonstrating that he actually made a trip to China.

Chinese leaders were excited about the possible financial support from the United States to fight the Japanese. In response to increasingly aggressive Japanese behavior in East Asia, the U.S. government notified Japan on July 26, 1939, that it would terminate the 1911 U.S.-Japanese commercial treaty in six months. America's decision had an enormous impact on the Chinese, who believed this would "make China's victory [over Japan] certain." The *New York Times* reported that China considered America's decision "a 'break' in international affairs favorable to their cause, for which they have been waiting since the beginning of hostilities." "The Chinese," the *Times* continued, "hope for further American action in the way of an embargo on trade with Japan before the end of the six months required before termination of the Japanese-American treaty."[66]

On August 22, after it became clear that President Roosevelt would not be able to compel Congress to grant him the discretion to change the neutrality law and place an embargo on the export of American war matériel to Japan, William drafted a twelve-page letter to Ambassador Hu Shi in Washington. He cautioned that "the only power in America able to 'make China's victory certain' is the driving power of the American people." William explained that not only Congress, but the American people, had decided not to grant the president the authority to apply further sanctions against Japan; Congress simply reflected American popular opinion. Although a Gallup Poll showed that "an overwhelming majority of the American people favor[ed] China [in its war with Japan]," William pointed out that "favor" was different from "support." Only when the American people were willing to support China would they be able to "demand" that Congress act.[67]

Meanwhile, William emphasized that since President Roosevelt would not be able to provide China with any additional assistance, the Chinese government itself should think about what it could do to exploit "the driving power of the American people" to help achieve its victory. He concluded that a conventional propaganda campaign directed at the American public would pay few dividends. Rather, China must await some "extraordinary events" that "would immediately result in a highly stirred public opinion which would quickly take the form of irresistible pressure on Congress." Perhaps, he argued, the American public would look favorably upon an act of generosity by the Chinese government toward the European Jews. Since the president was currently involved with the Evian Inter-Government Committee on Refugees and had, according to William, an "intense interest" in the plight of German Jews, he concluded that it would be a "brilliant psychological and moral triumph for the Chinese government if it were the first to demonstrate to the American people" that China was willing to accommodate desperate Jewish refugees. "What an electrifying effect such an announcement would have on the American people!" he wrote. "The mere offer alone would quicken the heart of America and call forth a reaction which would prove irresistible. All the rest would follow as day follows night." The American people and Congress then could not help but support the Chinese cause.[68]

William especially emphasized that the Chinese government should announce its settlement plan before Jakob Berglas arrived in the United

States and before President Roosevelt and the Inter-Government Committee's White House meeting on September 4, 1939. According to an article from the *New York Herald Tribune*, Jakob Berglas was then on his way to America to obtain assistance for his project to settle German Jews in Yunnan. William predicted that the Berglas plan would no doubt win substantial popularity and might even draw attention from President Roosevelt. If so, William assumed that China might lose entirely the "psychological advantages" of its plan.[69]

Confident that President Roosevelt would "quickly recognize in China's generosity an opportunity to advance China's cause with the American people," William brought his plan to the Department of State in a personal attempt to convey the Jewish settlement plan to the president.[70] On August 31, 1939, with the help of White House adviser Benjamin Cohen, William met with Robert T. Pell of the State Department's Division of European Affairs. After explaining his plan in detail, William told Pell that he had suggested that the Chinese government invite Jewish representatives from the United States to investigate the settlement plan there. Also, he continued, "this invitation should come from China on the eve of President Roosevelt's White House meeting to discuss the problem of refugees and that it should be given the greatest possible éclat in the American press." At the end of the meeting, William expressed his hope that the Department of State would "recommend his idea favorably to the president." Pell, however, suggested that first, William should contact the President's Advisery Committee, a body that offered the president advice on refugee issues. He wrote William a letter of introduction.[71]

Although William proudly informed Einstein on October 31, 1939, that his "negotiations with the Chinese Government regarding German-Jewish refugees have been most successful," and that "we are, at last, faced with an exceptional opportunity to render a much needed service to our suffering co-religionists," no further record on the Jewish settlement plan from either the Chinese or U.S. side has been found.[72] Along with the Maurice William plan, the Sun Ke plan and the Jakob Berglas plan all abruptly disappear from public records.

At this stage, the lack of support from the American government was at least in part responsible for the failure of these Jewish settlement plans. Historian David Wyman argues that America's leadership and example were vital to the resolution of the Jewish refugee problem during the crucial years 1938 to 1941.[73] In this period, before Hitler blocked their means of escape, European Jews were still able to leave Nazi-controlled areas. Nevertheless, most of the world closed its doors to the Jewish refugees, and only a relatively small number of them found sanctuary overseas.

Although the majority of the American people and their president, as Wyman argues, despised Nazi persecution of the Jews, most of them "opposed widening the gates for Europe's oppressed."[74] So, through their policy of indifference, the Americans failed to play an active role in assisting the European Jews during this crucial period.

In early July 1938, the Evian Conference convened in France. Called at the insistence of U.S. President Roosevelt, the conference hoped to stem the growing Jewish refugee crisis in Europe. Thirty-two nations attended, including the United States, Great Britain, France, Canada, and Australia. Like other participants, the United States did not agree to accept additional European Jewish refugees.[75] In addition, from late 1938 to early 1939, polls demonstrated that American public opinion was inhospitable to the admission of "Jewish exiles," and the majority of the American people opposed refugee immigration. First, concerns with unemployment and then the fear of a subversive political "fifth column" shaped anti-immigration sentiment in the United States during this period. Congress therefore responded to the refugee problem based on the will of the majority of the American people.[76] Without public support, even the Wagner-Rogers bill, which aimed to rescue Jewish children, never made it to the floor for a vote in either house of Congress in the summer of 1939.[77]

By the fall of 1939, Roosevelt was "preoccupied with the war in Europe and the politics of the home front." In the growing climate of fear produced by the war, the prospect of foreign subversives, who might infiltrate the refugees, seemed to have deeply disturbed the president and his country.[78] On the other hand, another presidential election was looming in 1940, and Roosevelt could not afford to neglect the importance of public support. As historians Richard Breitman and Alan M. Kraut argue, Roosevelt "accurately assessed the mood in Congress and, beyond that, among the public generally." He consequently tightened immigration regulations in 1939–1941 to reduce the influx of refugees to the United States.[79]

The Roosevelt administration distanced itself from endeavors to rescue European Jews beginning in 1939. The general indifference of the administration to the plight of the Jews was reflected in its unwillingness to support the Chinese government's Jewish settlement plans. As a result, the Chinese officials may also have lost interest in those plans because of the lack of American aid. The Chinese were eager to impress the Americans since they desperately needed help in their war against Japan. If the U.S. government was not able to provide help, the Nationalist government could not finance the settlement plans by themselves. The Chinese were still at war with Japan. If the Jewish settlement plans could not be made to benefit China, it would be prudent to simply abandon the plans since the Chinese had many other pressing concerns.

Chinese Visas to Shanghai

Although Jewish refugees were able to land in Shanghai without completing entry procedures, and in fact the majority of Jews came to the city without visas, from 1938 to 1940 Chinese diplomats in Europe issued visas to refugees wishing to go to China. The Chinese visas served as evidence of their intention to leave Nazi Europe, as did ship tickets to Shanghai, during the time of forced migration. Shanghai survivors later recalled that they were required to show Nazi officials evidence of their plans to depart before receiving formal permission to leave Germany or Austria.[80] Those who were unable to obtain foreign entry visas to leave their countries might find themselves put into concentration camps.[81]

The story of the Chinese consul general in Vienna, He Fengshan, is generally well known, especially among the Shanghai survivors and in Austria. He was one of only two Chinese named "Righteous among the Nations" by Yad Vashem. According to Yad Vashem's official website, "Ho refused to abide by the instructions of his superior, the Chinese ambassador in Berlin, Chen Jie. Chen Jie, hoping to cement closer ties between China and Germany, had forbidden Ho to issue visas on such a large scale, estimated to run into the hundreds, perhaps even thousands."[82] This has led to a considerable misunderstanding that he issued visas to Jewish refugees on his own initiative and in defiance of the policies of the Chinese Nationalist government. In reality, the Chinese consulate general in Vienna was not the only consular office that provided visas to Jewish refugees to China. The consulate general in Vienna never challenged the order of the Chinese government. On the contrary, the consular officers there scrupulously followed the instruction of the Foreign Ministry to issue European Jews visas to China.

As early as in February 1939, the local Shanghai English-language newspaper, the *Shanghai Times*, reported that Chinese diplomats in European countries had been issuing visas to Jewish refugees. In an article complaining about the flood of Jewish refugees into Shanghai, the paper noted that "Chinese consulates in Europe are granting visas to all those applying with their passports for permission to come to Shanghai."[83] Although in August 1939 the Japanese occupation authorities and the Shanghai Municipal Council (SMC) announced immigration regulations restricting further European Jewish refugees from entering Shanghai, some shipping companies in Europe cabled the SMC to inquire whether or not they could transport refugees who had obtained Chinese visas.[84]

A closer examination of six Chinese visas from Shanghai survivors reveals much about the activities of the Chinese consuls in Europe. These visas were issued by Chinese diplomats in four different countries: (1) visa 1451, issued to Paul Adler on October 7, 1938, by consul Zhou Qixiang of the consulate general in Vienna to Shanghai; (2) visa 1681, issued to Margarethe and Lotte Lustig on October 18, 1938, by consul Zhou Qixiang of the consulate general in Vienna to Shanghai; (3) visa 1808, issued to Walter Immergut on October 6, 1938, by consul general Huang Zheng of the consulate general in Paris to Shanghai; (4) visa 59/39, issued to Arthur and Margarete Lubinski on April 3, 1939, by Zhang Gengnian (position not mentioned) of the consulate general in Hamburg to Shanghai; (5) visa 60/39, issued to Susanna S. Lubinski on April 3, 1939, by Zhang Gengnian of the consulate general in Hamburg to Shanghai; (6) visa 1118, issued to Oscar Schenker on August 19, 1940, by attaché Wu Guanghan of the legation in Sweden.[85]

Most important, the passport covers of visas 1, 2, 4, and 5 were clearly marked with an upper case "J" (the passport covers for visas 3 and 6 were unavailable). This demonstrates that these Chinese diplomats were clearly aware that they were granting visas to Jews. Since multiple Chinese diplomats issued Jewish refugees visas in multiple European cities, it is unlikely that they were all acting on their own initiative. Rather, it appears that they were following the orders of the Chinese government and that granting visas to Jewish refugees was not a personal decision.

Documents from the Executive Yuan indicate that the Nationalist government at the time kept records of the visas granted to European Jews. At the beginning of July 1939, when the Chinese officials were studying the Jakob Berglas plan, they seriously considered the reports from Chinese consular offices overseas that demonstrated the majority of the Jews who had come to China maintained their nationalities and that only a few of them were stateless.[86] These diplomatic reports prove that, first, Jewish refugees obtained visas from various Chinese consular offices. Therefore, the Chinese consuls kept records concerning subjects like the nationalities of the Jews who received visas. Second, the Chinese government was clearly aware that its diplomats overseas were issuing visas to European Jews. If China did not have a policy on the issuance of visas to European Jews, if these visas were issued purely at the discretion of individual diplomats acting on their own consciences, there would be no such consular records created and used by the Chinese government.

Documents from the Chinese diplomatic missions in Europe further substantiate this. In the report of May 22, 1940, from acting consul general

Yao Dingchen (Yao Ting-chen) in Vienna regarding the activities of his post, under the item "passports and visas," Yao explained that since the *Anschluss* with Austria two years earlier, many Austrian Jews came to the consulate for visas to China to escape Nazi persecution. "Between April 1938 and 1939, a large number of people came [to the consulate general] to obtain visas to China every month. Sometimes the number reached 400 or 500 per month."[87]

Also, in January 1941, the Chinese consul in Amsterdam contacted the Foreign Ministry regarding the issuance of visas to Jewish applicants. In its reply to him, the Foreign Ministry noted, "Referring your telegram No. 63 if applicants are Jews they should comply with conditions contained in our telegram No. 177, [March 1,] 1939."[88] Although telegram No. 177 has not been located in the Foreign Ministry's archives, it clearly contains instructions for Chinese diplomats regarding the treatment of Jewish requests for visas. This confirms that the Nationalist government maintained a policy that specified how Jews were to be issued visas and expected its diplomats to abide by it.

Consul general He Fengshan himself also stated explicitly in his memoirs that the Chinese consulate general in Vienna was obeying the order of the Foreign Ministry in providing visas to European Jews. This primary source concerning the Nationalist government's Jewish policy has long been neglected while the story of He Fengshan's heroic personal efforts to save the lives of Austrian Jews has frequently been repeated.

In his memoirs, He Fengshan pointed out that

> [at the time] our government was not consistent in its policy on issuing visas to Jews. Therefore, an incident [concerning visa policy] happened later. For instance, the order our consulate general received from the Foreign Ministry was to be generous to Jews who wished to come to China and not to reject [their requests for visas]. Also, Kong Xiangxi, president of the Executive Yuan, even publicly expressed his sympathy for the plight of the Jews. It is said that [he] would specially open up Hainan Island to accommodate Jews. However, under the same government, the Chinese ambassador to Germany at the time, Chen Jie, had a different attitude. He believed that in order to maintain China's [good] diplomatic relations with Germany, we should not oppose Hitler's anti-Semitic policies. Once during a long distance call, he ordered us to restrict issuing visas [to Jews]. I immediately rebutted him and told him that the Foreign Ministry had a different "liberal visa policy."[89]

After this, consul Zhou Qixiang, who took charge of passport and visa business in the consulate, continued to follow the Foreign Ministry's order regarding the handling of Jewish visas. He Fengshan first seemed to believe that the Foreign Ministry might issue a new visa policy and waited for instructions. However, he never received new instructions from the Foreign Ministry. At the same time, ambassador Chen Jie in Berlin was outraged when he learned that the consulate general in Vienna continued to grant visas to Jewish refugees. Since there was also a rumor that consul Zhou Qixiang was selling visas, Chen Jie immediately sent an investigator to Vienna. Except for proving that the consulate general faithfully obeyed the Foreign Ministry's "liberal visa policy" toward Jewish refugees, the investigator could not find any evidence of wrongdoing by Zhou.[90] Although consul general He Fengshan disobeyed the orders of his superior in Berlin, he did not contradict the wishes of the Nationalist government. Rather it was the ambassador, himself, who contradicted his government's official visa policy.

Meanwhile, although Consul Zhou Qixiang in Vienna was proven innocent of the accusation that he sold visas to Jewish refugees, consul general Huang Zheng in Paris did profit from issuing Chinese visas in the summer of 1939. Gu Weijun (Wellington Koo), one of the most important and influential diplomats in China's modern history and the ambassador to France at the time, recalled the incident in his memoirs:

> Apparently an agreement was signed between a travel agency and the visa office of the Consulate-General to secure Chinese government passports for Jews who had fled by the hundreds, if not the thousands, from the Fascist and Nazi-dominated parts of Europe… [and] the applicants were charged 800 francs upon receiving a visa, which was well above the regular fee, and, as was reported to me, the money was divided between one certain travel agency, through which only the Jewish applicants could get passports from the Consulate-General Annex, and the Chinese Consulate-General. It was, evidently an illicit, unauthorized and unjustifiable attempt by the issuing group to exploit the situation of the Jews.

Gu Weijun also received a list of more than two hundred European Jews who had obtained such visas from consul general Huang Zheng.[91] The Chinese Foreign Ministry informed the ambassador that those visas were invalid and ordered Huang Zheng to return to China immediately.[92]

Although the Foreign Ministry announced in June 1939 that the Huang Zheng visas were invalid, representatives of the Jewish community in Paris came to the Chinese embassy to ask Gu Weijun if Jews could still go to China with valid visas. The Jewish representatives also told the ambassador that they had received information from the annex of the Chinese consulate general, where the visa office was located, that German Jews who wished to go to Shanghai could all obtain visas. Meanwhile, since Shanghai was then occupied by the Japanese, the Chinese consuls could not guarantee that the refugees would be able to land in Shanghai. The Chinese consulate general also explained to the Jews that if they wanted to go to the interior of China, they would be able to get their visas soon. After learning of the Chinese government's plan to settle European Jewish refugees in Yunnan Province from local and English-language newspapers on June 22, 1939, Gu Weijun cabled the Foreign Ministry and requested confirmation of the Nationalist government's policy toward the entry of Jews into China.[93]

It happened that Jews in France also received the information about the Chinese government's Jewish settlement plan. According to the Jewish Immigration Association in Paris, consul general Huang Zheng met in early May 1939 with Edouard "Roschild" (presumably "Rothschild"), the prominent French financier, and told him that Chiang Kai-shek was very sympathetic to the plan to transplant Jewish refugees to southwestern China. Representatives from the Jewish Immigration Association immediately contacted Huang Zheng. The Jewish representatives agreed to decide details about how to carry out the settlement plan and then submit them to the Chinese government through the consul general. The Jewish Immigration Association also decided to hold a board meeting on August 22 to further discuss the plan. Huang Zheng, however, had already left Paris before the meeting. Ambassador Gu Weijun therefore cabled the Chinese Foreign Ministry on August 18, 1939, on behalf of the Jewish representatives and urged the Chinese government to clarify its attitude toward the Jewish settlement plan.[94]

The Foreign Ministry informed the ambassador that consul general Huang Zheng had never forwarded any information from the Jewish community in Paris to the government. The Foreign Ministry also ordered the Chinese embassy to continue following its normal procedures in processing the visas of European Jews. The Nationalist government was still preparing for the Jewish settlement plan, which had not yet been launched.[95]

After August 1939, however, because the Japanese authorities and the Shanghai Municipal Council restricted the entry of Jewish refugees, recipients of Chinese visas were not allowed to enter the city unless they possessed sufficient funds, had relatives there, or held employment contracts. Nevertheless, the Foreign Ministry's records show that Chinese diplomats in Europe continued to issue Jews visas, albeit with the stipulation that the recipients had adequate financial resources and relatives in China.[96]

Although the Japanese drove the Nationalists out of Shanghai in late 1937, the Chinese government obviously never considered the city "lost territory." Throughout the discussion regarding the Jewish settlement plans, the Foreign Ministry never expressed concern over the legitimacy of Chinese visas to Shanghai. Their belief that Shanghai remained the territory of the Republic of China reveals the Nationalists' determination in their war against Japan. Furthermore, China's visa policy served as a vehicle to pursue de facto, or even de jure, recognition by the Western countries of its claim to this "lost territory."

Conclusion

When European Jewish refugees began fleeing Nazi persecution to Shanghai in the summer of 1938, the Sino-Japanese War was at a crucial stage for both China and Japan. Until late 1938, the Japanese occupied Northern China and drove the Nationalists out of all major commercial, industrial, agricultural, and cultural centers of the eastern part of the country. It was a moment of life and death for China. Both China and Japan formulated plans to use Jewish financial power to achieve final victory in the war.

In early 1939, Sun Ke's plan to establish a settlement in southwestern China for European Jewish refugees received the support of the Nationalist government. The Chinese officials intended to use this plan to attract Jewish capital and to obtain the sympathy of the American and British people for China's resistance against Japan. On the other hand, since China at the time was still nominally an ally of Germany, the Chinese also had to be cognizant of their plan's reception by Berlin. China could not afford to make Germany another enemy. Therefore, China's Jewish settlement plan initially aimed to assist "stateless" Jews. Meanwhile, after American Jewish leaders enthusiastically participated in the settlement plan and pledged to convince the Roosevelt administration to support China financially, Chinese officials gradually abandoned their concerns about Germany. Although the Nationalist government did not want to exacerbate its already troubled relations with Germany, China's highest priority during this period was to win international assistance in its war against Japan.

On the other hand, although the Chinese devoted themselves to the anti-Japanese war and did not want to upset the Germans, they never blindly believed, as the Chinese ambassador to Berlin did, that "in order to maintain China's [good] diplomatic relations with Germany, we should not oppose Hitler's anti-Semitic policy."[97] Instead, the Nationalist government adopted a "liberal visa policy" regarding the entry of European Jewish refugees into China. It decided to use the same regulations to handle the entry and residence of Jewish refugees with nationality as all other foreigners.

For stateless Jews, the Foreign Ministry ordered its diplomats abroad to grant special passports or visas to assist them in entering China. Chinese consular officers in Europe faithfully obeyed the order and granted Jewish refugees visas to Shanghai.

The Nationalist government was enthusiastic about the plan to settle a large number of European Jewish refugees in southwestern China in 1939. However, they were unable to obtain assistance, especially financial assistance, from the United States to carry out the plan. The U.S. government itself imposed a restrictive quota on Jewish immigrants at the time, and public opinion was against providing further help to European Jews. Without funds, the Chinese government simply could not implement the scheme. Furthermore, the Jewish settlement plan was unable to help win the sympathy of the American people for China and its war against Japan, as the Nationalist government originally expected. As a result, the Chinese themselves lost interest in the plan to settle European Jews in China.

The Chinese government carefully prepared, discussed, and kept records of its settlement plans, but a thorough examination of the archives reveals no intention by the Nationalists to retaliate physically against the refugees if they failed to help implement these arrangements. In contrast, as we shall see later in this book, there is ample evidence in the Japanese record that the "Jewish experts" regularly threatened the safety of the refugees if they refused to play the role assigned them in Japan's settlement plans. Although both the Chinese and Japanese wished to exploit the Jewish refugees for their own ends, the Nationalists did not make the safety of the Jews contingent on their cooperation. Rather, they appeared resigned merely to put their plans aside without repercussions for the refugees if financial assistance from the international Jewish community was not forthcoming.

Although the Nationalist government's settlement plans were ill-fated, they are still important to our understanding of Chinese politics and diplomacy during the Second World War. First and most important, these plans reveal the Nationalist government's basic proclivities toward its war of resistance against Japan in general and toward the Jewish refugee issue in China in particular. In fact, these two elements were inseparable. As Nationalist officials contemplated the settlement plans, they clearly understood that, despite the economic considerations involved, it was in China's best interest to improve its relationship with the Western democracies. In this sense, the Nationalist government's efforts to settle European Jewish refugees anticipated China's emergence as an important actor in the Grand Alliance during World War II.

Second, these settlement plans also underscore a more general dilemma that the Nationalist government encountered during the early stages of the war. They illuminate the gap between China's intentions and capacities in handling important international issues. Facing the challenge from Japan, China's top priority was to fend off the aggressors and to survive. At the same time, the Chinese government also realized that it was necessary to build up its international reputation and prestige and cultivate its image as a country that deserved to stand among the ranks of the "great powers." Thus, Chinese leaders constantly found themselves developing ambitious plans that they were frequently incapable of executing. Nevertheless, projects such as the Jewish settlement plans are important, not only because they stand as missing chapters of modern Chinese history but also because they clarify the nature and ambition of Nationalist China as an emerging international power during the war years.

CHAPTER 3

Yasue Norihiro, Inuzuka Koreshige, and Japan's Policy toward the Shanghai Jewish Refugees, December 1937–December 1939

After Japan drove the Chinese Nationalist government from Shanghai in late 1937, it became a major power controlling the city along with the Shanghai Municipal Council, led by Great Britain and the United States, and France. Although Japan and Germany signed the Anti-Comintern Pact on December 25, 1936, and became allies, the pragmatic Japanese treated the Jewish refugees in Shanghai less harshly than the Nazis. Instead of exterminating the Jews, the Japanese tried to take advantage of purported Jewish financial and political power to support Japan's conquest of China and East Asia.

From the late 1920s to the early 1930s, through a series of violent actions in Manchuria and at home, the Japanese military, the army in particular, assumed control over Japan's foreign policy. The military's leading role in determining Japan's foreign policy made it possible for army and navy "Jewish problem experts" to convert their ideas into national policy. In fact, Japan's Jewish policy in the late 1930s and the early 1940s was initiated by the military and reflected its convictions.

In the Japanese military decision-making structure, field grade staff officers, primarily colonels, lieutenant colonels, and majors, who worked on the General Staffs in Tokyo or in Japanese-occupied China, rather than their commanding officers in the central government, drafted the military's policies. Army colonel Yasue Norihiro and navy captain Inuzuka Koreshige in Manchuria and Shanghai, the so-called "Jewish experts," were among this group. The two men were either individually or jointly responsible for making Japan's Jewish policy in 1938 and 1939.

Colonel Yasue, of the Kwantung Army in Manchuria, believed that Japan should "embrace" Jews under the country's national spirit of "Hakkō Ichiu,"[1] or "universal brotherhood." Yasue was a faithful supporter of the Kwantung Army's plan to introduce foreign, especially American, capital to develop Manchuria. The Japanese Army considered the Soviet Union its most immediate potential enemy and prepared for war with the Russians in Manchuria. At the same time, the army needed additional funds for its growing offensive against China. As a result, Yasue promised the Jews in Manchuria safety in exchange for their cooperation and pliability. The colonel attempted to use his "kind" treatment of the Manchurian Jews to impress Jews in central China and around the world, and to obtain capital from their wealthy coreligionists in Shanghai and the United States. As a key element of this strategy, Yasue initiated a policy of "embracing" the Jews. This policy was eventually presented to the Five Ministers' Conference on December 6, 1938, and was accepted as Japan's first official Jewish policy.[2]

Meanwhile, Captain Inuzuka controlled the destinies of the Jewish refugees in Shanghai. Inuzuka believed that the tens of thousands of European Jewish refugees under the Japanese Navy's control in Shanghai were, in a way, hostages. As long as the international Jewish communities agreed not to conduct anti-Japanese activities and American Jewish leaders were willing to pressure the Roosevelt administration on Japan's behalf, the refugees' well-being would be assured. Although leaders of the local Jewish communities approached Inuzuka and tried to establish a cordial relationship with him, the captain insisted that the Japanese government always keep the Shanghai Jews under its thumb. Exploiting the Jews, he argued, would be like eating the delicious, but potentially poisonous blowfish, fugu. If prepared properly, it could bring Japan great benefits. However, if it were done improperly, the risk would be very high; Japan might even be used by the Jews.[3]

Both Yasue's invocation of "Hakkō Ichiu" and Inuzuka's fugu metaphor were grounded in anti-Semitic ideas. For their own survival, Jews in China did not have any choice but to cooperate with the Japanese. The bizarre theories of the Japanese "Jewish experts" eventually saved the lives of European Jewish refugees during World War II. Under their plan, the more refugees that came to Japanese-occupied China, the more opportunities the "experts" had to exploit them. Yasue and Inuzuka were not interested in restricting the arrival of Jews. Nevertheless, reality forced them to alter their approach. The swelling number of the Jewish refugees in Shanghai became an enormous burden for the war-torn city. The Shanghai Municipal Council, and even the local Jewish communities, appealed to the Japanese authorities to regulate the influx of refugees. Under great pressure from the various local authorities, Yasue and Inuzuka eventually established a new Japanese Jewish policy in August 1939 to prohibit further entry of Jewish refugees into Shanghai. While implementing their policy, Inuzuka did not want to upset the wealthy local Jews from whom he wanted to obtain capital.

The First Far Eastern Jewish Conference, December 1937

From December 26 to 28, 1937, the First Far Eastern Jewish Conference convened in Harbin. Seven hundred people, including twenty-one Jewish representatives from six northern Chinese cities and Kobe, Japan, attended the conference. The Jewish representatives to the meeting expressed their appreciation to the governments of Japan and Manchukuo for their "impartial" and "humanitarian" treatment of the Jews in East Asia and averred that they would cooperate with both governments.

The Jewish Conference represented the first major effort to unify leadership for the East Asian Jews. At this forum the Jews of East Asia, primarily for the purpose of self-protection, publicly indicated their support for the Japanese and their puppet regime for the first time. After the outbreak of the Sino-Japanese War in 1937, Jewish leaders in northern China had become aware of Japan's military capacity, and begun to appreciate that Japan had greater influence in East Asia than the Western powers. The Jewish communities therefore decided that it would be wise for them to solicit Japan's patronage.[4] A Japanese intelligence report at the time noted that although the Jews had earlier kept their distance from the Japanese and Manchukuoan governments, they had recently approached the army intelligence department, the Special Service Agency in Manchuria, and attempted to improve their relationship with the Japanese. To better manage this new situation, the Ministry of the Army sent Colonel Yasue Norihiro, one of the military's "Jewish experts," to Manchuria to assist General Higuchi Kiichirō, the head of the Special Service Agency of the Kwantung Army in Harbin.[5]

Harbin had formerly hosted the largest Jewish community in East Asia. In the late nineteenth and early twentieth centuries, the construction of the Chinese Eastern Railway and the Russian October Revolution of 1917 brought waves of Russian Jewish, as well as White Russian, immigrants to the city. At its peak in 1929, the Jewish population in Harbin reached twenty thousand.[6] Jews established "an entire Jewish social system—schools, a hospital, a bank, an old people's home and a cemetery"—in the city, and considered Harbin a Jewish "paradise" in the 1920s.[7]

The situation changed after Japan's invasion of Manchuria in 1931. As Marvin Tokayer and Mary Swartz note, although the leaders of the Kwantung Army tried to create "a utopia of Manchukuo," the Japanese civilians who followed the army simply dreamed of enriching themselves there. Kidnappings for hundreds of thousands of dollars ransom became frequent, and the Jews were common targets. Harbin soon turned into a place of "living death" for Jews, and the climax of their tragedy was the kidnapping of young Simon Kaspe in 1933.[8] Simon Kaspe's father was a prosperous businessman in Harbin, but because he was a naturalized French citizen, not a stateless Jew, the French consul urged that he not pay the ransom in order to preserve France's honor. Despite their best efforts, in early December 1933, more than three months after the kidnapping, the police found the boy's body. "He had been starved, beaten and tortured. The nails of...the fingers had been torn out. Both his ears had been cut off."[9] After Simon Kaspe's funeral, thousands of Jews fled Harbin for the International Settlement in Shanghai or other Chinese cities. In the following years, almost 70 percent of them left the city.[10] By 1938, approximately six thousand Russian Jews had settled in Shanghai, establishing a large Jewish community.[11]

The remaining Jews, in order to survive the cruel reality of life in Manchuria, had no other choice but to seek the further protection of the Japanese authorities. On the eve of the first Jewish conference, Abraham Kaufman, leader of the Jewish community in Harbin, visited the Kwantung Army's Special Service Agency and met with a "Major Kawamura." Kaufman made it clear to the major that the Jews "acknowledged Japan's stature in the Far East and had decided to become Japan's wards." From then on, the Jews would "adapt themselves to the national policies of Japan and Manchukuo in order to survive." Kaufman wished to obtain an understanding from officials of both governments concerning the organization of the East Asian Jews. Kawamura responded that if the Jews and the Japanese acted secretly, it might invite misunderstanding from other countries. He promised that Japanese and Manchukuoan officials would back the Jews and suggested that the Jews should be openly receptive to the Japanese. Kaufman was greatly encouraged and was ready to call the First Far Eastern Jewish Conference.[12]

The Kwantung Army welcomed and supported the Jewish conference. It constituted a valuable opportunity for the military authorities since they had long hoped and expected to obtain Jewish collaboration and capital for the development of Manchuria. General Higuchi offered to deliver a congratulatory address at the conference in an unofficial capacity.[13] Although the Kwantung Army also asked consul general Tsurumi Ken in Harbin to give a similar speech, Tsurumi rejected the request after discussing it with foreign minister Hirota Kōki. The consul general was apprehensive that his speech might complicate Japan's relations with Germany, since the two countries had recently signed the Anti-Comintern Pact, and Germany had expelled the Jews. On the other hand, Tsurumi was also concerned that not giving such a speech would adversely affect Japan's relationship with the Jews in Manchuria, who played important roles in the area's economy. However, the foreign minister believed that Japanese-German relations were more significant.[14] Eventually, consul general Tsurumi sent a vice consul to the conference.[15]

The First Far Eastern Jewish Conference served the purposes of both the Jews and the Japanese, and all achieved their original goals. At the conference, the Japanese military occupation authorities promised that because Manchukuo was founded in the spirit of "universal brotherhood," it would provide the same protection to the "diligent and kind Jews" as Japan would, allow them to live a peaceful life and establish an "Arcadia" together.[16] Consul General Tsurumi described in a telegram to the foreign minister that Japan's participation in the conference was enthusiastically welcomed by the Jewish communities. Lew Zikman, a wealthy Jewish businessman who served as vice president of a sugar refinery in Harbin, volunteered to spend his own money to publish articles praising Japan's goodwill in a local Jewish newspaper in order to help spread the word to the whole world.[17]

The representatives of the Jews attending the conference proclaimed that they would take seriously their obligations to cooperate with Japan in building a "new order" in Asia. The conference also organized a "National Council of Far Eastern Jews" and proposed to convene each year in Harbin.[18] The conference would serve as an institution to reconcile the different perceived needs of the Jews and the Japanese authorities.

Although the Kwantung Army appeared satisfied with the results of the Jewish Conference in Manchuria, 1,500 miles to the south, in Shanghai, Navy Captain Inuzuka remained cautious about the Jews. The captain agreed that the conference served as a successful propaganda vehicle for Japan. However, he noted the absence of representatives from the Jewish communities in Shanghai and Hong Kong. Since intelligence reports later confirmed that the Shanghai Jewish leadership was "indifferent" to the conference, Inuzuka argued to his government that it was important to render the Shanghai Jews cooperative as well.[19]

Before large numbers of Russian Jews resettled in Shanghai in 1938, there was already a Jewish community of Baghdadi origin in the city. Notable Baghdadi Jewish families such as the Sassoons, the Hardoons, and the Kadoories played an important role in developing Shanghai's economy. Led by the Sassoons, these Baghdadi Jews first immigrated to Bombay in the early nineteenth century to escape political and religious persecution. In Bombay, they created flourishing commercial empires. In the wake of the Treaty of Nanjing in 1042 and the opening of Shanghai as a treaty port, the Baghdadi Jews explored new business opportunities in the Chinese city. The Jewish-owned companies in Shanghai acquired great wealth through the cotton and opium trade by the turn of the twentieth century, and they succeeded in the real estate market thereafter. By 1925, an American tourist in Shanghai claimed that "almost half the business and residential districts were owned by Baghdadi Jews."[20]

The Baghdadi Jews in Shanghai were, as historian Maisie Meyer notes, "Anglophiles and intensely patriotic to Great Britain," especially after the British occupied Baghdad in early 1917. When British imperial power was at its peak, being identified as British was advantageous for the Jews. British nationality guaranteed prosperity and security for the Jewish business elite, and "opened the doors to economic, political, legal and social privileges."[21]

The wealthy Baghdadi Jews were not only well connected in upper class British circles in Shanghai but also "welcomed into British society." Victor Sassoon and Ellis Kadoorie received knighthoods, and a branch of the Sassoons who immigrated to Great Britain in the late nineteenth century became close friends of King Edward VII.[22] To Captain Inuzuka, the Baghdadi Jews, who numbered only about one thousand but formed a financially and politically influential group in Shanghai, were potentially of greater value to Japan compared to the stateless Russian Jews in Manchuria.

The captain was also uninterested in the Ashkenazi Jewish community in Shanghai. Even the Baghdadi Jews "preferred to differentiate themselves from their Ashkenazi coreligionists."[23] Before the arrival of the Jews from Manchuria in the early 1930s, thousands of mostly indigent Russian Jews had already settled in Shanghai. The number eventually reached six thousand to eight thousand by the end of the decade.[24] However, as Meyer observes, the "different cultural, political, and socio-economic background of the Ashkenazi Jews gave them little in common with the well-established" Baghdadi community, and this caused friction between the two Jewish groups. Unlike the many successful Baghdadi Jewish businessmen, the Ashkenazi Jews were often "ex-soldiers, political exiles, and adventurers and some were involved in highly questionable enterprises."[25] Marcia Ristaino notes that, for their part, "Ashkenazim often expressed resentment of [the] wealthy and socially prominent" Baghdadi Jews who seemed to have "little interest in the Ashkenazi welfare."[26] Following the First Far Eastern Jewish Conference, Captain Inuzuka in Shanghai strove to win over the Baghdadi Jewish businessmen as part of his plan to exploit alleged Jewish financial power.

Although the Japanese military occupation authorities in China attempted to use the favorable results of the conference as propaganda to combat international sanctions on the Japanese economy and anti-Japanese protests, the conference did not draw as much attention from the rest of the world as the Japanese wished. Foreign Minister Hirota ordered consular offices overseas to investigate international reactions to the conference in early February 1938. Ambassador Tōgō Shigenori in Berlin informed the foreign minister that German newspapers did not report on the Jewish Conference since the German government believed that articles concerning the conference would be "unfavorable" to Japan.[27] On the other hand, an embassy report from Poland stated that although Polish newspapers did not cover the conference, Jewish newspapers in the country published several editorials concerning a Japanese military officer's congratulatory address to the assembled delegates. The embassy was disappointed that the Jewish editorials were "skeptical" and "mocking," and characterized the speech as an example of "Japanese cunning."[28]

The Military and the Making of Japan's Foreign Policy in the 1930s

In order to appreciate the influence that Yasue and Inuzuka wielded in China and to understand how two mid-level officers came to shape the policy of Japan toward the Jewish refugees in Shanghai, it is necessary to examine the complex dynamic between the Japanese military and the civilian government in Tokyo as well as the intricate relationships between factions within the Japanese military establishment.

Political scientist Yale Maxon argues that Japan from 1930 to 1945 had a "double-headed government in which civil and military power contended for supremacy in the formulation of foreign policy."[29] He contends that the Meiji Constitution, which gave privileges to both civil and military elements, sowed the seeds of chaos in the civil-military struggle for superiority during the 1930s.[30] Under the Meiji Constitution, the war (army) and navy ministers had direct access to the emperor and were beyond the control of the prime minister. On the other hand, the foreign minister was generally ranked junior in the cabinet. The position of the foreign ministry further declined later in the 1930s. At the time, the Foreign Ministry "had to share with others its role in determining the lines of foreign policy," especially its China policy. In fact, the army and the navy completely "leapfrogged over" the Foreign Ministry in Japan's foreign policy making.[31]

On June 4, 1928, a group of young officers in the Kwantung Army assassinated Manchurian warlord Zhang Zuolin. They were dissatisfied with the government's policy of collaborating and negotiating with him. The army leaders always claimed that Japan's interest in Manchuria was built on the army's sacrifice in the Sino-Japanese and the Russo-Japanese Wars, and that Manchuria was strategically important for the Japanese Army as it prepared itself for a potential war with the Russians. They were disappointed by the government's failure to take a hard-line foreign policy toward north China and occupy it forcibly.[32] Eventually, as navy minister Okada Keisuke pointed out, the "Kwantung Army proved by this event that it was more powerful than the Japanese government in Tokyo"[33]

The assassination of Zhang Zuolin, as well as the later Manchurian Incident of September 18, 1931, which led to Japan's seizure of Manchuria, was planned and conducted by field grade staff officers of the Kwantung Army. In the years before the beginning of the Pacific War in 1941, the middle echelon staff officers who held significant positions in the Army Central Command, such as the Army General Staff and the Army Ministry, played key roles in the army's decision-making process. These field grade staff officers were responsible for initiating and drafting important national policies that needed to be presented to the Imperial Headquarters-Cabinet Liaison Conference, one of Japan's principal policy-decision making bodies.[34]

Historian Fujiwara Akira, who himself experienced the Second World War as an army captain, explains that at the turn of the twentieth century, the army followed the German model, which emphasized the importance of the staff officers' roles in making and implementing policy, to train its officers. This practice resulted in gekokujyō, junior officers dominating senior officers in the army. The army commanders "hardly ever judged, decided or ordered anything by themselves." It was considered a "virtue" that commanders leave all decisions to their staff officers and take only the final responsibilities.[35] At the time of the Manchurian Incident, the Kwantung Army General Staff officers Itagaki Seishirō and Ishiwara Kanji exercised greater influence than their commanding officers in Manchuria. Therefore, the assassination of Zhang Zuolin in 1928 indicated the extent of not only the army's but also the field grade staff officers' involvement in Japan's national and foreign policy making.

By the end of 1931, the Kwantung Army gained complete control over Manchuria and, in March 1932, established Manchukuo. On July 26, Prime Minister Saitō Makoto submitted a plan to the cabinet to unify various institutions in Manchuria. The prime minister proposed that the commander of the Kwantung Army should also serve as the ambassador to Manchukuo and that the ambassador should receive orders from the foreign minister and take charge of foreign affairs in Manchuria.[36] The Manchurian Incident and the establishment of Manchukuo further confirmed the army's role in determining Japan's foreign policy, especially in China.

Meanwhile, the conclusion of the London Naval Limitations Treaty in 1930 provoked many naval officers' dissatisfaction toward the civilian government. The naval chief of staff, Admiral Katō Kanji, stubbornly confronted the cabinet and opposed the disarmament. Nevertheless, with the support of moderate senior naval officers, the government was able to prevail over the chief of staff.[37]

However, the London Naval Treaty triggered internal divisions within the navy leadership. Traditionally, the "administrative group," mostly staff officers, held important positions in the Navy Ministry; the "command group," generally operation officers, controlled the Navy General Staff. The "administrative group" comprised the key players in the navy's policy making and always stimulated operation officers' sense of rivalry. In 1930, the "administrative group" was willing to accept the London Treaty. They believed that Japan should depend on diplomatic efforts to solve problems in Japanese-U.S. relations and tried to avoid a naval race with the United States that might bankrupt Japan. The "administrative group" emphasized that Japan should never confront the United States. Nevertheless, the "command group," led by Admiral Katō Kanji, challenged this theory after the conclusion of the London Treaty. The limitation and reduction of naval armament increased the operation officers' strong dissatisfaction toward the United States since they considered heavy cruisers and submarines vital assets in any future war against the Americans. Although Admiral Katō and the "command group" were defeated at this time, the London Naval Treaty increased the influence of the hard-liners in not only the General Staff but also the Navy Ministry.[38]

On May 15, 1932, a group of young naval officers, with support from their army counterparts and radical civilian politicians, killed Prime Minister Inukai Tsuyoshi. The May 15 Incident was not merely one of many attempts to establish a military government in the early 1930s. As Maxon argues, it "caused a fundamental change in the character of the Japanese government. 'Normal constitutional government' (party government), as it had existed since 1924, was now abandoned."[39] After the May 15 Incident, the military increased its political pressure in an effort to establish a pliable cabinet. It also worked to ensure that the army and navy ministers gained a stronger voice in both domestic and foreign affairs.[40]

In September 1933, shortly after Hirota Kōki was appointed foreign minister, the prime minister, foreign minister, army minister, navy minister, and finance minister began to convene the Five Ministers' Conferences. Their purpose was to determine Japan's policy on issues of foreign relations, national defense, and finance. Imai Seiichi argues that the creation of the Five Ministers' Conference indicated that the prime minister and the foreign minister were no longer able to decide Japan's foreign policy by themselves; they had no choice but to acknowledge the military's influence over the formulation of foreign policy.[41] Eventually, the military took over political initiative within the government as a result of the February 26 Incident of 1936, a revolt led by radical young officers who briefly seized power in Tokyo.[42]

In sum, from the early 1930s, the military, the army in particular, successfully increased its influence over and eventually controlled foreign policy making through a series of military actions in Japan and East Asia.[43] Field grade staff officers in the army and navy were actively involved in initiating and determining Japan's foreign policy. This was especially obvious in the Kwantung Army's case. Compared to their commanding officers in Tokyo, the middle echelon officers stationed in China played a vital role in forming Japan's East Asian policy.

During the years following the Manchurian Incident, in Manchuria and North China, Maxon notes, "the control of foreign policy had passed to the field."[44] He describes the army's policy-making process this way: after junior officers on the spot initiated a policy, they sent it to the Army General Staff in Tokyo; the General Staff, believing that "forces on the spot are best able to decide," would formulate and submit the policy to the war minister; the war minister would act as "transmitting agency" to propose the policy to the civil government as the "will of the Army"; eventually, the government, without any actual control and "motivated by fear," would accept the draft policy, originally prepared by field grade officers, as an official foreign policy.[45]

The military's control over Japan's foreign policy in the 1930s made it possible for the army and naval "Jewish problem experts" to push through their policy toward the Jews in Japanese occupied China. Staff officers Colonel Yasue in Manchuria and Captain Inuzuka in Shanghai, who worked at, and had strong connections with, the Ministries and the General Staffs of the Army and Navy, enthusiastically formulated, promoted, and conducted Japan's Jewish policy. Because Japan's foreign policy in the 1930s, and its

East Asian policy in particular, was motivated by military considerations, the country's Jewish policy also reflected the will and needs of the military. Furthermore, the military nature of Japan's Jewish policy ensured that when the strategic situation changed regionally and internationally, the policy would eventually affect the fate of the European Jewish refugees.

The Five Ministers' Conference of December 6, 1938, and Japan's First Official Jewish Policy

After Hitler came to power in 1933, he initiated an anti-Jewish program in Germany, and later in Austria and other Nazi-occupied territories. The Nazis were determined to force the Jews to leave these countries by taking away not only their property but also their jobs and sending Jewish men to concentration camps. As early as 1933, a small group of Jewish professionals fled Europe to Manchukuo.[46] Thereafter, the Paris-based HICEM (HIAS ICA-Emigdirect), an organization sponsored by three Jewish immigration associations, helped arrange to send more refugees, mostly professionals, to the Japanese puppet regime.[47] Subsequently, twelve families and approximately one hundred European Jews arrived in Shanghai in 1933. The numbers gradually grew to several hundred by summer 1938. Similarly, most of them were professionals and had property.[48]

In the late 1930s, when the world was closing its gates to desperate European Jewish refugees, the number of Jews who fled to East Asia, the Japanese-occupied areas in particular, increased. Nevertheless, the Japanese government did not immediately shut out the Jews, who were expelled by Japan's allies. Tokyo was certainly aware of the anti-Jewish movement in Europe launched by Germany and Italy. Japanese diplomats overseas faithfully conveyed news about the Nazi persecution of Jews and the world's condemnation to Tokyo throughout the 1930s.[49] If so, why did Japan not take any immediate measures to restrict the entry of Jews to its territories? One possible reason is that since "the Jewish issue" had never before been an "issue" for the Japanese, the government did not have any experience "handling" the Jews. At the time, Japan did not have any policy regarding the influx of Jewish refugees, and its leaders lacked knowledge of Jews and Europe's anti-Semitism. Although Yasue and Inuzuka had devoted themselves to Jewish research, they were exceptions. Eventually, in early 1938, officials in Tokyo began to realize that Japan must cope with the European Jewish refugees systematically.

The Ministry of Foreign Affairs took the initiative. On March 31, 1938, in his message to the vice ministers of the army and navy, vice minister of foreign affairs Horinouchi Kensuke emphasized that in light of the current international situation and the problems in the occupation areas, Japan needed to study and formulate its own policy toward Muslim and Jewish issues. On January 17, 1938, shortly after the First Far Eastern Jewish Conference, the chief commissioner of the Metropolitan Police reported to the minister of interior affairs that the head of the Tokyo Muslim Association, a White Russian who immigrated to Japan in the early 1920s from Manchuria, had made an inflammatory anti-Semitic statement following General Higuchi's speech at the conference.[50] Horinouchi informed the two ministers of the establishment of the Committee on the Muslim and Jewish Problem, sponsored by the Ministry of Foreign Affairs, and asked for approval and participation from the two ministries. He also explained that the Committee on the Muslim and Jewish Problem aimed to help the Ministries of the Army, Navy, and Foreign Affairs to better communicate and cooperate with one another regarding these issues. Therefore, the committee should meet at the Foreign Ministry whenever a problem occurred. Horinouchi soon received support from the military, and the three ministries all appointed high-ranking officials to the committee. The vice minister of foreign affairs himself served as the committee chair.[51]

Colonel Yasue and Captain Inuzuka welcomed the establishment of the Committee on the Muslim and Jewish Problem. The two "experts" were relieved that the central government eventually took the Jewish issue as seriously as they had long wished. In addition, the committee meetings provided them perfect opportunities to convince the leaders in Tokyo that Japan should take advantage of Jewish refugees for its own sake.

On September 19, Yasue delivered a speech to the committee members. He emphasized that since Jews in Manchuria had already decided to cooperate with the Japanese and Manchukuoan governments in exchange for Japan's protection, Japan should take this opportunity to further expand its influence over Jews in northern and central China, and eventually the world. As a matter of fact, Yasue never considered the Jewish issue in Manchuria to be a separate one from the Jewish issue in other regions of China, especially in Shanghai. He attempted to use the close connections between Manchurian and Shanghai Jews, led by wealthy Baghdadi Jewish families such as the Sassoons, to control the affluent Jews of Shanghai. Yasue believed that Japan's war in East Asia made it clear that the Western governments, the British and French in particular, were powerless to defend the Jews, and the Jews would eventually realize that Japan was the only country they could depend upon to protect them. He also hoped that pro-Japanese propaganda by Jews in East Asia would help curtail the boycott of Japanese goods in the United States. Yasue emphasized that Japan should not follow Germany's anti-Semitic policies. Rather, it should treat Jews in the spirit of *Hakkō Ichiu*. He believed that since the Jews had great influence over world politics, economy, and media, it was counterproductive to make the Jews enemies of Japan.[52]

Captain Inuzuka's talk to the committee on October 12 focused on the Jews in Shanghai. Compared to Yasue's passion, Inuzuka expressed more caution about using the Jews. Inuzuka understood that the Shanghai Jews were concerned about Japan's Jewish policy and were eager to approach the occupation authorities; it was a perfect chance for Japan to take advantage of them. However, he cautioned the committee that the last thing Tokyo should do was to be too "friendly" to the Jews. Instead, Japan should completely subdue the Jews and always "keep our hands around their throats." Nevertheless, like his fellow "Jewish expert" Yasue, Inuzuka tried to persuade his audience that Tokyo should not expel the Jews, since Jewish economic power in China, Shanghai in particular, could definitely benefit Japan. Inuzuka also urged the central government to consider immediately and establish "practical measures" to enable Japan to exploit Jews.[53]

The officials from the Ministries of Foreign Affairs, Army, and Navy did not immediately accept the opinions of the "experts." The Ministry of Foreign Affairs commented that Colonel Yasue's argument still "left room for discussion." Disagreements came even from the army itself.[54] The controversy over Yasue's theories might explain his absence from the next committee meeting on October 5. Although Captain Inuzuka was among the attendees, the army sent a Colonel Saitō instead of Colonel Yasue.[55] The reaction of the Committee to the contention of the "Jewish experts" revealed a lack of understanding between officers deployed in China and officials in the central government.

The committee meeting of October 5 focused on the entry of the Jews, especially the Jewish refugees, into Japan.[56] This was the first time that Japanese officials discussed the Jewish refugee issue at the governmental level. As a result, both the military and civilian members agreed that it was undesirable under the current circumstances for Japan to accept Jewish refugees who were expelled by the German and Italian governments. Furthermore, Japan was unable to admit these refugees because of its ongoing war with China. Based on the committee's decision, prime minister and foreign minister Konoe Fumimaro cabled all consular offices on October 7, 1938, and clearly instructed that although the Jewish refugees were allowed to transit, they were not welcome to enter Japan and its colonies. Since Japan at the time was being criticized internationally for its military invasion of China, Konoe did not want the Jewish refugees to become another inflammatory issue. Further, he emphasized in his instructions to the consuls that they should publicly use the term "refugees" rather than "Jewish refugees" in order to avoid possible international criticism.[57]

The decision of the Committee on the Muslim and Jewish Problem did not discourage Colonel Yasue from pursuing his plan to take advantage of the East Asian Jews. After returning to Manchuria, he ordered the SMR on October 27 to initiate research on Jewish-related matters regionally and internationally. Yasue assigned the Special Research Team several significant research topics concerning the Jews.[58] An intelligence officer himself, Yasue certainly understood the important role that the military's intelligence reports played in determining of Japan's foreign policy. The result of the SMR's research helped Yasue to establish a Jewish policy, presented to the Five Ministers' Conference by the army minister on December 6, 1938. This became Japan's first official policy concerning the Jews.

Yasue requested first that the Special Research Team explore the policy that Japan should take toward the Jews as well as concrete plans to carry it out. "Since the imperial government currently doesn't have a clear policy toward the Jewish issue," he explained, "different policies are being taken at each party's own convenience."[59] In order to establish a standardized Jewish policy, Yasue required information on how Japan should accept, treat, and exploit Jews who lived in East Asia.

The second research topic he assigned was to examine "the advantages and disadvantages of the introduction of foreign, especially Jewish, capital [to Manchuria]." He wanted to know, further, under what conditions and by what means Japan could introduce this capital without it being accompanied by harmful Jewish influence. Yasue emphasized that because Japan was in a state of war, it required "a rapid exploitation of natural resources and military facilities."[60] The introduction of foreign capital eventually became a vital issue for Japan.

Yasue's third topic concerned the "fundamental principles" of the Jewish policies that Japan should take. According to Yasue, "Japan does not, and does not necessarily have to, take Germany's and Italy's anti-Semitic policies toward the Jews. It should rather follow its national policy of *Hakkō Ichiu*, cooperation and harmony among peoples, and embrace the Jews."[61] Meanwhile, he contended, some Japanese people and government officials had followed Germany and Italy's example and espoused anti-Semitism after the conclusion of the Anti-Comintern Pact with the two countries in 1937. In order to create a national consensus, Yasue asserted that it was crucial to explain the reasons Japan adopted a Jewish policy different from Germany's and Italy's.[62]

Although Yasue repeatedly emphasized that Japan should "embrace" the Jewish refugees, there was a significant precondition for this: Jews should contribute their financial power to Manchuria's economic development. The Japanese Army traditionally considered Russia its major potential enemy. Therefore, Manchuria served as an important strategic buffer zone between the Soviet Union and Japan. The Japanese Army needed to develop and stabilize Manchuria so that it could be well prepared to confront the Russians.

As a result of the Russo-Japanese War of 1904–1905, Japan took over from Russia the lease of Kwantung Territory, the tip of the Liaodong Peninsula and the area around the South Manchuria Railway, and control of the southern branch of the Chinese Eastern Railway. Maintaining and developing Japan's rights and interests in China, Manchuria in particular, became an important foreign policy issue. The Japanese government established an administrative body of the Office of the Kwantung Governor General in 1906. Although the Kwantung Army was originally put under the authority of the governor general, it established its own command in 1919.[63]

This period coincided with the era of German defeat in World War I. The disintegration of German power convinced some Japanese Army officers that "for their Asian empire, the lessons of the European conflict were ominous. Future wars would be fought not only with guns but with the entire resources of nations.... Without these requisites of *economic* security, the mightiest army would be paralyzed."[64] They considered "a modern industrial base" the most important prerequisite for Japan during the era of modern war. Michael Barnhart argues that these "total war officers" further concluded that a nation would never be "truly secure" if it could not fulfill its economic needs during the wartime.[65] In Manchuria during the 1930s, therefore, economic security became an important concern of the Kwantung Army. Ishiwara Kanji, in fact, was one of the leaders of the "total war officers."[66]

After Tanaka Giichi, a former army general, became prime minister in 1927, he advocated a Manchurian policy "focused on military expeditions and aggressive development" of Japan's rights and interests in the region. He also considered Manchuria a "strategic barrier" between Japan and the Soviet Union.[67] Tanaka's hard-line policy received support from a group of prominent field grade staff officers in the Kwantung Army who tended to believe that "the exercise of force was inevitable for the settlement of Manchuria."[68] They eventually became involved in the Manchurian Incident in late 1931.

Senior staff officers Colonel Itagaki Seishirō and his subordinate, Lt. Colonel Ishiwara Kanji, both belonged to this group. Itagaki and Ishiwara especially believed that Manchuria could serve as a base from which to supply Japan's future aggressive ventures in Asia.[69] At the same time, Ishikawa Kanji strongly advocated for the industrialization of Manchuria and envisioned creating a self-contained industrial center in the region to support the expansion of Japan's military.[70]

The army proposed in June 1937 to introduce foreign, especially American, capital into Manchuria, and in October the Japanese government formalized a "General Plan for the Establishment of Heavy Industries in Manchuria," which made the pursuit of foreign capital an official goal. Ayukawa Yoshisuke, president of the Nihon Industrial Company (Nissan), shared the Kwantung Army officers' opinions. At the end of a trip to Manchuria in 1937, Ayukawa met with Itagaki and discussed the industrialization of Manchuria. Ayukawa emphasized that this project should "depend for at least one-third and preferably one-half...upon foreign capital (principally American dollars)." The Nihon Industrial Company was officially relocated to Manchuria and was reconstituted as the Manchuria Heavy Industries Development Corporation in December 1937.[71]

Cho Yukio points out that improving relations with the United States was another important reason that the Japanese government, the army in particular, was eager to bring American capital to Manchuria. Although that effort was unsuccessful, the Japanese Army attempted to "secure American recognition of Japan's vested interests—acquired through aggression—in Manchuria and China."[72] The army clearly stated in "The Army's Hopes Regarding Current Foreign Policies" in July 1938 that Japan's diplomatic efforts toward the United States should concentrate on "persuading the United States at the very least to retain a neutral attitude, if possible to adopt a pro-Japanese attitude, and especially to strengthen friendly economic relations." "The Army's Hopes" also emphasized that such diplomatic efforts should include conducting "appropriate propaganda" to "correct" the American view of Japan, promoting trade with the United States, and importing American capital.[73]

The Jews in East Asia, many of whom the Japanese believed to have relatives and friends in the United States, therefore became targets of the Kwantung Army. Represented by Yasue Norihiro and Ishiwara Kanji, the Kwantung Army officers planned to use the Jews and their connections in the United States to attract American investment and to ease tensions with the Americans. Ishiwara Kanji stated in "Opinions on Diplomatic Policy" in November 1938 that since much of the American public held anti-Japanese feelings, Japan needed to make every effort to maintain a good relationship with the United States. Ishiwara regretted that although the First Far Eastern Jewish Conference was a great success and had a positive influence on Jews, Japan was unable to take advantage of this because of its concerns about Germany. Nevertheless, Ishiwara proposed that Japan should not only use the Jews but also suggested that Japan help them establish a Jewish homeland in East Asia. Doing so, he concluded, would have an important impact on the American media.[74]

Although Itagaki Seishirō at the time served as the army minister in Tokyo, it is very likely that through his close ties with the Kwantung Army, he was aware of the plan. The result of the SMR's research obviously also helped Yasue set up a Jewish policy by the beginning of December 1938. After consulting with Captain Inuzuka, Yasue flew to Tokyo to meet with Itagaki, a friend and classmate from the military academy, just before the Five Ministers' Conference on December 6.[75] Itagaki then presented Yasue's draft to the conference.[76] The Five Ministers' Conference determined the "Outlines of the Jewish Policies" on December 6, 1938, as Japan's first official policy toward Jewish refugees.

On December 7, foreign minister Arita Hachirō sent the "Outlines" to the Japanese ambassadors to Germany, the United States, and Manchukuo, as well as to the Japanese consuls in China. In the introduction, the foreign minister explained that since maintaining a good relationship with Germany and Italy was at the core of Japan's foreign policy, Japan should basically "avoid actively embracing" the Jews who were banished by allied countries. However, it would contradict Japan's advocacy of "racial equality" if it persecuted the Jews as its allies had done. Also, Arita emphasized that Japan, under a "state of emergency," needed "the introduction of foreign capital" in order to pursue economic construction as well as its war aims. At the same time, Arita noted, Japan had to "avoid worsening" its relations with the United States.[77]

The Five Ministers' Conference established three Jewish policies:

1. [Japan should] treat Jews living in Japan, Manchukuo, and China equally with other foreign nationals. No special measure would be taken to expel the Jews.
2. [Japan should] impartially deal with Jews who are arriving in Japan, Manchukuo, and China under the general regulations admitting foreigners.
3. [Japan should] avoid actively inviting Jews to Japan, Manchukuo, and China. However, people such as investors and technicians who can be used [by Japan] should be exceptions.[78]

Although Japan's first official Jewish policy guaranteed that the Japanese would not persecute Jews, it was not, as David Kranzler argues, a pro-Jewish policy.[79] Japan's policy was based on the Kwantung Army's greed and desperation for international capital; the Jews were the targets of exploitation. Although the "Outlines of the Jewish Policies" brought about a closer relationship between the Japanese occupation authorities in China and the East Asian Jews, the Jews were not in a position to decide their own fate. Their lives were in constant danger if they could not fulfill Japan's requests or would not cooperate with the Japanese. Meanwhile, the establishment of the "Outlines of the Jewish Policies" further confirmed the position of Colonel Yasue and the military "experts" in formulating Japan's Jewish policy.

In late December 1938, Kaufman informed the Kwantung Army that the Jews in East Asia would like to convene a Second Jewish Conference. The Second Far Eastern Jewish Conference was prepared completely under the direction of the Kwantung Army and Colonel Yasue.[80] The Kwantung Army devoted itself to this conference. In his telegram to the chief of the Army Ministry's Military Affairs Bureau, Isogai Rensuke, the chief of staff of the Kwantung Army stated that the occupation authorities were working to make it easy for the Jewish representatives in East Asia to enter northern China and Manchukuo to attend the conference. Meanwhile, Isogai also took Japan's relationship with its allies into serious consideration. He promised the chief of the Military Affairs Bureau that although the Kwantung Army officers would allow the Jews express their appreciation to Japan and Manchukuo in the resolution of the conference, they would not permit them to do anything that might provoke Germany's and Italy's ire.[81]

Two months before the Second Far Eastern Jewish Conference, obviously with Colonel Yasue's influence, Kaufman submitted a report concerning the life of the East Asian Jews to both the American Jewish Congress and the World Jewish Congress. In his report, Kaufman introduced the political, economic, social, and religious situation of the Jews in the Japanese-occupied areas and Manchukuo. He emphasized that there was no anti-Semitism at all there and that the Jews enjoyed the same rights as other people in those areas. Although White Russians had earlier published an anti-Semitic newspaper, *Nash put'*, in Manchuria, Kaufman added, it was soon shut down by the Japanese military authorities. The Japanese authorities forbade all anti-Semitic sentiment from being published. Kaufman concluded, "We are responsible for emphasizing heartily that Japan and Manchukuo are righteous countries." According to Yasue, Stephen Wise, president of the American Jewish Congress, had agreed to include Kaufman's report in the record of the American Jewish Congress and to publish it in American newspapers.[82]

Wise also responded personally at the end of the year, expressing his joy for his fellow Jews in East Asia. A Japanese source reported that Wise was "in an influential position among American government circles" and that he even received New Year's greetings from President Roosevelt.[83] In addition, Yasue received information from Paris that Kaufman's report was favorably considered at the World Jewish Congress.[84] It seemed that Yasue's propaganda strategy was successful. The Japanese had apparently impressed favorably the American and international Jewish communities.

From December 26 to December 28, 1938, approximately one thousand people attended the Second Far Eastern Jewish Conference in Harbin. Unlike the First Far Eastern Jewish Conference, the Shanghai Jewish communities sent their representatives to this meeting. Captain Inuzuka, who had earlier complained about the absence of the Shanghai Jews at the First Far Eastern Jewish Conference and who was at the time in charge of Jewish matters in Shanghai, clearly played an important role in "persuading" the Shanghai Jews to attend.

Before the conference, Colonel Yasue assembled all the Jewish leaders and delivered a speech in a private capacity. In his speech, Yasue pointed out that he expected the Jewish leaders to display their leadership prudently and properly since the current international situation was getting "complicated." "If [the principles of] your leadership contradict Japan's and Manchukuo's holy ideals," he warned, "it will definitely cause sorrow for your fellow Jews." Therefore, Yasue concluded that the guiding principles of the Jewish leaders would directly affect the destiny of the Jews in East Asia. He "eagerly wished" that the leaders would recognize fully Japan's and Manchukuo's "mission" of establishing a new order in East Asia and would collaborate with the two governments.[85]

The Jewish leaders correctly interpreted his none too subtle message. The resolution of the Second Far Eastern Jewish Conference reemphasized that the Manchukuoan and Japanese authorities assured Jews a peaceful life, that Jews enjoyed racial equality and rights, and that the Jews would cooperate with Japan and Manchukuo in establishing a new order in East Asia. The resolution further declared that the Jews in East Asia should appeal to "every Jew around the world" for their support to Japan and Manchukuo. Under the instructions of the Kwantung Army, the conference's proceedings and final statements were sent to Jewish associations in New York, London, Paris, and Shanghai, as well as to thirty-one English and Jewish newspapers in the United States, and seven English and Jewish newspapers in Britain.[86]

The Influx of the Jewish Refugees into Shanghai and the Restrictions on Their Entry, December 1938–August 1939

Although the "Outlines of the Jewish Policies" tried to "avoid actively" inviting Jews to East Asia, the Japanese-occupied areas in particular, it did not prohibit Jews from landing in China, especially the treaty port of

Shanghai. Yasue and Inuzuka were clearly not interested in preventing the European Jews from arriving because the more Jewish refugees came to East Asia, the more opportunities the Japanese had to control and exploit them. Other Japanese officials at the time expressed no interest in the so-called Jewish issue, allowing the experts to dominate the decision making. According to Shanghai Municipal Police reports, at the beginning of December 1938, approximately five hundred German and Austrian Jewish refugees had arrived in Shanghai since early August; on January 11, 1939, the total number of Jewish refugees was fourteen hundred; at the end of January 1939, the number further increased to approximately twenty-two hundred.[87]

The unexpectedly and steadily increasing number of Jewish refugees made Shanghai's foreign, especially Jewish, communities nervous and became a great burden for them. By January 1939, the local Jewish communities established four refugee relief organizations: the Committee for the Assistance of European Jewish Refugees (CAEJR), Relief Society for German Austrian Jews, International Committee for Granting Relief to European Refugees, and Shanghai Jewish Youth Association. According to the relief committees, only 10 percent of the refugees were from middle-class backgrounds and were able to make a living in Shanghai by themselves. The rest of them needed immediate assistance, and it cost the committees as much as $90,000 per month for refugee relief.[88]

The arrival of the destitute European Jews worsened the already desperate refugee situation in Shanghai's International Settlement and French Concession. By the end of 1938, about 1.5 million Chinese refugees had poured into these two Western communities.[89] On December 20, 1938, Michel Speelman, chairman of the CAEJR, and Ellis Hayim, director general of the CAEJR, met with G. Godfrey Phillips, the British consul general and secretary and commissioner general of the Shanghai Municipal Council (SMC), and discussed the recent refugee problem in Shanghai. In his report to C. S. Franklin, chairman and secretary general of the SMC, Phillips noted, "I obtained the impression that both these gentlemen were extremely anxious....I formed a strong impression that they would very much welcome any practical means to limit the number of Jewish refugees who are admitted here." Phillips also emphasized that

[I]t seems entirely wrong that Shanghai...should, because of the circumstances of the moment of completely free entry, be expected to bear far more than its share in the work of finding a home for refugees from Central Europe. The foreign community of Shanghai is by no means prosperous at the present time, and it would seem that this community could not possibly absorb any really large further number of foreign refugees. A further large influx of such people will only result in depressing further the present standard of living of the existing foreign community. It is further unfair and undesirable that yet a new call should be made in Shanghai for funds which are badly needed for those to whom Shanghai's first duty is owed.

The commissioner general urged that the SMC should begin considering ways to control the entry of Jewish refugees into Shanghai.[90]

It seemed that Phillips's report was persuasive to the SMC. Three days later, obviously under the SMC's instruction, Godfrey Phillips cabled the Jewish relief and emigration organizations in London, Paris, and New York, notifying them that Shanghai was facing a "most serious refugee problem," and that the Municipal Council "request[s] [their] assistance in preventing any refugees coming to Shanghai." He also noted that the Municipal Council might be forced to take action toward the prohibition of the entry of Jewish refugees.[91]

On the same day, December 23, 1938, the chairman of the SMC sent out Circular 399-G-VII to member countries concerning the "desirability of preventing further influx" of Jewish refugees into Shanghai. The chairman also attached an urgent letter to the circular to all senior consuls in the International Settlement. In his letter, the chairman expressed the Municipal Council's great concern over the arrival of the European Jews and requested that "the interested Consuls may take any steps within their power to prevent any further arrival of Jewish refugees in Shanghai." He also claimed that if the problem worsened, it would be the "Council's duty to protect the community of the International Settlement by taking steps to prohibit the landing ... of any further Jewish refugees without adequate means of subsistence or promise of employment."[92] In addition to the circular of December 23, 1938, the chairman sent letters again on January 16, 1939, to the German and Italian consuls and asked for special cooperation from the two governments to discourage such emigration to Shanghai. The consuls agreed to urge their governments to "do everything possible" to prevent further Jewish emigration.[93]

The Japanese consulate in Shanghai also received the SMC's circular. Acting consul general Gotō Itsuo cabled Foreign Minister Arita to request instructions. Arita replied on December 30, emphasizing that the Japanese consulate should definitely avoid taking any measures that might have a negative effect on German-Japanese relations. He also warned Gotō that if the way Japan treated the Jewish refugees in Shanghai irritated American Jewish businessmen it would affect Japan's relationship with the United States government as well. According to the foreign minister, the American news media had "falsely reported" about the Japanese and Manchukuoan officials' treatment of European Jews who had just arrived in Manchuria through Siberia. Arita worried that if Gotō took the SMC's request too seriously, Shanghai's Japanese consulate might be put in the same unfavorable situation. At this moment, Arita suggested that Gotō should clearly inform the Municipal Council that Japan "does not desire a growth in the number of elements, regardless of their nationality or origin, which disrupt the improvement of security inside the International Settlement." Japan would cooperate with the SMC "within the practical and possible limits" on the measures taken for this reason.[94]

There was no opposition from the military and the "Jewish experts" to the foreign minister's order. First, since the member countries of the Municipal Council, and even the local Jewish communities, supported the council's decision, it would be wise for Japan not to confront the entire international community in Shanghai. Second, since Japan's allies, Germany and Italy, did not protest against the council's decision, Japan could not act differently.

On the other hand, the number of Jewish refugees in Hongkou, the area of the International Settlement controlled by the Japanese Naval Landing Party, increased rapidly because the cost of living there was much lower than in other parts of Shanghai. Now the Jews competed for housing, employment, and business with the Japanese and other local residents.[95] The unanticipated situation upset the local communities and challenged Japan's existing Jewish policy. Although Captain Inuzuka still worked at the Navy General Staff in Tokyo, he began to spend more time in Shanghai doing field research on the Jewish refugees. As early as the beginning of January 1939, Inuzuka proposed that the Army, Navy, and Foreign Ministries should set up a three ministries' joint committee to fully study the Jewish issue for future policy making. However, the local authorities were not enthusiastic about this.[96]

Like his fellow "expert" Yasue in Manchuria, Inuzuka was relentless. He, too, worked to use his research to win his government's support for his ideas. After returning from a research trip to central and northern China, Captain Inuzuka delivered a speech to the Committee on the Muslim and Jewish Problem on January 18, 1939, outlining his "Personal Opinions on Current Situation of and Measures Taken toward the Shanghai Jews." Inuzuka explained that his research trip had four purposes: (1) to tighten the communications between the central government and the local officials; (2) to sound out the Jewish *Zaibatsu* in Shanghai on their current attitude toward Japan and the possibility of introduction of Jewish capital;[97] (3) to investigate the current situation of the Jewish refugees on the spot and to consider necessary measures for handling the problem; and (4) to collect and study materials that would help the future policy-making.[98]

In Shanghai, Inuzuka made contact with Jewish leaders and businessmen who made it clear to him that they were willing to do business with Japan. The head clerk of a Shanghai Jewish *Zaibatsu* explained to Inuzuka that Jews were moneylenders and merchants, therefore they would not choose between Japan and China as long as the business was secure and permanent. Ever since Japanese officials' statements that "Japan does not discriminate against Jews" were carried in the local Jewish newspaper on December 16, 1938, the general mood of the Shanghai Jews toward the Japanese authorities appeared relatively favorable. Further, some Jews collected articles from Jewish newspapers concerning the historically friendly Jewish-Japanese relationship and sent them to Inuzuka to demonstrate that they felt no hostility toward Japan and wanted to live in harmony with the Japanese.[99]

Meanwhile, Inuzuka warned the officials of the Committee on the Muslim and Jewish Problem that Japan should not be fooled by the Jews since their friendly attitude toward Japan was rooted in their own self-interest; they had been expelled from their homes all over the world and urgently needed places to resettle. Therefore, the Jews turned "pro-Japanese" simply because their current plight prevented them from doing otherwise. "In order to keep this situation permanent," Inuzuka emphasized that the Japanese government must restrain the Jews constantly and effectively. He believed that this was an important point that people who advocated "the use of the Jews" had not yet taken into account.[100]

Nevertheless, the captain insisted that the current situation forced Japan to use Jews even though the risk was expected. "Just as the dish of *fugu*," he explained, "although it is delicious, it will take your life if you don't know how to prepare it."[101] Inuzuka then concluded his report by requesting that the Ministry of Foreign Affairs conduct an immediate on-the-spot investigation and build up local institutions that would help to do research on and decide policies toward the Jewish refugee issue.[102]

Although Inuzuka's fugu theory seemed different from Yasue's theory of "*Hakkō Ichiu*," their policies of using the Jews in East Asia for Japan's sake were grounded in the same anti-Semitic ideas. Both Yasue and Inuzuka clearly expressed to the Jews that the only way for them to survive in the Japanese-occupied areas was to obey Japan and contribute to its war effort. Even though the Jews chose to collaborate with Japan, there was never an equal relationship between them, since the Japanese were able to decide the fate of the Jews.

It seemed that Inuzuka's report was well received, and it did not take the three ministries long to make their final decision. On March 20, 1939, on behalf of the Committee on the Muslim and Jewish Problem, the Ministry of Foreign Affairs distributed a memorandum concerning the investigation of the refugee situation in Shanghai. In order to examine concrete measures toward the Jewish issue in accordance with the policy established by the Five Ministers' Conference in December 1938, the Ministry of Foreign Affairs proposed to the Army and Navy Ministries that they should each dispatch investigators to do field research in China. The Ministry of Foreign Affairs also cited specific items to be investigated such as the establishment of a settlement for the Jewish refugees from Europe and measures concerning introduction of Jewish capital. The Foreign Ministry was especially interested in finding out how to use Jews in China to help mobilize American public opinion, alter American East Asian policy, and persuade the advisers to the American president to be more pro-Japanese, or at least to remain neutral toward Japan.[103]

The army and navy soon adopted the Foreign Ministry's proposal. Colonel Yasue from the Ministry of the Army, Captain Inuzuka from the Ministry of the Navy, and Consul Ishiguro Shirō in Shanghai from the Ministry of Foreign Affairs were appointed members for the joint committee to investigate the Jewish refugee issue in Shanghai. They first gathered in the city in May, then began their respective investigations. While in Shanghai, they met with prominent figures of the Jewish communities and the local Japanese officials.[104]

On May 25, the joint committee held a meeting with Sir Victor Sassoon and Ellis Hayim, Sassoon's political adviser and director general of the CAEJR. At the meeting, Sassoon and Hayim once again complained that the CAEJR's relief activities were under great pressure because of the shortage of funds and the increasing number of refugees. The Jewish leaders explained that because they were unable to convince foreign consuls to prevent Germany from dumping more Jewish refugees in Shanghai, the Japanese became their last hope for an effective negotiation with the Germans. They also guaranteed that local Jewish communities in general would understand that the restrictions on the entry of refugees would improve the lives of those who were already in Shanghai.[105] The mounting pressure from the Jewish communities forced the Japanese officials to reconsider their refugee policy. Most important, Inuzuka did not want to upset the wealthy local Jews whom he attempted to exploit.

By the beginning of June 1939, a total of ten thousand Jewish refugees had arrived in Shanghai, and more than five thousand of those lived in Hongkou.[106] The joint committee and the local Japanese authorities were under great pressure to resolve the refugee problem. A month later, on July 1, Inuzuka, Yasue, and Ishiguro submitted "Emergency Measures for

Managing the Shanghai Jewish Refugees" to the central government. The Emergency Measures served as provisional steps to ban the further flood of Jewish refugees into Hongkou until the new policy had been established and implemented. They basically prevented the Jewish refugees not only from living or doing business in the area, but also from entering it. The joint committee also asked Tokyo to negotiate with the Germans and Italians not to send any Jews to Shanghai or Japanese-occupied China in the future.[107]

In addition to the Emergency Measures, the joint committee presented a sixty-page "Joint Report of the Investigation on the Jewish Issue in Shanghai" to the Committee on the Muslim and Jewish Problem a week later.[108] According to the Joint Report, Britain's betrayal on the Palestine issue provoked the resentment of Jews all over the world and pushed them closer to the United States. The Shanghai Jews were no exception. Recently, the U.S. secretary of the treasury, Henry Morgenthau, had invited the chairman of the CAEJR to visit the United States to discuss America's contributions for refugee relief. Inuzuka, Yasue, and Ishiguro assumed that American Jewish leaders were attempting to "pull Shanghai Jews away from British influence and put them under the control of American Jews."[109] Nevertheless, the joint committee argued that the Shanghai Jews' American connections could actually benefit Japan. Since the secretary of the treasury was a Jew, and "many [other] influential" members of President Roosevelt's brain trust were believed to be Jewish, the committee hoped that they could help to at least preserve U.S. neutrality toward Japan.[110]

Meanwhile, Inuzuka, Yasue, and Ishiguro contended that since the United States was a capitalist country and since "capitalists" helped presidents win elections, "capitalists" wielded great influence over American politics. Eighty percent of the "capitalists" in the United States, however, were Jews. The committee also charged that Jews controlled 80 percent of the media, which molded public opinion in the United States, a country where public opinion significantly mattered. Inuzuka, Yasue, and Ishiguro believed that although Jews were scattered across the world, they were closely tied together. Therefore, the officials believed that as long as the Japanese exercised control over the Shanghai Jews, they could use American Jews to change popular opinion and the policies of the United States toward Japan.[111]

Regarding the introduction of Jewish capital, the Joint Report devoted much attention to Sir Victor Sassoon, the leading British-Jewish *Zaibatsu* in Shanghai. The joint committee was confident that it was able to ease Sassoon's original anti-Japanese attitude and to keep him neutral, at least. However, as a British citizen, Sassoon remained reluctant to invest in

Japan's business ventures in Shanghai. Nevertheless, a pro-Japanese Jewish leader notified the committee that if the Shanghai Jews secretly persuaded Jewish *Zaibatsu* in New York, American Jews might personally offer loans to Japan. If American Jews agreed to the loans, Inuzuka, Yasue, and Ishiguro expected that this would also affect the decision of Jewish *Zaibatsu* in Shanghai. They further expected that these actions by American Jews would encourage Jewish capitalists in Europe to invest in the Japanese-controlled portion of China. In return, the Joint Report noted that Japan should provide the Jewish refugees in Shanghai certain rights or a settlement.[112]

Concerning the Jewish settlement, Captain Inuzuka and Colonel Yasue believed that in providing Jews a "safe refuge," the Japanese government could use this opportunity to (1) favorably change American public opinion toward Japan; (2) make Jewish loans and investment more easily accessible; (3) increase the sympathy of American and European Jews for Japan; and (4) obtain the absolute cooperation of the East Asian Jews with Japan.[113]

The military "experts" once again succeeded in determining Japan's Jewish policy. On August 10, 1939, the Japanese government officially accepted Inuzuka, Yasue, and Ishiguro's "Emergency Measures for Managing the Shanghai Jewish Refugees" as its new Jewish policy. At the same time, the Ministry of Foreign Affairs ordered the Japanese consulate general in Shanghai to inform the German and Italian consuls general that the Japanese government would prevent Jews from entering Shanghai after August 10, 1939. The Foreign Ministry also notified Japanese stream ship companies to stop transporting Jewish refugees to East Asia.[114]

Consul general Miura Yoshiaki in Shanghai then met with the CAEJR leader, Hayim, and presented him a memorandum regarding the restrictions. Miura informed Hayim that after careful consideration, the Japanese authorities concluded that they "should take such steps as are within their power to stop temporarily a further increase of European refugees." One temporary measure that the Japanese authorities took was to request refugees who lived in Japanese-occupied Hongkou as of August 22, 1939, to fill out the "Directory of Jewish Refugees" and send copies to the Japanese authorities through the CAEJR. The Japanese authorities would return one copy of the registration to the refugees after investigation. Refugees who obtained returned copies would be allowed to stay where they were; those who did not receive the copies would be required to leave. The consul general also requested that the CAEJR cooperate with the Japanese in carrying out a "satisfactory registration" and barring newcomers from entering the area.[115]

After conferring with the Japanese authorities in Shanghai, Godfrey Phillips sent letters on August 14, 1939, to the CAEJR, members of the consular body, and three leading shipping companies informing them of the council's decision "to forbid any further entry into the International Settlement of refugees from Europe." Phillips also wrote the French consul general and expressed his hope that the French Municipal Administration could take a "common policy" to "forbid any further influx into the French Concession of refugees from Europe" as well.[116]

B. S. Barbash & Company, an import-export shipping group operating in Shanghai, contacted the secretary of the SMC twice in August 1939 to ask for his instructions about how to handle refugees to Shanghai who possessed official Chinese visas. Phillips's answer was prompt and straightforward. He replied that "emigrants who have a Chinese visa are not excluded from the Council's prohibition."[117]

On the other hand, although the Japanese authorities clearly indicated "Jewish refugees" in official documents concerning the restriction of entry, the Municipal Council used the ambiguous term "European refugees" instead. Since the "European refugees" arriving in Shanghai during World War II were mostly Jews who escaped Nazi persecution, the SMC obviously tried to avoid applying the term "Jewish" to avoid accusations of anti-Semitism.

However, the Municipal Council's ambiguity confused shipping companies that were expected to assist the SMC in stopping "European refugees" from coming to Shanghai. On August 16, 1939, Butterfield & Swire attempted to seek "the precise definition of the term 'Refugees from Europe'" from the secretary of the SMC. The agents of Butterfield & Swire wondered whether the term was "applicable to any specific nationality" or if "it applied only to destitute person."[118] The secretary simply replied, "I hope that it will be possible in the near future for the Council to announce precise regulations covering the various points which you raise."[119]

Meanwhile, a Combined Committee was established on August 18 to cope with the Jewish refugee issue. The committee consisted of four members: vice consul M. G. Cattand, who represented the French Concession, Eduard Kann, for the CAEJR, Consul General Ishiguro of the Japanese consulate general, and E. T. Nash, assistant secretary of the SMC. The committee's mission was to "decide on the status of refugees" and "draw up rules and regulations governing the further influx" of Jewish refugees into Shanghai. In addition, secretary Godfrey Phillips made special comments indicating that cases such as refugees who were already in Shanghai and wished to invite their families from Europe would "receive the most sympathetic consideration of the committee."[120] In his interview with *North*

China Daily News on August 18, the secretary also emphasized that the committee would "specify clearly who will be considered a refugee and who will not."[121]

Although the Combined Committee was able to draft a "Provisional Arrangement regarding Entry into Shanghai of Central European Refugees" in September after a monthlong discussion, the definition of a "refugee" remained unsettled.[122] Despite the members' various efforts, they eventually took the advice of Eduard Kann to simply abandon the term "Jewish refugee" thereafter and use the expression "Central European refugees" for those "who were declared to be Jews in Germany, Italy and other countries."[123]

Meanwhile, the German and Italian acting consul generals in Shanghai quickly responded to Godfrey Phillips's letter of August 14 and protested against the council's decision to ban further entry of the European Jews into the city. Both consul generals stated that the Municipal Council's decision had no "validity" since it did not have "the full agreement of the Consular Body," at least from Germany and Italy. Nevertheless, they showed an understanding of the difficulties that the council was facing in Shanghai as a result of the influx of Jewish refugees. In addition, E. Bracklo, acting consul general for Germany, encouraged the council to allow those who had already boarded for Shanghai from Europe, those who were able to support themselves financially, and those who had families that already resided in Shanghai to enter the city.[124]

On October 22, 1939, two months after the Japanese authorities and the Municipal Council decided that they were to ban further entry of the European Jewish refugee into Shanghai, the two authorities reached an agreement to announce new immigration regulations. The Municipal Council declared its new policies, clearly taking German acting consul general's "advice" into account, in its press communiqué that the prohibition rules announced in August would not apply to refugees who belonged to the following categories: (1) people who had, "available for use in Shanghai," not less than $400 U.S. dollars for each adult, or not less than $100 U.S. dollars for each child who was younger than thirteen years old; (2) people who had "immediate family relations . . . of refugees of certified financial competency resident in Shanghai; or have a contract of employment with a resident in Shanghai; or intend to contract marriage with a resident in Shanghai." However, the communiqué also noted that these regulations were applicable only to refugees who attempted to enter "South of the Soochow [Suzhou] Creek," the portion of the International Settlement not controlled by the Japanese, and that refugees who wished to live in the Japanese-occupied areas needed to "comply with the regulations of the Japanese authorities."[125]

In response to refugees' pleas to bring their families from Europe, Japanese Consul General Miura notified the CAEJR that for "humanitarian" reasons, the Japanese authorities might make exceptions and allow the entry of such refugees "in limited numbers." In his letter to Ellis Hayim on October 28, Miura stated that only those who had entry permits "issued by the Japanese Consulate-General will be permitted to enter the Japanese-occupied part of the International Settlement." The new regulations also emphasized that applications for entry permits "by reason of family relations or other considerations should be made by a refugee of financial competency" who lived in the Japanese-controlled areas and was "registered with the Japanese naval authorities."[126]

On the other hand, the French Council, as the *Shanghai Times* reported on October 13, 1939, contended that they would grant no permits of any kind to "holders of German passports—Jews or Christians" to enter the French Concession because of the ongoing war between France and Germany.[127] Although the French authorities eventually decided to issue Jewish refugees immigration permits based on similar requirements of the Municipal Council from February 3, 1940, they soon closed the door of the French Concession to the Jewish refugees again in May 1940.[128] The investigators of the Shanghai Municipal Police believed that this was because the French Concession was "practically fully occupied" by refugees. They also hinted that the French authorities were to "prevent any 'fifth column' activities in the Concession that might be caused by the further influx of refugees."[129]

Although refugees who had sufficient funds "available for use in Shanghai" were able to receive entry permits from the SMC, David Kranzler explains that since most Jewish refugees from Germany were "penniless," they depended heavily on their relatives or friends in the United States and HICEM to prepare "such a large sum of money."[130] Meanwhile, the Special Branch of the Municipal Police, an intelligence unit, found this regulation was particularly "open to abuse." For instance, a family of four (including two adults and two children) might originally put up the required "landing money" of $1,000 in order to enter Shanghai. After several weeks of their arrival, they would use $400 of that money, which was supposed to support their lives in Shanghai, to apply for an entry permit from the Municipal Council for another person. The police investigators also discovered that many employment contracts were suspicious. The SMC's regulations were unable to effectively stop the further influx of Jewish refugees as it wished. As a result, by May 2, 1940, there were seventeen thousand Jewish refugees residing in the International Settlement, both north and south of Suzhou Creek, and the French Concession.[131]

Nevertheless, the entry permits to Shanghai, from both the SMC and the Japanese authorities, saved numerous Jewish lives. As the Municipal Police pointed out "Many refugees in Shanghai are in the unfortunate position of having relatives in Nazi occupied territories. . . . The issue of a permit has, it is realized, the effect of releasing men and women from concentration camps."[132] The entry permits, however, also had unexpected political uses. The Japanese authorities reportedly issued permits "quite freely" when they attempted to obtain more votes from Jewish residents during the election of the Municipal Council.[133]

The restrictions on the entry of Jewish refugees into Shanghai in the second half of 1939 indicated the considerable gap between the reality of the refugee problem in Shanghai and the ideal of the military "Jewish experts." Yasue and Inuzuka were unable to predict the difficulties in Shanghai that accompanied the coming of the Jewish refugees and the opposition from the international community, and even the local Jews. The Japanese authorities had no choice but to follow the decision of the international community to forbid the further influx of Jewish refugees and to reconsider their Jewish policy that had been decided by the Five Ministers' Conference in 1938.

Japanese-German Relations in 1938 and 1939: The Unrealized Dream of a Military Alliance

By mid- to late 1938, the Japanese military realized that the war in China was far from over, and that the Chinese could not be subjugated by military instruments alone.[134] At the time, the main concern of the Japanese government, as well as the army, was how to conclude "the China Incident." Escalation of the invasion of China and preparations for war against the USSR had already exceeded Japan's military capacities. The Japanese were hoping that an alliance with Germany would help to end the conflict in China soon. The Nazi regime, on the other hand, did not want to face Britain, France, and Russia simultaneously in Europe and was eager to cultivate Japan as an ally.[135]

The appointment of pro-Japanese Joachim Ribbentrop as the new German foreign minister in February 1938 played an important role in Germany's decision making toward East Asia. His predecessor, Freiherr von Neurath, was a product of the era of Sino-German cooperation. Neurath and his Foreign Office "had little sympathy for Hitler's pro-Japanese policy," and they attempted to stay impartial during the crisis in East Asia. Ribbentrop's pro-Japanese attitude, however, coincided with Hitler's.

Germany recognized Manchukuo diplomatically in 1938.[136] After Ribbentrop became foreign minister, the two of them overcame opposition from the Foreign Office and army and determined to ally with Japan.[137]

On November 25, 1938, the second anniversary of the Anti-Comintern Pact, Germany concluded a cultural agreement with Japan. The agreement was intended to advance Japanese-German cooperation and augment German influence over the Japanese in order to pave the way for a future military alliance.[138] The Japanese preferred that the alliance target only the Soviet Union. The Germans, however, desired a treaty aimed at the Soviet Union as well as the major Western democracies.[139]

The army, especially young and lower echelon officers, gave their full support to the alliance with Germany. Meanwhile, along with Foreign Minister Arita, navy minister Yonai Mitsumasa and vice minister Yamamoto Isoroku—moderate leaders who represented the navy's administrative group—resisted any alliance aimed against France and Britain. Unlike the army generals, the admirals appreciated that the United States backed the Western powers.[140] The Five Ministers' Conference held seventy-five meetings that addressed Germany's proposal for an unconditional military coalition; Yonai "risked his portfolio" and firmly opposed army minister Itagaki throughout these meetings.[141]

By spring 1939, the Japanese had seized Hainan Island and the Spratlys in the South China Sea. This expansion to the south further escalated tensions between Japan and the Western powers.[142] During the spring and summer of 1939, Japan and the USSR fought a "full-scale but unofficial" war at Nomonhan near the Manchurian-Mongolian border. Japan suffered a serious reversal in this battle. As historian Ernst Presseisen observes, it now became even clearer to Itagaki that "Japan could never hope to eliminate Russia's influence in Asia without the aid of an ally."[143] In addition, on June 14, the Japanese Army blockaded the British and French Concessions in Tianjin (Tientsin). This incident worsened Japan's already troubled relationship with the two nations.[144] Furthermore, on July 26, the U.S. government informed Tokyo that it would terminate the Japanese-U.S. Treaty of Commerce in six months. The increasing tensions between Japan and the Western powers in East Asia further drove the Japanese Army into a military alliance with Germany.

However, the Germans had other concerns during this period. Germany's rapprochement with the USSR was secretly under negotiation. On August 23, 1939, Germany's Non-Aggression Pact with Stalin's Soviet government shocked Tokyo. It clearly violated the spirit of the Anti-Comintern Pact between Germany, Japan, and Italy. Foreign Minister Arita called off meetings concerning Japan's military alliance with Germany. At this moment, even the army's enthusiasm for the alliance waned.[145] As Frank Iklé observes, the rest of 1939 and early 1940 "saw German-Japanese relations at their lowest ebb," and only Germany's military successes in Europe in May and June 1940 were able to "set the tide in the other direction."[146]

Although the army's attempt to establish a military alliance with Germany failed, the influence of the radical and pro-German groups in the military increased. Nevertheless, this unsuccessful attempt to establish a German-Japanese military alliance did not seem to have any immediate or significant impact on Yasue and Inuzuka's Jewish policy during the rest of 1939.

On October 28, 1939, Captain Inuzuka and Colonel Yasue spoke once again at the meeting of the Committee on the Muslim and Jewish Problem. Inuzuka emphasized that the prohibition on the entry of Jewish refugees into Shanghai did not hurt Japan's reputation; it actually worked in Japan's favor. He explained that, most important, the regulations could restrain world Jewry since the ten thousand European Jewish refugees under Japan's control in Shanghai were, in a way, hostages. Japan could also use the Jewish refugees as a bargaining chip with world Jewish leaders in the future.[147]

Regarding prominent Jewish leaders with British citizenship, Captain Inuzuka said he was satisfied with their cooperative attitude. Inuzuka pointed out to his audience that Japan was gradually taking control of Shanghai because Britain and France were busy fighting their war in Europe and were unable to intervene in East Asian affairs. In addition, Japan's control of China's hinterland and coastline caused a considerable decline in Jewish business. Inuzuka believed that all these factors made Jewish leaders in Shanghai realize that Japan was the only power on which they could depend. He said he had also met with senior members who were highly respected by the Shanghai Jewish community, such as Victor Sassoon's uncle, D. E. J. Abraham, and Sir Ellis Kadoorie. Inuzuka had promised these elders that although Japan's relations with Britain were deteriorating, the Japanese authorities considered Jews with British nationality simply Jews and would protect them. These strategies seemed to help him win the trust of the elders, and Abraham even invited Inuzuka to celebrate the Jewish New Year. The captain concluded his remarks by saying that Japan's economic schemes, including that concerning the introduction of Jewish capital, would not make any progress unless these psychological efforts succeeded.[148]

Captain Inuzuka also told the members of the committee that he seemed to have accomplished a great deal in the way of propaganda toward the United States. For the first time, he had an opportunity to meet with and influence prominent American Jewish businessmen in Shanghai. These businessmen, Inuzuka said, agreed completely with his plan to employ a barter system between Japan and the United States using Jewish companies as middlemen. Some of them even insinuated that as long as Japan could help to improve their trade with China, American Jewish businessmen would not complain. They also volunteered to talk to American Jewish leaders about this plan after their return to the United States. On the other hand, Inuzuka said he had attempted to use the Jewish media in East Asia to direct propaganda toward the United States. For example, the editor-in-chief of *Israel's Messenger*, the official monthly organ of the Shanghai Zionist Association, and some Zionist scholars cooperated with the Japanese. *Israel's Messenger* was circulated in the United States at the time, and it successfully implied to Americans that its opinions were the most authoritative from East Asia.[149]

Colonel Yasue's speech to the committee concentrated on the establishment of a Jewish settlement. Two days before this meeting, Yasue had discussed the settlement plan with the vice minister of the army. He was repeating his old tactic: drafting a policy himself and using the army official in Tokyo to convey it to the central government. The colonel pointed out that it would be of greater value to Japan to have the Jewish refugees petition the Japanese government for such a plan rather than have the Japanese provide them a settlement directly. Subsequently, Japan should accept their request with certain conditions attached.[150]

Yasue attempted to use the forthcoming Third Far Eastern Jewish Conference in Manchuria to facilitate his plan. Since Jewish leaders in East Asia would come to this conference at the end of December 1939, Yasue planned to draft a petition and let the conference present it as an official resolution. In addition, Yasue hoped to arrange for some Jewish representatives from the United States to attend the conference so that he could add to the resolution that American Jews, who had close ties with the Jews in East Asia, agreed with the settlement plan. He believed that this would be very effective propaganda with the Americans.[151]

The resolution of the Third Far Eastern Jewish Conference in December 1939 was subtly different in important ways from that of the previous conferences. It was the turn of the East Asian Jews to use their "friendly" relationship and cooperation with the Japanese to help their coreligionists. The East Asian Jews pleaded with the Japanese and Manchukuoan governments to try their best to help European Jewish refugees travel to East Asia, for instance, by issuing them transit visas.[152]

The Japanese authorities in Manchuria accepted this request. The Manchukuoan foreign minister's telegram to his ambassador to Tokyo proves that in late December 1939, Japan relaxed its visa regulations for Jews who had permits to Shanghai. The foreign minister wrote that until then Manchukuoan officials allowed only valued refugees, such as technicians, or those who were not involved in political movements, to enter, and they issued transit visas to those who had entry visas for other destinations. Meanwhile, in response to Japan's relaxation of the visa regulations in late December, 1939, the Manchukuoan government decided that it would also ease its policy for handling the transit visas. The Japanese, the foreign minister explained, requested Manchukuo's cooperation to issue transit visas to Jews who possessed the following: (1) entry permits obtained from the authorities of the International Settlement or the French Concession; and (2) Japanese transit visas (through Manchuria).[153]

Conclusion

Army colonel Yasue Norihiro and navy captain Inuzuka Koreshige, the "Jewish experts" in Manchuria and Shanghai, were the principal architects of Japan's Jewish policy in the late 1930s. Although grounded in anti-Semitic ideas, Yasue and Inuzuka's policy in 1938 and 1939 indirectly saved the lives of the Jewish refugees from Europe. In August 1939, the Japanese occupation authorities reluctantly decided to prevent the influx of Jewish refugees into the city under mounting pressure from Shanghai's international communities, and even the local Jews. Nevertheless, another three thousand European Jews, who were eligible for entry permits issued by the SMC, the Japanese consulate general, and the French Concession, successfully fled Nazi-occupied Europe to Shanghai after the regulations became effective.

The reason the military "experts" were able to treat Jewish refugees leniently and make Jewish policy contradictory to that of their ally, Germany, was partly that Japan and Germany had not yet reached an agreement on establishing an official military alliance during this period. In the spring of 1938, the Japanese Army realized that it was impossible for Japan to end the war with China immediately. The army attempted to create a military alliance with Germany and hoped to conclude "the China Incident" shortly with the help of Germans.

The German government, on the other hand, wanted Japan's assistance in order to avoid confronting all the major Western powers at once. The Germans then proposed to Tokyo an alliance aimed against the Soviet Union, Great Britain, and France. Although young and junior army officers gave their full support to an unconditional alliance with the Nazis, the civilian foreign minister and navy minister strongly opposed the plan and insisted that any such alliance should be directed primarily against the Soviet Union. The navy admirals were well aware that the United States supported the Western powers, and they attempted to avoid a conflict with the Americans.

In addition to the resistance from the Foreign Ministry and the navy, the conclusion of the German-Soviet Non-Aggression Pact on August 23, 1939, also played an important role in shattering the army's dream of a military alliance with Germany. The failure of this attempt also delayed radical and pro-German groups in the military from coming to power. Until the conclusion of the Tripartite Pact in September 1940, Yasue and Inuzuka were able to continue their original Jewish policy.

Because Japan's Jewish policy of 1938 and 1939 reflected the strategic needs of the military, the development of the war and the changing of war aims naturally affected the policy itself. After the conclusion of the Tripartite Pact with Germany and Italy in September 1940, pro-German factions in both the military and the government gained power. A war with the United State became inevitable; Japan's efforts to maintain a good relationship with the Americans no longer made any sense. Yasue and Inuzuka's Jewish policy thus became meaningless for Japan's newest plan for war.

CHAPTER 4

The Tripartite Pact and Japan's Policy toward the Shanghai Jewish Refugee Issue, January 1940–August 1945

In July 1939, Captain Inuzuka and Colonel Yasue proposed that the Japanese government establish a settlement for European Jewish refugees in Shanghai. Through this settlement plan, the "Jewish experts" attempted to favorably impress world Jewry (American Jews in particular), attract international Jewish capital, and improve Japan's relations with the United States. More specifically, they believed that American Jews were financially and politically influential and could help to change the U.S. government's attitude toward Japan. Essentially, the Japanese tried to create a Jewish settlement in the occupied city and use it to benefit Japan's imperial endeavors in Asia.

While the Japanese government contemplated this settlement for the Shanghai Jews, Japan's relationship with the United States further deteriorated. Tamura Kōzō, a Japanese businessman in New York, formulated a plan to settle thirty thousand German Jewish refugees in Japanese-occupied China, a project he hoped in part would improve the climate of Japanese-U.S. relations. American Jewish leaders promised that they would provide financial support for the project, and from late 1939 to summer 1940, Tamura worked closely with them and the Japanese "experts."

Meanwhile, the failure of the Japanese Army's attempt to form a military alliance with Germany in 1939 did not stop the increasing influence of radical and pro-German groups in both the military and the government. From late 1939 to early 1940, some military officials publicly challenged and criticized Inuzuka and Yasue's Jewish policy. Germany's victory in Western Europe in the spring of 1940 successfully revived the pro-German groups' passion for a military alliance with the Axis powers.

On September 27, 1940, Japan signed the Tripartite Pact with Germany and Italy. The alliance was necessary for the Germans because they believed that Japan would keep the Americans busy in the Pacific and distracted from the European battlefield. At the same time, the treaty enhanced—from Tokyo's perspective—Japan's capacity to gain access to Southeast Asia, a new source for the Japanese military of natural resources, and therefore allowed Japan to circumvent American economic sanctions.

Less than two weeks after the conclusion of the Tripartite Pact, the Japanese government immediately began revising its Jewish policy. The strategic situation in late 1940 was entirely different from that of late 1938, when Japan set up its original Jewish policy based on the counsel of the "Jewish experts." In late 1938, the opportunity still existed for Japan to improve its relations with the United States and Britain, and for that purpose Inuzuka and Yasue's plan for using the Jews made a certain sense. But Japan's alliance with Germany and Italy in late 1940 produced a different situation and made a U.S.-Japanese confrontation more likely than ever before. Also, since Japan's Jewish policy rested heavily on the requirements of the military, the changing strategic situation naturally resulted in a change in Japan's policy toward the Jewish refugees. Although the majority of Japanese officials had tolerated Inuzuka and Yasue's plans for using the Jews until then, they no longer wanted to oppose their German allies' long standing anti-Semitism. The "Jewish experts'" theories became unacceptable. Inuzuka and Yasue were removed from their positions one after another in 1940, and they were subsequently unable either to decide or influence Japan's new Jewish policy.

The conclusion of the Tripartite Pact ended Japan's hopes not only for a friendly relationship with the United States, but also for Tamura's Jewish settlement plan. The military alliance immediately provoked American hostility against Japan. From this moment, there was little Tokyo could do to salvage its relationship with Washington. Japan did not have a chance to use the Jews under their control to ease the tensions between the two countries. Consequently, the Jewish refugees in Shanghai lost their value to the Japanese. After Japan's Pearl Harbor attack, a ghetto in Shanghai, rather than a settlement, was established for the Jews.

Japan's Jewish Settlement Plan,
December 1939–September 1940

The Third Far Eastern Jewish Conference convened in Harbin December 23–26, 1939. The representatives of the conference accepted a petition, drafted by Colonel Yasue, to the Japanese government for a Jewish settlement in China as a secret resolution.[1] They sent a telegram, also drafted by the colonel, on December 30 to Jewish leaders in the United States and asked American Jewish organizations to appeal to the Japanese government for support for the settlement plan as well.[2]

As described in the previous chapter, the "Jewish experts" enthusiastically initiated their settlement plan beginning in the summer of 1939. However, as Japanese historian Maruyama Naoki observes in *Taiheiyō Sensō to Shanhai no Yudaya nanmin* [The Pacific War and the Shanghai Jewish Refugees], as early as in 1933, N. E. B. Ezra had already proposed that the Japanese government resettle oppressed European Jews in Manchuria.[3] Lew Zikman also presented a plan in early 1939 to transplant Jewish refugees to the area.[4] Both Ezra and Zikman attempted to use Jewish capital in exchange for Japan's accommodation of their coreligionists from Europe. They submitted their plans before the military "Jewish experts" systematically carried out their policies for exploiting the Jews; these schemes eventually failed partly owing to the lack of effective support from the "experts."

N. E. B. Ezra was the editor-in-chief and founder of *Israel's Messenger*. In his letter of September 15, 1933, to Japan's vice minister of foreign affairs, Shigemitsu Mamoru, Ezra explained that because of Nazi Germany's persecution of the Jews, world Jewry was facing a serious problem finding refuge for European Jews. Ezra proposed to help one thousand families or fifty thousand people immigrate to Manchukuo. If the Japanese government would agree to accept the refugees, he assumed that world Jewry would not have any problem financing the immigration.[5]

Ezra also sent copies of his letter to Shigemitsu to Jewish leaders in Britain and the United States in an appeal for support. On September 17, he wrote Israel Cohen of the World Zionist Organization in London. Ezra emphasized that Manchukuo would be a perfect place to establish a "Jewish Center" for future immigration, and that Japan had never persecuted Jews in East Asia.[6] However, Cohen responded a month later and opposed Ezra's plan. He pointed out that it was inappropriate to relocate Jewish refugees to Manchukuo, which was conquered by the Japanese. He was also concerned that the unsolved Soviet-Japanese conflict in the region would cause more instability. Cohen predicted that Jewish refugees would rather explore the possibilities of immigrating to other European countries, or the United States and Australia, before considering Manchukuo.[7]

When Ezra presented his Jewish settlement plan to world Jewish leaders in 1933, European Jews were still able to flee to neighboring countries or the United States. Therefore, it was natural that Jews would prefer other Western nations with which they shared a similar lifestyle and culture. East Asia was never the first choice for the refugees; they came to China beginning in 1938 simply because it was the last remaining place that would take them in.

In addition, Jewish leaders in the West, such as Israel Cohen and Rabbi Stephen Wise, president of the American Jewish Congress, initially opposed an approach by the Jews in East Asia to the Japanese. They believed Japan's invasion of China was immoral and that Jews should not be involved with the Japanese for any reason. Although Ezra also wrote Rabbi Wise about the settlement plan, there is no evidence that he ever heard back from the rabbi. Wise condemned Japan's invasion of China and actively supported a boycott of Japanese products in early 1937. As Pamela Rotner Sakamoto points out, "Wise viewed Germany and Japan as fellow fascists."[8]

In October 1933, Ezra had an opportunity to meet in Shanghai with Sugimura Yotarō, Japan's former under-secretary-general for the League of Nations. Sugimura avoided committing himself to support Ezra's settlement plan, but encouraged him to discuss it further with Vice Foreign Minister Shigemitsu.[9] However, the Jewish Telegraphic Agency in Tokyo reported to the *Jewish Daily Bulletin* in New York on August 6, 1934, that Sugimura Yotarō held a press conference at which he stated that "Japan is desirous of having 50,000 German Jewish refugees as settlers in Manchukuo."[10] The same report also appeared a week later in the Viennese daily *Neue Freie Presse*.[11]

Foreign Minister Hirota Kōki immediately denied the rumor. He stressed that it was likely that Ezra misunderstood Sugimura.[12] When Ezra visited Shigemitsu in late August 1934 in Japan, Shigemitsu also made it clear that the Japanese government "would not consider the proposal."[13] He explained to Ezra that Manchukuo had just been established and had a lot of internal problems that needed to be solved. Therefore, the government was not in a position to deal with the Jewish settlement plan.[14]

The Japanese government in the early 1930s was indifferent to the Jewish refugees. At least, the Japanese did not yet have any intention of using them. Only when Yasue and Inuzuka emerged toward the end of the decade as military "Jewish experts" and actively promoted the exploitation of the Jews did Japan take the Jewish settlement plan seriously. In March 1939, the central government decided to let the "experts" investigate the Jewish refugee issue in Shanghai and explore further a plan to establish a Jewish settlement.

In April 1939, Lew Zikman, the sugar merchant in Harbin, presented another plan to transplant two hundred families, about six hundred people, who were already in Shanghai, to Manchukuo. Zikman offered to "organize some sort of enterprise" in Harbin and use Jewish refugees as laborers. He emphasized that this enterprise would contribute to the development of Manchukuo's industry. Zikman also promised that if the Japanese government favored the plan, he would negotiate with American refugee relief agencies to solicit $150,000 to $200,000 for the region to support the plan financially.[15] However, Ueda Kenkichi, Japan's ambassador to Manchukuo, worried that the transplantation of two hundred families would result in the further influx of Jews, and that Zikman might not be able to obtain such a large amount of American capital. At the end of April 1939, he eventually declined Zikman's proposal.[16]

When Zikman presented his settlement plan to the Japanese authorities in Manchuria, Yasue, Inuzuka, and Ishiguro had just begun their investigation of the deteriorating Jewish refugee situation in Shanghai. The joint committee eventually submitted its final report to the central government on July 7, 1939. In this report, the "Jewish experts" officially proposed that their government establish a settlement for Jewish refugees in Japanese-occupied China. Zikman had missed his chance.

Before the joint committee submitted its report, the members held a meeting in early June 1939 with concerned officials from the Ministries of the Army, Navy, Foreign Affairs, and Kō-Ain,[17] or the Asia Development Board. Regarding the Jewish settlement, the joint committee suggested that the Japanese government consider establishing it either in areas adjacent to Shanghai, such as Pudong, or in locations away from Shanghai, such as Chongming Island, at the mouth of the Yangtze River, and Hainan Island in the South China Sea. The committee expected that not only the local Shanghai Jewish community but also world Jewry would contribute financially to the plan.[18] Certainly the settlement plan aimed to attract Jewish investment.

The parties concerned responded differently to the potential locations identified at the meeting. The navy preferred to establish the Jewish settlement in Shanghai and requested that militarily important locations, such as the islands of Chongming and Hainan, should be excluded from final consideration.[19] This modification was in fact convenient for Captain Inuzuka. Since the Naval Landing Party controlled the city at the time, Inuzuka would therefore be in a better position to control and exploit the Jewish refugees. Kō-Ain supported the navy's suggestion. Its officials also cautioned Tokyo that for security reasons, the government should always keep a close eye on the Jews so that they would not be able to conspire with third parties against Japan or challenge Japan's control over them in the future.[20]

On the other hand, officials from the Japanese "Central China Expeditionary Army" informed Colonel Yasue that since they wanted financial support from Jews for the reconstruction of Shanghai, instead of in Pudong, which was separated from the city by the Huangpu River, they would rather locate the settlement in areas that would soon be merged with the city and under the control of the Shanghai mayor of the puppet Weixin zhengfu,[21] or Reform Government. In case the settlement needed to be established in another location to accommodate more refugees, the Central China Expeditionary Army preferred to locate it in Pudong, Chongming Island, or Hainan Island.[22]

Colonel Yasue, however, suggested that if it were necessary to relocate Jews somewhere other than Shanghai, the settlement should be built in the form of a Jewish autonomous state similar to Birobidzhan, the capital of the Jewish autonomous state within the Soviet Union, and be placed under Japanese "protection" through the Weixin zhengfu.[23] Since the mission of the joint committee was to study the Jewish refugee issue in Shanghai and its solution, it was difficult for Yasue to claim that the settlement should be established under his influence in Manchuria.

After Inuzuka, Yasue and Ishiguro submitted their Joint Report to the central government on July 7, 1939, the Committee on the Muslim and Jewish Problem held several meetings to discuss it. At the meeting of July 18, the committee decided that it required further research on the Jewish settlement plan in Shanghai. Although the local authorities had agreed that it was necessary to establish such a settlement, there were still disagreements regarding its location.[24]

While the Japanese government was studying a settlement for Shanghai Jews in the summer of 1939, its relationship with the United States further deteriorated. In January 1939, the U.S. government decided to forbid the export of aircraft parts to Japan. In July the Americans notified the Japanese government they intended to abrogate the United States–Japanese Treaty of Commerce and Navigation. Maruyama argues that Japan's difficulty in obtaining supplies such as machinery was an important reason that motivated Tamura Kōzō's scheme for a Jewish settlement in late 1939.[25] Tamura, a longtime representative of Japanese canning manufacturer Tōyō Seikan in New York, assumed that "Jewish influence in the U.S. is very great and that the Jews could help create friendly relations between the U.S. and Japan."[26]

Tamura Kōzō's Jewish settlement plan garnered more attention from both the Japanese officials, the "experts" in particular, and the American Jewish leaders compared to the proposals of Ezra and Zikman. This was a result of the changing situation in Shanghai and in the world. First, the Japanese government accepted the idea of establishing a settlement for Shanghai Jewish refugees and launched a serious investigation by Inuzuka, Yasue, and Ishiguro. Second, because of the deterioration of U.S.-Japanese relations, the "experts" determined to use the Jewish refugees to pressure American Jews, who allegedly wielded great political power, to help ease the tensions between the two countries. Finally, the American Jewish leaders eventually realized that the European Jews were desperate to find refuge, and they were not in a position to reject any possibility.

In April 1939, Tamura had met in New York with the president of Long Island Machinery, Frank Garson, the chairman of the Refugee Committee, a "Mr. Grunbaum," and Rabbi Stephen Wise. When he returned to Japan later, Tamura delivered a message from American Jews to the Foreign Ministry, army, and navy. The Jewish leaders proposed that if Japan would allow thirty thousand German Jewish refugees to settle in Japanese-controlled territory during the next two years, American Jews would consider providing Japan with financial and material aid.[27]

The ministries were intrigued by the plan. On November 11, 1939, the Committee on the Muslim and Jewish Problem invited Tamura to a meeting. Through Tamura, the committee attempted to use the Jewish refugee issue in Shanghai to sound out the opinion of American Jewish leaders toward Japan. Following the meeting, Tamura traveled to Shanghai to meet with local army and navy officers. The military was reportedly "greatly enthusiastic" about the settlement plan.[28]

During his visit to Shanghai in November, Tamura personally wrote to Frank Garson, since he had not heard from the American Jews after April's meeting.[29] The American Jewish leaders, on the other hand, were also busy preparing for their negotiations with Tokyo. Bernhard Kahn, the honorary chairman of the American Jewish Joint Distribution Committee's executive council in Europe, reported to Paul Baerwald, the chairman of the "Joint" in New York, in late December that during his recent meeting with Garson, Kahn requested that Garson obtain the following information from Tamura before any negotiations had started: "1. How many refugees Japan would accept; 2. What type of people; 3. Where the Japanese government would like them to settle; 4. What assurances can be given for their undisturbed settlement." Kahn also informed Garson that as long as the Jewish leaders received this information, they would try to have the members of "Joint" in Yokohama, Japan, and "some representatives of Wall

Street, take up the question with the Japanese government."[30] Garson forwarded the questions to Tamura, making it clear that he could not send a delegation to Japan unless he received "satisfactory" replies to the questions and that the invitation should come from "the government or reliable organization."[31]

However, Foreign Minister Nomura was uncertain about Tamura's proposal. On November 16, 1939, he informed the Japanese ambassador to the United States, Horinouchi Kensuke, of the plan. The foreign minister pointed out that the Jewish settlement plan was an issue not only of receiving refugees but also of impinging on Japan's relationship with the United States. Nomura therefore ordered the ambassador to investigate Tamura's credibility and asked his opinion of the feasibility of the Tamura Plan.[32]

Ambassador Horinouchi replied a week later and confirmed Tamura's reliability. Nevertheless, he also raised a new matter that the foreign minister had neglected: it would be difficult to obtain the U.S. government's approval for the Jewish investment in the settlement plan.[33] The ambassador's judgment was sound. As discussed earlier, Maurice William's plan to establish a Jewish settlement in China in the same period failed because the American Jewish leaders were unable to gain support from their government. In any case, the American Jews were loyal to their country. Although they were willing to help their coreligionists, they recognized the need to obey their government first. As Bernhard Kahn stated, in fields other than religion, American Jews "would not react in any other way than as Americans."[34]

It appears that the Japanese government took Horinouchi's warning seriously. In spite of the army's and navy's preliminary "great interest" in Tamura's plan, they decided not to involve themselves "too deeply" in the problem.[35] Instead, the local army and navy authorities in Shanghai started questioning and complaining about Inuzuka and Yasue's Jewish policy as well as the settlement plan.

Consul General Miura in Shanghai reported to Foreign Minister Nomura on December 29, 1939, the result of a liaison conference among the Ministries of the Army, Navy, and Foreign Affairs concerning Tamura's proposal. Miura believed that the opinions expressed by army and navy officers at the meeting indicated the general opinion of the local military authorities. According to the report, Sakurai Shōzō, a unit chief of staff of the Central China Expeditionary Army, stated that he was informed by the Ministry of the Army of the settlement plan, and described it as "a complete surprise" to him. Although "it seems that someone pushed Tokyo to make such a decision," Sakurai continued, "I have no idea what it is about." In addition, he added that the plan to establish a Jewish settlement in the army-occupied area (in Shanghai) was "unexpected and extremely troublesome."[36]

Nakamura Toshiyuki, a vice chief of staff of the China Theater Fleet, also shared Sakurai's view. Nakamura demanded that the Jewish policy in Shanghai be discussed among, and decided by, the local authorities concerned. He also insisted that it was "absolutely impossible to allow" those who claimed to be Jewish problem "experts" to apply a Jewish policy "arbitrarily" to Shanghai. Nevertheless, Nakamura admitted that the Jewish refugee issue was important and should not be neglected.[37]

The situation became unfavorable for the Tamura Plan. Japan's Jewish policy was originally based on the strategic needs of the military, and the Jewish settlement plan was no exception. Therefore, if the military challenged or disagreed with the current Jewish policy, it would be difficult for the Japanese government to pursue it further.

Foreign Minister Nomura then cabled Ambassador Horinouchi in Washington once again on January 6, 1940. Nomura explained, "Not only did you express in your last telegram that there was little possibility for this plan [to succeed], but also that both the Army and Navy changed their minds." According to the foreign minister, military officials in Tokyo, Shanghai, and Manchuria were now reluctant to consider the Tamura Plan, and their negative opinions on the exploitation of the Jews became stronger. Even the Jewish communities in Shanghai, the expected location for the settlement, were unenthusiastic.[38] The foreign minister's message reflected the fact that the Japanese government's original interest in Tamura's proposal had evaporated.

Meanwhile, Colonel Yasue did not give up his hope for a Jewish settlement in Manchuria. The colonel once again required help from researchers at the SMR in implementing his Jewish policy. Returning from the Third Far Eastern Jewish Conference at the beginning of 1940, Yasue assigned the SMR's Special Research Team to investigate issues concerning the establishment of a Jewish settlement. The Special Research Team completed a report in May 1940 and sent it to the central government in June. The report anticipated that the settlement required an area that should be able to accommodate between thirty thousand and seventy thousand refugees, since the researchers believed that in addition to newcomers, the current twenty thousand Jews themselves would "increase naturally" in the future.[39] The settlement was also expected to be "an autonomous city" while at the same time "a developing satellite town of an existing metropolis." It was intended to have its own commercial and industrial zones as well.[40]

In October 1940, consul Shimomura Hitsujirō in Suifenhe, a city in northeastern Heilongjiang Province on the Chinese-Russian border, sent a top-secret telegram to the Japanese ambassador to Manchukuo concerning "The Current Situation of the Jewish Autonomous State [in the Soviet Union]." The report provided information on the autonomous state's medical and education system, media, and the Second and Third Five-Year Plans for Industry. The report also drew a brief picture of everyday life in Birobidzhan. Unlike the May report, which was sent to the Foreign Ministry by Colonel Yasue through the consul general in Shanghai, the name of the Special Research Team did not appear in this telegram. Instead, Consul Shimomura noted cryptically that the research information was "obtained by a certain institute in the area."[41] In Manchuria in the early 1940s, this institute could only be the Special Research Team of the SMR.

Although Yasue had once again used the SMR's research to help him convince the Japanese government to set up a Jewish settlement in Manchuria, he did not succeed this time. After Japan concluded the Tripartite Pact in September 1940 with Germany and Italy, Tokyo decided to change its existing Jewish policy; pro-German groups in both the government and military would not allow a Jewish settlement in Japanese-occupied China. The research report of October 1940 seemed to be Yasue's last attempt at this issue. Being aware of the pressure from the pro-German groups, perhaps Yasue ordered the Special Research Team not to reveal in the report itself and its relationship with the Colonel.

Meanwhile, Captain Inuzuka was transferred from active duty to the naval reserve in January 1940. Still, he worked on Jewish matters and stayed in Shanghai as a part-time naval employee. Foreign Minister Nomura strongly suggested that Consul General Miura in the city should hire Inuzuka to work part time for the consulate general as well, so that it would expedite communications between the two ministries.[42]

While still in Shanghai, Inuzuka did not miss any opportunity to promote his Jewish policy. On January 19, 1940, under the captain's leadership, the Office of the Naval Attaché in Shanghai submitted two investigative reports to the consul general. In "Explanation of Several Questions on Maneuvers with Respect to American Jews," Captain Inuzuka responded to the criticisms of Tamura's settlement plan for Jewish refugees. He pointed out that the criticisms and suspicions came from the "lack of knowledge" of Jews and their current situation. As an "expert" who had long been doing research on Jews, Inuzuka once again emphasized the importance of making use of the refugees. According to Inuzuka, since Japan was at a crucial moment in the war, "if we accept thirty thousand Jews within our sphere of influence, it is like we are holding them hostage." "In addition to taking advantage of their wealth," the captain believed that Japan would be able to "use their own weapons to point at the chests" of world Jewry. Inuzuka concluded that the acceptance of thirty thousand Jews would increase Japan's national strength. Japan, on the other hand, would not have much to lose.[43]

However, Captain Inuzuka was not able to silence those who thoroughly opposed the exploitation of the Jews. An officer named Hamano, of the intelligence agency of the Central China Expeditionary Army, authored a classified study at the beginning of March 1940. He disagreed with the Tamura Plan and concluded that the Japanese authorities should forbid further Jewish refugees from entering the army-controlled areas in central China and transport those who currently resided in the region to other places. He called the "Jewish problem experts" "Jewishized Japanese" who had "gotten involved in Jewish propaganda and ideology without noticing it." He believed that it was a good example of "going out for wool and coming home shorn."[44]

Hamano's statement outraged Inuzuka. On March 27, the captain fought back. He labeled Hamano's argument "a wild remark based on shallow and superficial fantasy." Inuzuka first defended Japan's Jewish policy decided by the Five Ministers' Conference. He emphasized that Japan's policy should be neither anti-Jewish nor pro-Jewish; it should be established based on Japan's "unique and impartial position." "Although we claimed the so-called use of Jews," he added, "it is not a policy of temporizing the Jews. [We] extend a helping hand to the Wandering Jew so that they could voluntarily cooperate with us in building peace in the East. It will also serve Japan's great purpose to present guidelines domestically and internationally for solving the Jewish problem—a cancer on the world—and to contribute to world peace."[45]

Inuzuka also pointed out that Western countries took advantage of Jewish financial power on one hand and persecuted Jews on the other. Therefore, their Jewish policy was selfish, and they eventually suffered from the "Jewish Peril." The captain believed that Japan's approach toward the Jewish problem should be different. The Jewish refugees under Japan's control were like hostages from the point of view of their coreligionists. Because other Jews understood that as long as the Japanese did not persecute Jewish refugees in East Asia, if they conducted anti-Japanese propaganda in other parts of the world, Japan must take revenge on East Asian Jews.[46]

The example of how Jewish leaders in Shanghai reacted to an anti-Japanese speech by Victor Sassoon in New York on February 24, 1940, proved that Inuzuka was right. According to the captain, the local Jewish leaders, fully aware that Japan comprehended their weakness, were panicked and started to worry about what would happen to them in the future. They published an article expressing their appreciation for Japan's kindness in a local English newspaper less than a week after Sassoon's speech. The thanks from Shanghai Jews were "sincere." Michel Speelman and Ellis Hayim, joint chairmen of the Committee for the Assistance of European Jewish Refugees, not only proclaimed their gratitude at a conference with the Japanese press, but also sent cables and letters to the headquarters of the Jewish Relief Committees in New York and Paris "with the suggestion that the offices not miss a chance to express their appreciation to Japan."[47]

Although Inuzuka desperately tried to justify his Jewish policy, he did not aim to save Jews. The captain was fighting to maintain the current policy so that he could continue to take advantage of the Shanghai Jewish refugees. Inuzuka never lost his faith in Jewish financial and political power and was determined to use it to benefit Japan's war effort. At the same time, the captain never abandoned his conviction that the Jews themselves constituted a "cancer on the world."

In the following months of summer 1940, as Consul General Miura noted in his secret report to foreign minister Matsuoka Yōsuke, Inuzuka and Yasue attempted to use a German-Jewish refugee, Karl Kindermann, in Tokyo to approach rabbi Stephen Wise, "the supreme leader of the American Jews," about the settlement plan.[48] It seemed that the "Jewish experts" were eventually able to change Rabbi Wise's attitude toward Japan. Although Wise firmly opposed any contact between the East Asian Jews and the Japanese until the late 1930s, he not only involved himself in the Tamura Plan from late 1939 but also expressed his willingness to cooperate with Japan thereafter.

In his letter of June 7, 1940, to a Japanese official named "Niwa," Kindermann repeatedly emphasized that Rabbi Wise was "one of the most influential" political figures in the United States and a "very close friend of President Roosevelt." Kindermann also believed that Wise could "be very useful for Japanese interests." He further explained that in a private letter from Wise to Clarence Pickett, executive secretary of the American Friends Service Committee, Wise stated "his resolution to become a [sic] open-declared friend of Japan if the Japanese government is really interested to start the refugee settlement in Manchukuo." It appeared to Kindermann that Soviet and Nazi propaganda had colored Wise's misgivings about Japan. Kindermann told the Japanese that he could do no more to help on this; it all depended on Japan's policy.[49]

Kindermann also attached a letter he had received from Rabbi Wise to "Mr. Niwa." Wise responded on June 10 to Kindermann's concerns over the issue of the Jewish settlement plan. The rabbi clearly stated that "any offer to settle Jewish refugees in Japan, which would come from authoritative sources in Japan, would certainly receive the fullest consideration of Jewish organizations." However, he also emphasized that "any negotiation to be undertaken by any American Jewish organization with regard to Jewish immigration to and settlement in Japan would first have to be submitted to the State Department in Washington for its approval or rejection."[50]

The "Jewish experts" were satisfied with Wise's letter and hoped that it would have a positive influence on local Jewish leaders and *Zaibatsu* in Shanghai.[51] It seems that between late 1939 and summer 1940 Rabbi Wise eventually realized the difficulties that European Jews were facing in seeking a haven, and he concluded that the most important order of business for Jewish refugees was to survive, even if this meant that the Jews had to deal with the Japanese. Although the rabbi himself was determined to help his fellow Jews, only the American government could make the final decision about whether or not to support the settlement plan. Nevertheless, Maruyama points out that it is hard to imagine that the State Department would actually allow such negotiations, tantamount to an American recognition of Japan's invasion of China, to happen.[52] Furthermore, any efforts from either the Japanese "experts" or the American Jewish leaders to resettle European Jewish refugees to East Asia appeared to be too late. One month later in September 1940, Japan, Germany, and Italy signed the Tripartite Pact and formally established a military alliance.

The Tripartite Pact and Revision of Japan's Jewish Policy

Although the army's attempt to establish a military alliance with Germany failed in 1939, the influence of the radical and pro-German groups in both the military and the government increased. The criticisms of Inuzuka and Yasue's settlement plan from the military at the end of 1939 and in spring1940 reflected this situation. The beginning of the Second World War in Europe in September 1939 and Germany's victory in Western Europe in the spring of 1940 greatly inspired the pro-German groups in Japan.

Inuzuka and Yasue's insistence that Japan should not follow the Axis powers' Jewish policy but should instead exploit the Jewish refugees in China was now inconsistent with Japan's strategic situation in the second half of 1940. Following Germany's military victories in the spring of 1940, the army and the navy in Japan were eventually able to overcome their disagreements and once again pursue a military alliance with the Axis powers. The military leaders considered Japan's relationships with Germany and Italy more important than that with the United States. As a result, they could no longer sanction Inuzuka and Yasue's Jewish policy.

The two military services in Japan, the army and the navy, were never a monolith in the first half of the twentieth century. There was constant competition not only between the services, but also within the ranks of the army and the navy. The two services always worked to build up their arsenals and competed for budgetary resources. From the early twentieth century, the army considered Russia, a great land power, its primary rival, while the navy perceived the United States, a great sea power, its most important potential adversary. Fujiwara Akira argues that the conflict between the two services and the lack of unified national defense policy allowed the military to pursue its irrational goal of preparing to confront both nations even though Japan was incapable, militarily or financially, of battling the two great powers simultaneously.[53]

Until the late 1930s, the main concern of the army was girding for another war with the Russians and for its invasion of China. The navy, on the other hand, was controlled by moderate leaders such as admirals Yonai Mitsumasa and Yamamoto Isoroku, who strongly opposed a war with the United States. Therefore, neither the army nor the navy planned for a direct confrontation with the Americans until late 1939.

Traditionally, the Japanese Army followed the German model of military training. The navy, however, learned from the British and also imported technologies and strategies from the United States.[54] The Japanese government sent its most accomplished young naval officers to study in Greenwich, England, and Washington, D.C. Nevertheless, navy officers were outraged by the way Britain and the United States treated Japan after the end of the First World War. Starting in the late 1920s, Germany became the destination of choice for naval training. At the time the Second World War started, more and more junior officers distrusted the Anglo-American powers and admired Germany. These German-trained officers were eventually recruited to the central government after returning to Japan. By 1940, the pro-German group held important positions that formed the core of the navy's policy making. Ultimately, in addition to the existing conflict between the "administrative group" and the "command group," the navy leadership was divided into two main factions: the hard-liners were anti-London Naval Treaty, anti-American, and pro-German, and they claimed that a Japanese-American War was inevitable; the moderates were anti-Axis, and they insisted that Japan should never wage a war against the United States and Britain.[55]

Meanwhile, the Hiranuma Kiichirō cabinet collapsed at the end of August 1939 following the shock caused by the conclusion of the German-Soviet Non-Aggression Pact. Admiral Yonai resigned from the Navy Ministry. Although he became the prime minister in January 1940, his cabinet fell after six months. In addition, as Asada Sadao contends, Germany's victory in Western Europe by the summer of 1940 greatly inspired the naval officers on the General Staff. Those who were cautious and opposed war with the United States were criticized as cowards. The fading passion for the idea of the Axis revived and soon spread.[56]

Germany never abandoned its idea of establishing a military alliance with Japan, because Ribbentrop believed that "such an alliance would be the best way to prevent American intervention in the European war."[57] After Germany occupied the Netherlands in early May 1940, Ribbentrop signaled to Tokyo that Germany had no interest in the fate of the Dutch overseas empire. The Japanese interpreted this as a green light to take the Dutch East Indies and a signal that Germany would support "any action Japan might be tempted to undertake." Frank Iklé argues that Ribbentrop was in fact attempting to entice Japan into conquering the Dutch colony and then joining Germany in its war against the British.[58]

The fall of France in June 1940 further inspired the Japanese military leaders, since Japan was then placed in a position to absorb the European colonies in Southeast Asia into its own sphere of influence. For this reason, Tokyo required additional understanding and cooperation from Berlin.[59] However, both Ribbentrop and the Japanese Army officials considered Admiral Yonai's cabinet unsuitable to negotiate with the Axis powers. In late July, the army overthrew it and replaced it with the Second Konoe Cabinet.[60]

For the negotiation of a military alliance, the Foreign Ministry of Japan proposed that Germany agree "not to interfere with Japan's political leadership over French Indo-China, the Dutch East Indies" and should "extend proper support for ending the China conflict."[61] Tokyo also hoped that an alliance with Berlin would lead to a stable relationship with Moscow. The alliance with Japan offered Germany many similar benefits. Most important, the United States would have to divide its attention between the wars in the Pacific and the Atlantic. It also seemed that Japan was capable of "harming the British Empire."[62] On September 27, 1940, Japan, Germany, and Italy signed the Tripartite Pact.

The growing influence of the pro-German groups in Japan and the conclusion of the Tripartite Pact happened faster than Inuzuka and Yasue could have imagined. The more aggressive the Japanese military and its war plan became and the closer the relations between Japan and Germany grew, the less acceptable the Jewish policies of the military "experts" became. Following Captain Inuzuka's removal from active duty in early 1940, Colonel Yasue also lost his position as the head of the Dalian Special Service Agency, and he also moved to the reserve in the middle of December

1940.[63] The Fourth Far Eastern Jewish Conference, scheduled at the end of the year in Manchuria, had to be cancelled because of German pressure.[64]

Nevertheless, Captain Inuzuka made several last-ditch efforts in late summer 1940, all unsuccessful, to oppose the establishment of a German-Japanese alliance, to seek support to improve Japan's relations with the United States, and to continue his Jewish policy. First, on August 7, 1940, he submitted a sixty-three-page report on "The Handling of the [China] Incident and the Measures toward Jews" to the Foreign Ministry.

Captain Inuzuka's report explained the relationship between the Shanghai Jewish refugee issue and the solution to "the China Incident," the purpose of the "Holy War of Japan" in Asia, and the establishment of a New Order in the region. He pointed out that for the moment military preparedness, recovery of national strength, and the formation of an East Asian economic bloc were Japan's key tasks. Inuzuka argued that the United States should be the principal trading partner that would help Japan in these matters. However, Japanese-U.S. relations were, in reality, worsening. The captain concluded that the most expeditious way to force the United States to change its anti-Japanese attitude and to cooperate with Japan militarily and financially was to use the Jewish refugees under Japan's control to put pressure on American Jews, who "occupied important positions in all fields in the United States." Therefore, the solutions to the war with China and policy toward Jewish refugees were actually closely related to a successful conclusion of Japan's "Holy War" in general. Inuzuka claimed that the result of his work on the Jewish refugees in Shanghai for the last eighteen months showed that there was a strong possibility that Japan could reach a successful conclusion to its war.[65]

Meanwhile, Inuzuka was suspicious of the real intentions of Japan's new ally, Germany, in East Asia. He pointed out that Germany had sold Chiang Kai-shek's government new and powerful weapons on a massive scale. The captain also argued that Germany and Italy simply tried to use Japan to reduce British influence in East Asia so that they could position themselves better in the war in Europe.[66]

Captain Inuzuka also directly requested the Shanghai Jews to contact their coreligionists in the United States on Japan's behalf. A. H. George, the British consul general in Shanghai, reported to the British ambassador to China in early September 1940 that Captain Inuzuka had lately made extensive efforts to force the "large and defenseless Jewish community" to use its influence for Japan's sake. Ellis Hayim, joint chairman of the CAEJR, told the consul general that the committee had been approached repeatedly by Captain Inuzuka in August "with the request that they telegraph a message to the Government of the United States of America expressing their gratitude and appreciation for the 'kindly attitude of the Japanese authorities to the refugees.'" Hayim's refusal outraged the captain. Inuzuka then addressed a letter to Michel Speelman, chairman of the CAEJR, on August 27 "with thinly veiled threats" asking the committee to reassess its decision not to cooperate with Japan. The captain emphasized that (1) the refugees should appreciate that "no country in the world" would allow aliens to take refuge unless they provided services to help enrich their host country; (2) the refugees should understand the fact that "every inch of Kongkew and Yangtsepoo [Yangshupu], areas in which the Jewish refugees are now enjoying peaceful life was secured by the blood shed by Japan's armed forces"; (3) in order to survive the rising tide of anti-Semitism he suggested would sweep the region, it would be in their best interests if the refugees living within Japanese-occupied areas refrained "from any expressions of opinion likely to prove irksome to the Japanese Authorities and people, and to endeavor at all times to make the best possible impression upon them."[67]

Inuzuka's efforts continued. On September 13, 1940, two weeks before the conclusion of the Tripartite Pact, the captain delivered a radio address over the Tokyo Radio Broadcasting Station to the Jewish community in Shanghai. *Israel's Messenger* reported that Captain Inuzuka, claiming to represent the Japanese Navy, Foreign Office, and Kō-Ain in Shanghai, "revealed the attitude of official Japanese quarters" toward the Jewish refugee issue in Shanghai.[68]

Israel's Messenger praised the captain as "a true friend of the Jewish people" and declared that he had gained the "wide admiration of refugee Jews." Since the editor-in-chief of the periodical was cooperating with the Japanese at the time, there is no doubt that Inuzuka was behind the report. It is probable that the captain arranged for the publication of his speech and represented his opinion as the official Japanese one.

In his speech, Inuzuka explained that although the refugees were "homesick" and wanted to "return to Europe" in the beginning, they then "recognized that East Asia is their new home country, for they have realized that the equality of all races and the freedom of religion is one of the chief principles of the Japanese people." "The influx of such a great number of Jews to Asia," Inuzuka concluded, "means that these people are eager to see the establishment of a new order in Asia, so that they should cooperate with the Japanese and help in bringing about such a consummation. Japan will always deal with the Jews according to the principle of equality if they remain loyal to that great country."[69]

At the same time, Inuzuka was clearly aware that he would not be able to continue his Jewish policy if Japan militarily allied itself with the Axis powers. When the captain delivered his radio speech, the influence and the mounting pressure of the pro-German groups in the military and the government was difficult to ignore. Toward the end of the speech, the captain surprisingly defended Germany by referring to the persecution of Jews in Spain and pointing out that "the Nazis were not the first to imitate anti-Jewish persecutions" in Europe.[70]

There is no evidence that any other officials supported Inuzuka's radio statement. Yoshii Hiroshi argues that the formation of the military alliance immediately provoked America's bitter hostility against Japan. Therefore, the conclusion of the Tripartite Pact was extremely disadvantageous to Japan's diplomacy, especially with the United States.[71] There was nothing the "Jewish experts" could do to rescue Japanese-U.S. relations, which also meant that the value of Shanghai Jews was significantly reduced.

The Japanese government moved promptly to reverse its Jewish policy. On October 10, foreign minister Matsuoka Yōsuke cabled Japanese consular offices overseas concerning "The Issue of Visas to Foreign Refugees." According to Matsuoka, recently, quite a few "European refugees" had been denied permission to enter or transit Japan because they either did not posses the requisite entry documents for their destination countries or enough travel money. The foreign minister pointed out that it would be impossible for Japan to return these refugees if they had already arrived. In addition, Japan's current situation in the war would not allow it to accept more foreign refugees. Therefore, he ordered the consular officers to apply new regulations to "refugees" who wanted an entry or transit visa to Japan. The foreign minister explained that usually it was one of the ministry's "internal regulations" to require a fee from "stateless foreigners" in order to permit entry and transit; these old regulations did not apply to "refugees." After discussions with the minister of internal affairs, both ministries agreed to correct the inconsistency of this policy. The ministers decided that from then on "foreigners" who were also "refugees" must hold on arrival not only travel tickets to their final destination countries but also at least 25 yen per person per day in order to stay in Japan during the transit period, the period during which they waited for an entry visa to a different country. The foreign minister instructed his consuls, "No matter if they were Jewish or not," if the "refugees" could not fulfill the above requirements, "do not issue them entry visas or travel certificates to Japan."[72]

Although the foreign minister explained that he did not apply the new regulations only to "Jewish refugees," the majority of the "refugees" who needed Japan's entry or transit visas at the time were obviously European Jews. The foreign minister attempted to use the travel money requirement to limit, or stop completely, the coming of Jewish refugees, since he was certainly aware that the Jews would be unable to bring the required money out of German-controlled territories.

The Ministry of Foreign Affairs also received a request, shortly after the conclusion of the Tripartite Pact, to change Japan's policy toward Jewish refugees in East Asia. The European and Asian Divisions of the Foreign Ministry issued a circular prepared for a meeting on November 14, 1940, to discuss the request. However, there is no further evidence confirming who presented the original request or whether it was officially accepted.

Two documents were attached to the circular: "Proposals for a [New] Basic Jewish Policy" emphasized that Japan, henceforward, should not "positively" use the Jews and should pay special attention to "hostile plots" of international Jewry. It proposed that Japan should abandon its original policy of supporting Jews in East Asia (for instance, allowing them to convene the Far Eastern Jewish Conference under the Japanese authorities' auspices). Therefore, Japan should no longer expect to use Jews to break the deadlock in its relations with Britain and the United States.[73]

The second document, "Reasons for Proposing a [New] Basic Policy toward the Jews," listed three reasons that Japan should pursue a new policy toward the Jewish refugees. (1) When the Five Ministers Conference on December 6, 1938, decided the "Outlines of the Jewish Policies," Japan was not yet certain about its alliance with Germany and Italy. At the time, there was still a possibility that Japan could improve its relations with Britain and the United States. Therefore, Japan's policy emphasized the use of the Jewish refugees to attract American capital to East Asia. (2) However, since Japan then had formed an alliance with Germany and Italy, it would eventually cause the deterioration of Japanese-British and Japanese-U.S. relations. As a result, Japan lost almost every opportunity to use the Jewish refugees to ease the tensions in its relations with the two countries. In addition, Jews were cooperating with the British and Americans globally to confront the increasingly harsh anti-Jewish policies of the Axis powers in Europe. Consequently, the Jews, British and Americans would augment their anti-Japanese policies as well. (3) Under such conditions, the policy of using Jewish refugees to improve Japan's relations with Britain and the United State became baseless. "Although some officials still insisted that Japan should sustain and even strengthen such a policy," it would only benefit the Allies' scheme to drive a wedge between Japan and other Axis countries. Therefore, the document concluded, for the above reasons, Japan must reconsider its policy toward the Jews in light of the new international circumstances.[74]

The foreign minister's new instructions on issuing visas to Jewish refugees in October and the proposals for establishing a new Jewish policy in

November clearly demonstrate the change of attitude toward the Jews in the Japanese government after the formation of the alliance with Germany and Italy. The Foreign Ministry attempted to use every possible reason to ban Jewish refugees from coming to Japan and the Japanese-controlled territories in China, and the general mood within the government was anti-Jewish. Before the conclusion of the Tripartite Pact, although there was disagreement over Inuzuka and Yasue's Jewish policy, the majority of the Japanese officials, in both the government and the military, tolerated it. The Japanese officials also joined the "Jewish experts" in trying to use Shanghai Jews to attract American capital and improve Japan's relationship with the United States. However, the Tripartite Pact ended Japan's hopes for better relations with the Anglo-American powers. The strategic situation convinced the Japanese government that it was more important to maintain and strengthen its good relationship with its ally Germany. To that end, the Japanese could not and should not oppose Germany's Jewish policy as the "experts" had done. A new relationship with Berlin thus required that Tokyo establish a new policy toward Jewish refugees in Shanghai.

Sugihara Chiune and the Polish Jewish Refugees: From Kobe to Shanghai, Summer 1940–Summer 1941

The alliance with Germany and Italy also affected Jewish refugees already in Japan. The Japanese government decided after signing the Tripartite Pact to transport more than one thousand Polish Jews, who were temporarily seeking refuge in Kobe, to Shanghai. These refugees all received Japanese transit visas in the summer of 1940 from Sugihara Chiune, Japan's acting consul in Kaunas, Lithuania.

In November 1939, Sugihara Chiune received his orders from the Foreign Ministry and arrived at his new post in Kaunas, the capital of Lithuania from 1920 to 1940.[75] Since the Sugihara family were the only Japanese residents in Kaunas, and no other Japanese citizens there might require diplomatic support, his real task was to collect intelligence information and monitor the movements of the Germans and the Russians.[76] Sugihara Chiune, as Pamela Sakamoto describes him, was an "extraordinary diplomat," since "many Japanese diplomats issued visas that saved Jews, but only a few like Sugihara saved Jews by issuing visas."[77] In summer 1940, Sugihara granted 2,132 transit visas to Polish Jews without documents to destination countries and adequate transit money to come to Japan. This number was more than one-third of the transit visas that Japanese consuls in Europe granted between January 1940 and March 1941.[78]

Sugihara Chiune was born in 1900. While studying at prestigious Waseda University in 1919, Sugihara passed the Ministry of Foreign Affairs entrance exam and was then sent to study Russian as an exchange student at Harbin Academy, an institute established by the Japanese government and the South Manchurian Railway Company to train Russia specialists. Sugihara soon mastered the language and began teaching Russian at the academy. The Ministry of Foreign Affairs acknowledged his linguistic talents later and appointed him clerk to the Japanese consulate in Harbin. In 1932, Sugihara was transferred from the Foreign Ministry to manage the Russia Section in the Manchukuo Affairs Bureau. However, he returned to Japan and the Ministry of Foreign Affairs in 1935. Although Sugihara was then appointed to act as an interpreter at the Japanese embassy in Moscow, he was unable to obtain a visa from the Soviet government. It seemed that Sugihara, an expert on Russian affairs, made the secretive communist state nervous. Eventually, Sugihara was reappointed in 1937 to serve in the Japanese legation in Helsinki, Finland.[79]

In the final months of 1939, after Germany invaded Poland, more than ten thousand Polish Jews escaped to the tiny Baltic state of Lithuania. However, the Soviet Union invaded the country in June and annexed it on August 4, 1940. Although Lithuania served as a temporary haven for Polish Jews, who sought sanctuary there until the war was over or until they were able to immigrate to other countries, the Soviet occupation increased the anxieties of Jews. Since the USSR did not allow its citizens to emigrate freely, and the deadline for accepting Soviet citizenship in Lithuania was January 1941, thousands of Polish Jewish refugees attempted to flee the country. Many of them believed that "escape had become a matter of 'now or never.'"[80]

After Germany closed the Baltic Sea to air and sea transportation in April 1940, the only escape route left for Polish Jews from Lithuania was to travel eastward on the Trans-Siberian Railroad, cross the Eurasian continent to Vladivostok—Russia's gateway to the Pacific—and take ship to Japan. The refugees planned to travel to other destinations or get visas to other countries while in Japan. This new route remained open until June 1941.[81] Sugihara had issued Jews Japanese transit visas until he was forced by the Soviets to close his consulate in September 1940.[82]

Yukiko, Sugihara's wife, noted from her husband's diaries that on the morning of July 27, 1940, the consul was surprised to discover that hundreds of people had surrounded the Japanese consulate in Kaunas. They were Jews escaping the Nazis from western Polish cities and attempting to obtain Japanese transit visas so that they could travel through the Soviet Union and Japan en route to third countries. Facing the desperate crowd,

Sugihara decided to invite five people representing the refugees to enter the consulate and meet with him. The Jewish representatives requested the Japanese consul's assistance. They also told him that it was the Dutch consul in Kaunas, Jan Zwartendijk, who advised them to seek Japanese transit visas. Consul Zwartendijk was the only Western diplomat in Kaunas sympathetic to the Jews, and he agreed to issue the Polish Jews permits to enter the island of Curaçao in the Dutch West Indies.[83] It was a Dutch student at the Telshe Yeshiva who learned from the consul that one did not need an entry visa to Curaçao; only a "landing permit" from its governor was required. Since the Russians required that the Polish refugees obtain official permits in order to leave Soviet-controlled territory, the Dutch consul decided to "stamp the refugees' passports with an official 'permit' reading: 'Entry into Curaçao does not require a visa.'"[84] The refugees then needed Japanese transit visas in order to get to the island. Sugihara did not immediately respond to the request by the Polish Jews. Yukiko recalled that since the refugees required several hundred, even thousands, of transit visas, Sugihara must first ask for permission from the Foreign Ministry.[85]

The next day, Sugihara cabled Foreign Minister Matsuoka. However, there is a discrepancy between Yukiko's story and Sugihara's message. In his telegram of July 28, 1940, Sugihara simply described the terror associated with the Soviet occupation of Kaunas and the situation that "some one hundred Jews daily came to our consulate to apply for transit visas in order to travel to the United States through Japan."[86] He did not ask for Matsuoka's permission to provide transit visas to Polish Jews to travel to Curaçao. This discrepancy might simply be Yukiko's mistake. It is also possible that Sugihara sent such a message on purpose. Since Sugihara issued visas to Polish Jews who were not qualified to obtain Japanese transit visas, he may have intentionally hidden the fact that there were a great number of Jewish refugees requiring visas in Kaunas and that they were heading to a suspicious destination. Therefore, Sugihara simply informed the Foreign Ministry of the possibility that some Jews might receive Japanese transit visas in order to reach third countries.

The second time Sugihara referred to any Jews was in his cable to the foreign minister on August 9. Sugihara asked for Matsuoka's permission to extend the ten-day-long Japanese transit visa to one month for sixteen Jewish industrialists from Warsaw. These people were immigrating to South America and passing through Japan, and they wanted to meet some of their Japanese counterparts and do some business after they landed in the country. Sugihara believed that there was no reason to deny their request.[87] Matsuoka responded on August 13 and emphasized that Sugihara should issue transit visas only to those who had completed entry procedures to destination countries. Also, the duration of their stay should be decided when the Jewish businessmen arrived.[88] Although Sugihara still did not mention the Polish Jewish refugees, he had actually issued more than seventeen hundred transit visas, mostly to them, by then.[89] It seemed that Sugihara intended to draw the foreign minister's attention to something else and send as many Jews as possible out of Kaunas before Matsuoka noticed.

However, the Foreign Ministry soon discovered that some Polish Jews arriving in Japan, who had obtained transit visas from the Kaunas Consulate, did not possess enough travel money and complete entry documents for final destinations. Apparently Dutch Consul Zwartendijk in Kaunas issued twelve hundred to fourteen hundred entry permits to Curaçao and Sugihara issued a total of 2,132 transit visas in the summer of 1940.[90] Sugihara also granted visas to Jews without Curaçao permits. On August 16, 1940, Matsuoka informed Sugihara that the Foreign Ministry had difficulties in handling these Jews and could not let them land in Japan. The foreign minister once again ordered Sugihara that he should not grant transit visas to "international refugees" unless they had finished their destination procedures and possessed enough travel money for their stay during the transit period in Japan.[91]

In late August, Sugihara reported to Matsuoka that since the Central and South American countries had withdrawn their diplomats from Kaunas, Jews were applying for Japanese visas; Japan had become the only possible transit country. The Japanese transit visas were absolutely necessary for the refugees to leave the Soviet Union and travel to the United States. Sugihara claimed that he had issued transit visas only to those with reliable references, under the condition that the refugees should (1) obtain entry visas to destination countries by the time they boarded ships in Vladivostok; (2) make ship reservations to Japan and points beyond; (3) arrange to transfer overseas funds to Japan [to cover their travel expanses and the costs of their stay in Japan]. Sugihara also urged the Foreign Ministry to take urgent measures to protect those who had not yet completed these procedures from being rejected by Japanese shipping companies in Vladivostok.[92]

Although Matsuoka ordered Sugihara again on September 2, 1940, to follow the Foreign Ministry's instruction to issue Jews visas, the foreign minister assured the consul that Japanese shipping companies would not refuse to transfer the refugees to Japan. Matsuoka explained that if the shipping companies refused the Jews, it would only compromise the credibility of Japanese visas. He also claimed that it was "in fact impossible" for the shipping companies to contradict the Russian authorities' order to transport the Jews out of the Soviet Union since the Russians acknowledged Japanese transit visas as exit documents.[93] The foreign minister was facing a dilemma, and he chose to defend the empire's honor. As Sakamoto points out, "If Japan treated its own visas as suspicious, the faith of others in the Foreign Ministry, its representative, and their guarantees would suffer. By extension, the reputation of Japan and the Emperor would be tarnished."[94]

It is unclear whether Sugihara intentionally took advantage of the foreign minister's difficult position, but his transit visas eventually led to the escape of more than two thousand Polish Jews to Japan. In his accessible account of Sugihara's experience in Lithuania, sociologist Hillel Levine probes the Japanese diplomat's motives and finds them unstained. Rather, he characterizes Sugihara as the initiator of a "conspiracy of goodness" and a humanitarian.[95] Nothing in the historical record suggests that Sugihara was connected to the Japanese "Jewish experts" or that he supported their endeavors to manipulate Jewish money and influence. As Sugihara expressed it himself, "I acted according to my sense of human justice, out of love for mankind."[96]

Two local relief organizations in Japan, the Relief Aid Committee in Yokohama and the Jewish Community in Kobe, were organized to assist the arriving European Jewish refugees. The American Jewish Joint Distribution Committee also provided significant help. Ernst Baerwald of the Relief Aid Committee in Yokohama wrote the Japanese Foreign Ministry at the end of October and optimistically guaranteed that the coming of the Jewish refugees to Japan would not become a "public burden." Baerwald emphasized that "enormous amounts in USA currency have been remitted...to Japan and we have been always on the best of terms with the authorities in Kobe and Yokohama and with the shipping companies."[97]

From early 1940 to the spring of 1941, a total of 3,044 European Jewish refugees landed in Japan with transit visas. About seventeen hundred were still there, at least temporarily, as of April 1941. In addition, more than twenty-five hundred refugees who had received transit visas had not arrived yet.[98] Most of the remaining Jews in Japan were Polish Jews without destination visas. The Jewish Community in Kobe's report indicates that by April 15, 1941, a total of 1,478 Polish Jews had entered Japan, and only 49 of them left for third countries.[99]

The growing population of Jewish refugees caused both social and political problems for the Japanese government. Since the Polish Jews did not possess required travel money, they naturally became a "public burden" for both the refugee relief committees and Japanese society. For instance, by March 1941, the monthly relief amount climbed to $18,000, up from $900 in July 1940.[100]

Most important, the Japanese officials grew concerned that the presence of the Jewish refugees would unfavorably affect Japan's relations with its new allies, Germany and Italy. European Jews with transit visas began flooding into Japan at the most inconvenient time for Tokyo. Not only had the pro-German groups in the military increased their influence, but the Konoe Cabinet, especially Foreign Minister Matsuoka, was attempting to maintain a good relationship with the other Axis powers.

Matsuoka also intended to recapture for the Foreign Ministry control of Japan's foreign policy from the military. In summer 1939, the military, the army in particular, pushed a negotiation for an alliance with Germany. Foreign Minister Arita, however, strongly opposed it. One year later, Matsuoka enthusiastically took the initiative in negotiations with Germany. Furthermore, at the end of August 1940, Matsuoka, in consultation with the pro-Axis officials in the Foreign Ministry, removed more than forty ambassadors and senior diplomats who were considered "pro-Anglo-American" in order to assure the success of the alliance.[101]

In early 1941, Matsuoka scheduled a trip to Europe to meet directly with the Soviet and German leaders. He left Tokyo on March 12, 1941, and arrived in Berlin on March 27.[102] Before his departure, the foreign minister was concerned about the Germans' reaction to the unexpected influx of Jewish refugees to Japan. Just before leaving, Matsuoka met with Kotsuji Setsuzō, a Japanese scholar who supposedly spoke Hebrew and who had previously worked for him at the SMR as an adviser on Jewish matters. Kotsuji was also engaged in refugee relief in Japan at the time. Matsuoka told Kotsuji that the Germans were "getting very unpleasant" since Japan had let thousands of Jews transit through.[103] The fact that there were still almost two thousand Jewish refugees remaining in Kobe and Yokohama probably disturbed the foreign minister and complicated his agenda.

While Matsuoka was on his trip to Europe, prime minister Konoe Fumimaro acted as foreign minister. Konoe clearly wanted to ensure the success of Matsuoka's meeting with Hitler, and he realized that Japan must do something to tighten its control over the arrival of European Jews. On March 14, well before Matsuoka reached Berlin, Konoe instructed Japanese consular offices in Europe that for the time being only the embassy in Moscow could issue transit visas. Konoe also asked the embassy in Moscow to report to the Foreign Ministry the numbers of visa applicants who fulfilled the requirements every two weeks. Moreover, the Foreign Ministry would decide the numbers of visas that the embassy could grant.[104]

Although Matsuoka gave new instructions two weeks after the conclusion of the Tripartite Pact regarding visas issued to Jewish refugees and tried to stop European Jews from coming to East Asia, he could never have predicted that afterward thousands of Polish Jews would come and stay in Japan. Obviously, at the moment when Japan needed to establish closer ties with Germany, nothing could be more damaging to Japanese-German relations than Japan accommodating Jews who had been expelled by the Germans. The political situation became increasingly awkward.

Later, on March 19, the Japanese officials prohibited seventy-four Jewish refugees from landing in Japan and sent them back to Vladivostok because they lacked destination visas.[105] Most of them had received visas from Sugihara in Kaunas. However, the Russians refused to accept the Jews since they were not Soviet citizens and had already left the country.[106] The seventy-four refugees boarded the same Japanese ship on March 23 and attempted again to enter Japan. Although they did not possess destination visas, they had permits to enter the Dutch island of Curaçao. After the local Jewish community appealed to the Dutch embassy in Tokyo, the Japanese Foreign Ministry decided to make an exception for these refugees.[107]

When Japan occupied southern French Indochina in July 1941, the United States responded by freezing Japanese financial assets. The refugee situation in Japan further deteriorated, since the U.S. sanctions cut off the flow of the Joint's relief funds to the Jewish Community in Kobe.[108] However, the curtailment of relief funds provided Japan with a perfect excuse to get rid of the Jews. Also in July 1941, the Third Konoe Cabinet convened, and Toyoda Tejirō was appointed foreign minister. Toyoda inherited Matsuoka's policy and decided in August to transport the remaining Polish Jews in Japan to Shanghai.

On August 13, 1941, consul general Horiuchi Tateki in Shanghai complained to Foreign Minister Toyoda that 163 Jews were sent to the city from Kobe at the beginning of the month without prior notice.[109] Toyoda responded on August 20 informing Horiuchi that Hyōgo prefectural authorities had sent approximately 290 additional Jewish refugees to Shanghai that day.[110] Toyoda explained that this was because the Jewish refugees would not be able to receive relief funds from the United States and that the Japanese shipping companies traveling between Shanghai and Japan would cease business by the end of the month.[111]

The local authorities in Shanghai were doing their utmost to prevent more refugees from coming to the city and were unhappy about the central government's decision, even though the foreign minister pretended that the idea originated in the Hyōgo prefectural government. Consul General Horiuchi immediately replied to Toyoda's telegram and greatly "regretted" that the authorities in Hyōgo had decided to send Polish Jews to Shanghai "on their own authority." Horiuchi believed that such a decision should be discussed by the Committee on the Muslim and Jewish Problem and by the local authorities in Shanghai. Nevertheless, Horiuchi expressed his understanding and agreed to accept the refugees. Reports from Japanese shipping companies to the consul general also noted that there would be another three hundred refugees arriving in Shanghai on August 30 and eight hundred more thereafter. Horiuchi urged the foreign minister to inform him in advance of subsequent transportation of Jewish refugees to the city.[112]

The transportation of the Polish Jews to Shanghai in the fall of 1941 was unexpectedly interrupted by Captain Inuzuka. According to Ellis Hayim of the CAEJR, he had received a telegram on August 30 from the Jewish Community in Kobe informing him that 350 Polish refugees were on their way to Shanghai and would arrive the next day. Hayim and the Committee for the Assistance of European Jewish Refugees therefore devoted themselves to seeking shelter for the Kobe Jews. However, on August 31, Captain Herzberg, executive officer of the CAEJR, received a phone call from Captain Inuzuka three hours before the arrival of the Japanese ship. Inuzuka told the committee that "under no circumstance would the Japanese Landing Party allow the Polish Refugees an asylum in Hongkew." The captain explained that the "Japanese authorities were very strict that no person may reside in Hongkew without a permit" and that "the housing problem was already acute and the arrival of further refugees in Hongkew would further aggravate the situation." In addition, he pointed out that it was also because the Jewish community in Shanghai "had not co-operated with the Japanese in certain proposed commercial ventures and hence the Captain had no grounds to appeal to the authorities for leniency on behalf of Jewish Refugees."[113] Inuzuka proposed to the Shanghai Jewish *zaibatsu* in summer 1940 to create a real estate company using both Japanese and Jewish capital "as an expedient for the solution of the housing problem in Hongkew." The project required Jewish investment but was clearly for Japan's benefit. Therefore, there was "no active co-operation from the Jewish side."[114]

The CAEJR were eventually able to accept the Polish Jews after direct negotiations with Inuzuka's commanding officer, the chief of the Japanese Landing Party. However, on September 3, the CAEJR once again received a message from Captain Inuzuka claiming that although four hundred refugees would arrive on September 8, the Japanese Naval Landing Party would not allow them to enter Hongkou, either.[115] This time, the desperate relief committee threatened the captain that "in such a case we would not send our representative to meet the steamer and the Japanese authorities could act as they thought fit."[116] Since the committee suggested before that if the Landing Party would not allow the refugees to stay in Hongkou, "the only other alternative was for the refugees to remain on the Japanese steamer which brought them, or take them back to Japan," the CAEJR properly understood that the last thing Tokyo wanted was for the Jews to return to Japan.[117] On September 17, 1941, the last 199 Polish Jews from Kobe reached Shanghai.[118]

Also on September 17, Captain Inuzuka delivered a memorandum to Ellis Hayim describing the Japanese authorities' concerns about the residence of Jewish refugees in the Hongkou area. In the memorandum, the captain repeated his arguments regarding the accommodation of Polish Jews from Japan. According to Inuzuka, although the army, navy, and Japanese consulate general decided at a conference on August 21 to forbid further entry of Jewish refugees into Hongkou, it was his "interventions which enabled the Committee to find shelter for the many refugees at last moment, and helped the Committee out of a difficult situation." Therefore, the captain insisted that he had "the right in behalf of the Japanese Authorities to ask the Committee for further co-operations in the solution of the refugees problem." Inuzuka concluded that the "only solution of the matter" lay in the Jewish community's "active co-operation with the Japanese authorities."[119]

Inuzuka used the accommodation of Polish Jews to punish the Jewish community in Shanghai for not cooperating with the Japanese authorities, the captain himself in particular. Besides his complaint about the real estate company, Inuzuka was also dissatisfied with the Jewish committee's reaction to Tamura's settlement plan in 1939. The captain believed that the Japanese government provided "influential Jewish individuals in America" an opportunity to solve the refugee problem in East Asia; it was the Jews themselves who "ignored" the chance by doing nothing.[120]

Nevertheless, Inuzuka was unable to stop the transportation of Polish Jews to Shanghai. This simply indicates that Inuzuka was no longer able to decide and influence Japan's Jewish policy. The central government had made up its mind: they did not want any Jews to remain in Japan. The local authorities in Shanghai, although they protested at first, did not wish to oppose the government's decision.

Pearl Harbor and the Jewish Refugees in Shanghai

On December 7, 1941, Japan attacked the U.S. military installations on Oahu in Hawaii, thus launching its war against the United States. The Pearl Harbor attack further eroded the situation of the Jewish refugees in Shanghai. If the Jewish refugees significantly lost their value to the

Japanese after the signing of the Tripartite Pact, the outbreak of the war between Japan and the United States rendered twenty thousand of them in Shanghai nothing but a burden for the Japanese.

A month later, on January 17, 1942, foreign minister Tōgō Shigenori informed the Japanese consular offices in China and Manchukuo that the outbreak of the war in the Pacific made it necessary for the Japanese government to "fundamentally reconsider" its Jewish policy. Since the revision of the Jewish policy decided by the Five Ministers' Conference in 1938 was under consideration, Tōgō explained the "emergency measures" to the diplomats: Japan would treat German Jewish refugees as stateless refugees since Germany had claimed to deprive overseas Jews of their German nationalities starting on January 1, 1942. Also, it would keep stateless Jews and Jews from neutral countries under close observation, except for those who "Japan was using or would use in the future."[121]

By the middle of March 1942, the Japanese government completed the revision of its policy toward the Jewish refugees in Shanghai. Foreign Minister Tōgō notified consular offices in China of "Measures toward the Treatment of Jews under Current Situation," the decision of the Liaison Conference of March 11 between the government and the Imperial General Headquarters. According to this document, as a result of the outbreak of the Pacific War, the Japanese government decided to change its Jewish policy to the following:

(1) Except special occasions, Jews are forbidden to enter Japan, Manchukuo, China and all other Japanese occupied areas;

(2) As a general policy, treat Jews residing in Japan, Manchukuo, China and other Japanese occupied areas, as citizens of the countries of their nationalities. However, in consideration of the racial characteristic of the Jews, eliminate and oppress any hostile attempts while strictly *observing* their residences and businesses;

(3) Treat Jews who could be used by Japan (including those who could be used by allied countries who do not oppose Japan's policy) friendly. However, Japan does not support any of Jewish Zionist movement.

It also noted after these provisions that the Japanese government was to "abolish the Jewish policies decided by the Five Ministers' Conference of December 6, 1938."[122]

The "Measures" also stated that as a result of the eruption of the Pacific War and the consequent transformation of the international situation, it became meaningless for Japan to use Jews to attract foreign capital or to achieve breakthroughs in its relations with Britain and the United States.

Therefore, the document concluded, Japan no longer needed to consider its relationships with third countries while attending to the Jewish problem.[123]

Although Tōgō required the consular officers in China to keep a close eye on the Jewish refugees, the Japanese government had not yet agreed upon any specific plans concerning their treatment. A piece of advice came from Japan's ally, Germany, in May 1942. Ambassador Ōshima Hiroshi in Berlin reported to Foreign Minister Tōgō that during his meeting with Alfred Rosenberg, the head of the Reich Ministry for the Occupied Eastern Territories, the two had a conversation regarding Jewish refugees. Rosenberg warned Ōshima that since quite a number of Jews were residing in Shanghai, if their influence expanded to other areas in East Asia, it would cause an "annoying problem" to Japan. Rosenberg emphasized that Japan should segregate Jews in Japanese occupied areas as soon as possible so that they would not be able to make inroads in East Asia.[124]

Although it is unclear whether Rosenberg's "advice" was the decisive reason, it was the first time that the idea of segregating Jews appeared in Foreign Ministry documents, and the Japanese soon carried out the plan to put the Shanghai Jews into a designated area. In early November, the Japanese government transformed its Ministry of Colonial Affairs into the Ministry of the Greater East Asia in order to better supervise Japan's overseas territories in East and Southeast Asia and Pacific Islands. Aoki Kazuo was appointed the first minister. On November 18, 1942, consul general Yano Seiki in Shanghai cabled Aoki regarding the treatment of Jews. Yano informed Aoki that officials from the Japanese consulate, the Ministry of Greater East Asia, the army, the navy, and the SMC had organized a committee to study specific measures for dealing with the Jewish refugees in Shanghai. At the meeting of November 18, the committee drafted the following measures:

> (1) Set up a Jewish district in Yangshupu area north of Suzhou Creek and let Jews scattered throughout the city live in the district; (2) Stateless Jews, mostly German and European origin, were the main targets to be accommodated in the designated area. The Russian and other Jews would be handled later; (3) Military occupation authorities would observe and control Jews in the designated area.[125]

On February 9, 1943, Yano reported to Aoki the decision of the local authorities that the commanders-in-chief of the Japanese Army and Navy in the Shanghai area would soon jointly issue a proclamation concerning the treatment of the Jewish refugees. The proclamation would require "stateless refugees" in Shanghai to move into a designated area in three months from the day of the issuance.[126] Although the term "stateless refugees" remained unexplained in the proclamation officially issued on February 18,

1943, in Yano's telegram he clarified that it meant refugees who had arrived in Shanghai after 1937 from Germany, Austria, Czechoslovakia, Hungary, Poland, Latvia, Lithuania, and Estonia, and who were at present stateless.[127] The occupation authorities in Shanghai had studied and prepared for the case. The army officials argued that the decision of the Liaison Conference on March 11, 1942, almost a year previously, provided a "direct basis" for the segregation of the Jewish refugees.[128]

The twenty thousand Jewish refugees subsequently started their lives in the designated area, commonly known as the Shanghai Ghetto. However, as Maruyama Naoki points out, the area bore little resemblance to the Nazis' ghettos and concentration camps in Europe. Although Jewish refugees in the ghetto were under Japan's strict surveillance at the time, unlike imprisoned enemy nationals in Shanghai, they were allowed to leave the designated area bearing permits issued by the Japanese authorities. Also, unlike the Nazi concentration camps, the Shanghai Jews were never compelled to labor, nor did they face the threat of eradication. Conditions in the Shanghai Ghetto, which was located in the poorest area in the city, were far from ideal, but the Jews did not suffer their ordeal alone. The ghetto was also home to many Chinese and White Russians, who lived alongside the refugees.[129]

Although Maruyama also argues that the Japanese did not put the refugees into the ghetto under pressure from the Germans, both David Kranzler and Marcia Ristaino suggest that the Jews themselves believed that in the summer of 1942 "the long arm of the Gestapo" reached China, and that the Germans may have convinced the Japanese to implement their own "final solution" toward the Jews in Shanghai.[130] Kranzler and Ristaino both describe a meeting in the middle of June 1942, at which local Jewish leaders heard from a Japanese official, Shibata Mitsugu, who had once worked for the Jewish Affairs Bureau. According to Kranzler, Shibata told the Jewish leaders that

> under heavy pressure from the German Consulate ... to isolate the Jews, particularly refugees, from freedom of the city in Shanghai, the Japanese authorities were giving this matter consideration. ... It appears that at this point of the war, German influence was considerable and various ideas were being considered, including the sending of all refugees to one of the islands at the mouth of the Yangtze River near Shanghai.[131]

Laura Margolis, the head of Joint Distribution Committee in Shanghai between 1941 and 1943, related a different account of what appears to be the same series of events. Margolis composed a "Report of Activities in Shanghai, China, from December 8, 1941 to September 1943" from memory after returning to the United States because the Japanese forbade her to take any written materials with her when she left the country. She recorded in her report that in July 1942 "Mr. Peretz" (presumably Robert Peritz, according to Kranzler and Ristaino), of the International Committee for European Refugees, called the JDC representatives to his office and told them that "the Japanese were planning a catastrophic thing for the refugees" and that he needed their help. Peretz informed Margolis that "a plan was being evolved whereby the refugees would be loaded on ships, taken out to the ocean and drowned." He implored the JDC representatives to intervene to save the refugees. Margolis learned later from Michel Speelman that Peretz and "his Japanese friend, Mr. Katawa," rather than "Shibata," convened a meeting with Jewish leaders to alert them to the Japanese plan. Although Margolis recounted a different date and called the Japanese official by a different name, these might well be her mistakes.

Margolis described Peretz as a man with a "very bad reputation, who back in 1937, 1938, and 1939 was mixed up with the Japanese in Hongkew in a 'racket' to sell refugees permits for the immigration of their relatives to Shanghai," although permits were not yet required. At the time, "the Japanese working closely with Mr. Peretz in this 'racket'" was Katawa [or perhaps "Shibata"]. "Knowing the records of both Mr. Peretz and Mr. Katawa," Margolis continued, "we all think that they had hoped to get those men present ... [at the meeting] to pay some money to try to stop this action and that in these negotiations they would make their percentage."[132] Margolis, who personally knew the characters in question, clearly did not trust Peretz and his "Japanese friend" and was skeptical of their motives.

These are thus far the only accounts found relating to the issue of whether the Nazis exerted pressure on the Japanese to eliminate the Jews in Shanghai. Although no official document, at least from the Japanese side, has been found that can either confirm or disprove these reports, many local Jews were seriously frightened by the rumors that swirled around the city concerning their fate.[133] Later, Jewish leaders who attended the meeting decided to appeal the issue to higher Japanese authorities. They failed and were arrested for "spreading false rumors," although they were later released by the gendarmerie with an assurance that their fears were unfounded.[134]

Conclusion

Captain Inuzuka and Colonel Yasue consistently argued that Japan should not follow the other Axis powers' Jewish policy. Inuzuka, like all other moderate naval officers, opposed a military alliance with Germany and asserted that Japan should develop its relationship with the United States.

The captain believed that American capital was a key to Japan's military victory in China and the establishment of a new order in East Asia, and he expected assistance from the Shanghai Jews. Yasue, on the other hand, always worked to introduce Jewish investment to build up Manchuria—the army's sphere of influence and line of defense against the Soviet Union. Both "experts" sought to use Jewish refugees to help prevent a direct confrontation and ease tensions between the United States and Japan. However, following Germany's victory in Europe in spring 1940, the strategic situation in the Pacific was transformed. Japan was in a position to pursue a new source of natural resources in the European colonies of Southeast Asia, and the military decided to take the opportunity. The mutual needs of Germany and Japan eventually resulted in a military alliance, and this made conflict between Japan and the United States inevitable. Inuzuka and Yasue's Jewish policy, which was established in late 1938 when there was still room left for the amelioration of Japanese-U.S. relations, no longer fit the new strategic situation.

The conclusion of the Tripartite Pact was the turning point of Japan's policy making toward the Jewish refugees in Shanghai during the Second World War. The Japanese government immediately began modifying the Jewish policy that had been decided at the Five Ministers' Conference of 1938. The military leaders considered Japan's relationship with Germany more important than that with the United States and advised that Japan should abandon its current Jewish policy of supporting Jews in East Asia. Also, pro-German groups in both the military and the government gained power, and consequently Captain Inuzuka and Colonel Yasue were removed from their jobs at the beginning and the end of 1940, respectively. The "Jewish experts" were no longer in a position either to decide or influence Japan's new Jewish policy.

The Tripartite Pact also altered the fate of European Jewish refugees in Shanghai. Before that agreement, Inuzuka and Yasue were able to carry out their policy of using Jews without interference from Germany, and they tried to accept as many Jewish refugees as possible to the city. The Jews, on the other hand, at least had their lives guaranteed by the Japanese. However, the alliance with Germany and Italy ended all possibilities for Japan to establish better relations with the United States. Japan thus lost its opportunity to employ the presence of the Jewish refugees as leverage to ease the tensions between the two countries. As a result, Shanghai Jews significantly lost their value to the Japanese.

The Japanese government also decided to transport more than one thousand Polish Jews to Shanghai after the conclusion of the alliance. They considered it important to maintain and strengthen a good relationship with Germany. Therefore, Japan should no longer oppose the Axis powers' Jewish policy, as Inuzuka and Yasue had done. Tokyo did not want any Jews, expelled by its allies, to remain in Japan. The Polish Jews came to Japan with a ten-day transit visa issued in the summer of 1940 by Japanese consul Sugihara Chiune in Kaunas, Lithuania. Sugihara violated the order of the foreign minister and issued more than two thousand transit visas to Polish Jews who did not possess either visas to destination countries or enough travel money. These were also important reasons that the Jews eventually ended up staying in Kobe, Japan.

The transportation of Polish Jews to Shanghai illustrates the degree to which the alliance with Germany and Italy in 1940 had a tremendous impact on Japan not only strategically but also politically. Although the military, the army in particular, was enthusiastic about pursuing such a military alliance in 1939, they could not obtain support from the navy and the civilian foreign minister. However, in 1940, foreign minister Matsuoka Yōsuke took the initiative in negotiations with the Axis powers. Prime minister Konoe Fumimaro, before the foreign minister reached Berlin in spring 1941 for his first direct encounter with Hitler since signing the treaty, further tightened Japan's visa policy toward the European Jewish refugees in order to stop them from coming to East Asia. Therefore, after the conclusion of the Tripartite Pact, both the political and military climate in Japan was pro-German and anti-Jewish. The government and the military determined to share Japan's fortune with the Axis. The existence of the Jewish refugees in Japan and the Japanese-occupied Shanghai was in its way.

Although the Japanese government chose to send the Polish Jews to Shanghai, Captain Inuzuka attempted to prevent them from entering the Hongkou area. Realizing that the Jewish refugees had become useless to Japan, the captain, "a true friend of the Jewish people" who had gained "wide admiration of refugee Jews," intended to punish the Jews for not cooperating with the Japanese-proposed commercial ventures in Shanghai a year previously, and for not providing financial support to Tamura's settlement plan. Inuzuka's behavior once again proved that the "Jewish experts" never had any real intention of saving the Jewish refugees under their control.

Japan's December 1941 attack on Pearl Harbor, despite the contentions of some scholars, was not the reason that Japan decided to change its Jewish policy. What befell the Jewish refugees following Pearl Harbor resulted, ultimately, from the conclusion of the 1940 Tripartite Pact. In the spring of 1942, the Japanese government officially abandoned the Jewish policy decided at the Five Ministers' Conference, and, following the advice of their German allies, on February 18, 1943, the Japanese military authorities in Shanghai decided to force the Jewish refugees into the Shanghai Ghetto. There the Jews remained until the end of World War II.

Epilogue

The European Jewish Refugees and Shanghai

"We are finished people." The depressed voice of a Jewish woman refugee in Shanghai deeply shocked Anna Ginsbourg, secretary of the International League of Cultural Co-operation in China. In April 1941, Ginsbourg came to one of the refugee camps to interview the Jewish family that produced the first baby born in the Jewish Emigrant's Hospital in Hongkou. The baby was thirteen months old at the time. He was in good health and received sufficient milk from the International Committee's Milk Fund. His older sister, a student at Kadoorie's School for Refugee Children, had an enjoyable conversation with Ginsbourg in "faultless" English. Finally, their "thin, pale and fragile" mother participated in the interview. The mother told the secretary that her family had already spent two years living in the refugee camp, but she and her husband were still unable to find jobs. "But it does not matter," she concluded, "so long as the children are well. We all know that we are finished people."[1]

The term "finished people," according to Ginsbourg, demonstrated "the psychology of the mass."[2] The secretary considered that unemployment, poor health and living conditions, and "shattered nerves by past experiences prior to arrival in Shanghai" were the most important reasons responsible for the refugees' emotional deterioration.[3]

Without jobs and with few possessions, most of the refugees lived in conditions of great hardship during their years in Shanghai. As Berl Falbaum notes,

In making their decision to flee from impending extermination by the Nazis, they nevertheless left a highly civilized and sophisticated culture for a haven that could not have been more unlike the life they had experienced.... In Shanghai, they faced abject poverty, rampant disease, intense heat and humidity, periodic typhoons, a strange and difficult language, no running water, cramped quarters and, ultimately, a life under the occupation of a wartime enemy, the Japanese.[4]

The European Jews came to Shanghai not because they willingly chose the place to live; it was simply the last place to take them in.

This book has focused on the relationships between the policies of Chinese, Japanese, German, and American governments and the European Jewish refugees in Shanghai before and during World War II. The Jewish refugee issue was deeply involved with the complex strategic interests of the powers. Nevertheless, the daily experiences of the Jews in Shanghai are just as important. Previous studies, such as those by David Kranzler and James Ross, draw a detailed picture of the community life of the Shanghai Jews.[5] However, the relations between the Jews and the locals, the native Chinese in particular, have long been neglected by scholars of the field. The refugees' relationship with the local Chinese partly contributed to their decision to leave Shanghai after the end of the war. In fact, most refugees did not establish any relationship with their Chinese hosts. Unlike the earlier Kaifeng Jews, the Shanghai Jews were unable to integrate into either Chinese or Western society in the city, and they remained a lonely and separate group. Indeed, European Jews came to Shanghai under extraordinary circumstances, and the great majority had no intention of establishing a permanent community in China.

As Samuel Didner's and Horst Levin's experiences, discussed in the introduction, make clear, Shanghai had never been the Jewish refugees' first choice. When Jews began fleeing Nazi-controlled territories, their preferred destinations were other European countries or the United States. The refugees not only shared similar lifestyles but also culturally had much in common with other Europeans and the Americans. Some refugees, such as Samuel Didner, chose Shanghai because they were denied visas by every other foreign consular office. Others, such as Horst Levin, needed the ship ticket to Shanghai as proof they intended to leave Europe and to win their release from concentration camps.

Although the European Jews originally expected to immigrate to and start their new lives in Western nations, China was decidedly different, sometimes overwhelmingly so. The refugees had originally been unwilling to consider Shanghai since China in the late 1930s and early 1940s was a poor and underdeveloped society.[6] Obviously, their arrival in Shanghai itself, while a move that saved their lives, was deeply disappointing to many of the refugees. Shoshana Kahan, a Polish refugee from Lodz, recalled after arriving in China from Kobe, Japan, in October 1941, "What a disgusting city Shanghai is...now I understand why everyone fought with all their might to remain in Japan...Now I understand the terrible letters we received from those who had the misfortune to be sent here. A dirty disgusting city."[7] Irene Eber notes that Kahan "hated Shanghai from the moment she set foot in it."[8]

Not surprisingly at all, the reasons that the Jewish refugees came to Shanghai eventually shaped their decisions to leave China after the end of World War II. The end of the war brought them new possibilities of immigration to their preferred countries, and they were eager to depart. The months after August 1945, as Shanghai survivor William Schurtman recalls, were "a period of indescribable confusion and chaos....In the middle of all this confusion, the Hongkew Community was beginning to break up, as hundreds of refugees started to leave for America, Australia, Palestine, and Europe. People talked of nothing else but leaving the city."[9]

Nevertheless, there were a few exceptions. The poem "I love you, Shanghai," penned anonymously by "M," was published in the January 1948 farewell issue of *Future*, a journal put out by the Shanghai Jewish Youth Community. It reads as follows:

> I love you, Shanghai—as long as love lasts
> And until my heart will break
> A city so hot, a city so fast
> From Hongkew to Zikawei Creek.
>
> ...
>
> And a hundred times we shift the gear
> From take it to leave it, from hope to fear
> And we float and ply upon filth and smell
> We take it easy between heaven and hell.
>
> The gangway rolls back and my heart throbs
> The whistle is howling and mother sobs,
> Oh, mother and father, God bless you, Good-bye,
> I stay with Freddy in beloved Shanghai.[10]

Despite the fond sentiments of this poem, at the time this farewell issue appeared the American Jewish Joint Distribution Committee was significantly expanding and strengthening its effort to assist Jewish emigration.

The JDC was determined to settle the Jewish refugees in "new homes."[11] In 1946, it aided approximately twenty-seven thousand Jews from Europe, China, and other countries to immigrate to Palestine, the United States, and other areas.[12] Unlike the anonymous author of this poem, refugees who desired to spend the rest of their lives in Shanghai were fewer than 10 percent.[13]

Even that 10 percent was unable to stay longer, since the Communist revolution was then sweeping China. As Berl Falbaum points out, although a few refugees, "who had successful lives in Shanghai," considered staying in China and actually remained after 1948, they eventually chose to leave "not only because of the terrible conditions but also because of the next danger: The takeover [of the country] by Mao Tse-tung and the Communists."[14]

Pan Guang, on the other hand, contends that "the political situation in China at the time was not directly responsible for the refugees' decision to leave Shanghai." More important, they wanted to "go back to their home-lands and reunite with their families."[15] Tang Peiji further argues that in addition to the horrific and discouraging living conditions in Shanghai, many Jews had few or even no friends or relatives in the city and felt lonely and vulnerable, and they became hopeless for their future in China. Therefore, he concluded, the Jewish refugees simply considered Shanghai a temporary haven, and as soon as they were able to immigrate to their desired countries, most often the United States, they left China.[16]

Was Shanghai merely a "temporary haven" to the refugees? William Schurtman, who lived in Shanghai from 1938 to 1947 and then in Bolivia until 1950 before immigrating to the United States, observes that "most of them regarded their stay in Shanghai as an unpleasant, but at any rate temporary, interlude, and they lived only for the day when they could wander on to America and Australia or return to Europe."[17] Ernest Heppner also recalls in his memoirs,

> We had been living in limbo, in an alien world. No matter how many friends I had made among the Chinese, ours had been an artificial existence. We had struggled to survive the murderous climate, hoping not to succumb to some tropical disease as...thousands of others had done. After our liberation, all...I could think of was getting out of China to the United States. After all, Shanghai was supposed to have been a temporary stopover until our quota number was called.[18]

The younger generation of refugees also expressed their feelings toward Shanghai in the farewell issue of *Future*. As a refugee named Hank editorialized, "We hope, that the Shanghai stage of our lives will soon be at an end and that we will soon be able to make our start in a new and better environment."[19] While many of the younger generation, such as "M," remained sentimental about the city, for the majority their years in Shanghai were at most one stage of their lives, and they were eager and ready to move on. For most of the young refugees, "a better place" meant the United States. In fact, the United States was an endless topic of discussion between the readers and writers of the journal. Readers would wish "the best regards from beautiful America," while the writers would frequently finish their stories with a phrase such as "We hope we will soon be across the Pacific."[20]

Schurtman also points out another significant difference in the attitude toward their host countries between the European Jewish refugee community in Shanghai and other refugee communities in the world. He notes that Jewish refugees in other places "often became completely integrated into the life of the country. They learned the language and the customs." Nevertheless, while in Shanghai, "Few of them ever learned to speak Chinese, and even fewer tried to understand the local customs."[21]

Instead of learning Chinese language and customs, the refugees were more enthusiastic about learning English so that they could be well prepared to immigrate to the United States given the chance. The refugees also discovered enjoyable means to master the language. At the time, "there were three or four Chinese movie theaters in Hongkew, which specialized in American pictures, and these were quickly patronized by refugees—eager not only for entertainment, but also for an opportunity to learn English."[22]

In order to better understand how the refugees regarded Shanghai, it is especially important to examine the relationships between the Jews and the locals, both the Westerners and, especially, the Chinese. Historians and Shanghai survivors most often considered the European Jewish refugees a unique and separate group in the city during the Second World War. Felix Gruenberger, a former Shanghai refugee, divides the city's population into three social groups in addition to the Japanese occupation forces: "(1) The foreigners. These were the wealthy white Europeans ... who looked down upon anyone who had to do work which was lower than the standard for the white population. (2) The refugees ... These people were forced by their condition to accept work usually considered unfit for the 'whites.' (3) The native Chinese."[23] Therefore, he concludes, the "Jewish refugees were practically excluded from contacts with the Foreign Settlement and most of them were forced to live in their own group in Hongkew, thus forming an exclusive group."[24]

Although Shanghai was an open port and dominated by the Western powers and Japan, it was first and foremost a Chinese city. Charles Klotzer describes their relationships with the local Chinese: "While we were surrounded by Chinese and interacted with them on a daily basis, I developed no close relationships with any Chinese. Their lives were much more circumscribed than that of the refugees."[25]

Nevertheless, there were some refugees who developed cordial, and even close, relationships with their hosts. Some Jews got to know and become friends with the Chinese, most often in three different ways: first, some refugees rented houses or apartments from the Chinese. Second, some conducted or shared business with the Chinese. Third, some European Jews were employed along with the Chinese. A few well-off refugee families even hired Chinese servants.

The refugees had increased opportunities to live with the Chinese after February 1943 when they were forced by the Japanese to move into Hongkou, the poorest area in Shanghai, which was heavily occupied by native Chinese. Lilli Finkelstein and her family found an apartment in the area and had Chinese neighbors. Her neighbors, Finkelstein remembers, "were very friendly. They understood that we also had a difficult time. They were the poorest in Shanghai and did not have much education. Nevertheless, I became friends with several women, and a family invited me to their place for the Chinese New Year Eve dinner."[26]

German refugee Ursula Bacon remembers that her father learned from the other refugees about "how foreigners do business in China" soon after they had arrived in Shanghai. According to Mr. Bacon, the foreigners would become bosses themselves and "find a Chinese partner, or a comprador—a sort of local frontman who can wheel and deal in his language with his people accordingly to local customs and business manners. He gets cumshaw (Pidgin English for commission) on each job. The more jobs he brings in, the more money he'll make."[27] It seemed to work very well for the Bacon family. Ursula's father met a Chinese man "who was eager to associate himself with" him and "his idea for a business," and he successfully operated a painting company in Shanghai.[28]

Israel Kipen served as the head of the soup kitchen, which was founded by the Kitchen Fund relief organization and provided refugees free meals in the Hongkou ghetto. He hired a Chinese chef, an "out-going amiable fellow," who was always ready to help. He observed that the Chinese, as a whole, "were seen as obliging, clever, enterprising, wise and self-effacing being bearers of an old culture."[29]

While in Shanghai, Ernest Heppner found a job in a toy store owned by a Russian Jew, Mrs. Rabinovich. She liked the way Heppner served the customers and soon made him manager of a new store of hers, called the "Home of Books."[30] It was in the bookstore that for the first time Heppner had an opportunity to work with the Chinese. He felt that he "was part of the bookstore staff" and often had lunch with them.[31] Heppner records the following in his memoirs:

> I had enjoyed the unusual opportunity to work closely with the Chinese. I got to know my co-workers quite well and grew extremely fond of them. I learned how easy it was to do business with the Chinese, as a handshake would seal any contract. Those with whom I came in contact were hardworking, intelligent, reliable, friendly, and honest with their business friends. I had become very comfortable in this environment, so I was pleased when Liu [a Chinese coworker] invited me to spend a day with him and his family at his home.[32]

Although these refugees enjoyed friendly relationships with their Chinese hosts, some others encountered certain xenophobic, sometimes even anti-Semitic, sentiment during their stay, especially after the end of the war. Nevertheless, most of the refugees reacted to this with understanding rather than hatred, since they were aware that the Chinese themselves were victims of discrimination in a city that had been ruled by foreigners. Shanghai survivor John Isaack explains that "the Chinese people hated all white people" since they had been subjected by the English to "almost inhumane standards" for a very long time, and the Chinese cared deeply about "human dignity and an individual's personal honor and self-respect." In addition, he points out that the Chinese were generally unable to distinguish between Jews and other Westerners in their midst. For the Chinese, they were "all white devils, and all were hated accordingly."[33]

Henry Culman's experience further proves Isaack's point. Culman found a job in a Swiss machine shop in Hongkou after he graduated from the local Jewish school. In the factory, except for Culman and another refugee boy, the workers were all Chinese. Culman was fifteen and had to work seven days a week, ten hours a day. He was doing exactly the same kind of work that his Chinese coworkers did, and believed that "the Chinese had never seen a European being put to such a menial task....All their frustrations and resentments of long mistreatment by colonial powers were vented on me," he recalls. "From the very first day to the last, I was always and only referred to as 'The Foreign Swine.'"[34] Notably, however, Culman was never called "a Jewish Swine."

This type of "xenophobic" behavior escalated after the war. William Schurtman reports that some Chinese "tried to humiliate and insult the refugees in public, secure in the knowledge that the immigrants were vastly outnumbered and could not fight back." "But I am convinced," he emphasizes, "that these Chinese were not motivated by any kind of anti-Semitism but were merely availing themselves of the opportunity to 'get back' at some Whites for the humiliations they themselves once had to suffer under the British and French."[35]

Perhaps the only notable public anti-Semitic incident that related to the local Chinese happened in May 1946. Chinese who claimed to have previously lived in Hongkou, and who insisted that they had been forced to move out of the area by the Japanese in order to create a Jewish ghetto, returned and asserted their rights to houses and apartments that were occupied by Jewish refugees. Further, the Chinese "strung up anti-Semitic banners, proclaiming 'The Japs and the Jews are our enemies.' Chinese also staged street demonstrations in the city, carrying anti-Jewish slogans and caricatures of bearded and hook-nosed Jews." Still, Shanghai survivors who remember this event explain that "the hostility was not directed solely toward Jews. It was part of a resurgence of nationalism that fanned hatred toward all foreigners. There were anti-American demonstrations and riots throughout China."[36]

From early 1946 to late 1950, the JDC successfully arranged for approximately sixteen thousand Jews to leave Shanghai.[37] More than five thousand of them immigrated to the United States.[38] Another fifteen hundred refugees chose to return to Germany and Austria, and twenty-five hundred of them left for Australia. After the establishment of Israel in 1948, the new Jewish homeland accepted more than five thousand refugees from China.[39] When the Chinese Communists took over Shanghai in May 1949, the majority of former Jewish refugees had already left the city. In 1953, there were only 440 Jews still in Shanghai. The number further diminished to 124 in 1956 and 84 in 1958.[40] Ultimately, the remaining Jews left the city after the beginning of the chaotic Cultural Revolution in 1966.[41]

James Ross believes that most of the former Shanghai refugees he met led "full and successful lives."[42] Those in the United States, especially, truly embraced their "American dream."[43] Ross points out that half a century after their Shanghai sojourn, "despite painful memories of poverty and disease, most [former refugees] recall their Shanghai days with a sense of wonder. It was the defining experience of their lives, a time when they learned to see themselves as survivors instead of victims."[44]

After the implementation of Deng Xiaoping's economic reforms and opening in the late 1970s and the establishment of diplomatic relations between the People's Republic of China and Israel in 1992, more and more Shanghai Jews brought their children and grandchildren back to the city.[45] Sigmund Tobias was among those who revisited Shanghai. After immigrating to the United States, Tobias became a renowned educational psychologist and served as president of the Northeastern Educational Research Association and the Division of Educational Psychology of the American Psychological Association. In fall 1988, he was invited to deliver lectures at the Shanghai Institute of Education.[46]

At the end of his last lecture, Tobias handed a personal note to his interpreter and asked him to translate it to his Chinese audience. Sigmund Tobias, one of the twenty thousand Jews that Shanghai saved, was also speaking for many of the others:

> I am happy to have been welcomed so warmly in today's Shanghai, much the way about sixteen thousand other Jews were welcomed here almost fifty years ago. Had we not found safe haven in China then, most of us would not have survived, the way six million of our relatives, friends, and other members of our people were killed during the Second World War. Even though our life here during the Second World War was not easy, we realized how lucky we were to have found shelter in Shanghai when we heard about the…concentration camps. I am grateful to the Chinese people for letting us live among them peacefully during that terrible time, and am happy to have been able to return.[47]

Guo Taiqi, the foreign minister of the Nationalist government, declared in 1928 that Jews "are always welcome to our shores." The sentiment was not an empty one, and Shanghai became the last haven for European Jews during World War II. In their modern history, many Chinese considered Jews with respect and sympathy: Jews were role models for numerous leading nationalists and intellectuals for their movement to save China in the early twentieth century, and fellow victims of Fascist powers in the late 1930s and early 1940s.

When the European Jews first arrived in Shanghai in the summer of 1938, the Chinese were desperately combating the Japanese invasion alone. The Nationalist government accepted Sun Ke's plan in early 1939 to establish a Jewish settlement for the refugees in southwestern China. By doing so, Chinese leaders hoped to attract financial support from world, especially American, Jewry so that they could continue, and eventually prevail in, their resistance against Japan.

As a part of the settlement plan, the Nationalist government also established a "liberal visa policy" to help Jews enter China. Although a visa was not needed to land in the free port of Shanghai, the Chinese policy seemed to aim to favorably impress Jews, and in fact the majority of the refugees came to the city without visas. Nevertheless, Chinese visas, as well as ship tickets to Shanghai, served as evidence of the refugees' intention to leave Nazi Europe during the time of forced migration. They also helped win numerous releases of Jews from concentration camps.

China's settlement plan eventually failed mostly owing to the lack of funds, especially from the United States. Although American Jewish leaders promised assistance, their government made few efforts to rescue the Jews. China's Jewish policy in the late 1930s aimed partly to attract Jewish capital. However, unlike that of Japan's in the same period, China's policy was never intended to harm the refugees. A careful examination of archival records shows no intention by the Nationalists to ever put the physical safety of the refugees in danger if they failed to help implement these arrangements. The Chinese were simply making every effort to survive an invasion by a fascist power.

The Japanese, on the other hand, "learned" from their imported anti-Semitism in the 1930s that the Jews were a "cancer on the world" who exercised worldwide financial and political power. However, the military "Jewish experts," army colonel Yasue Norihiro and navy captain Inuzuka Koreshige, did not merely absorb traditional anti-Semitism, nor did they blindly follow their Axis allies' Jewish policy. Yasue and Inuzuka attempted to use the connections of the Jewish refugees in the world, the United States in particular, to help bring Jewish investment into Japanese-occupied China and to improve Japan's relationships with the United States. The "experts," with the help of military intelligence agencies, did systematic and extensive research on the Jews. This research further confirmed their belief in "Jewish power" and their determination to exploit it. Yasue and Inuzuka deeply believed that the Jewish refugees under their control would be able to contribute to Japan's final victory in its "holy war" in Asia.

The military in the early 1930s successfully seized control of Japan's foreign policy. Therefore, the military "Jewish experts" in the late 1930s were in a position to transform their theories into national policy. After their Jewish policy was officially adopted by the Japanese government at the end of 1938, Yasue and Inuzuka devoted themselves to developing a plan to settle Jewish refugees in Japanese-occupied China in order to help better carry out their policy. If their Jewish settlement plan succeeded, the financial support from American and European Jews, which they believed they would garner, would be used to enhance Japan's military power.

Nevertheless, since Japan's Jewish policy in the late 1930s was initiated by and reflected the desires of the military, the changing strategic situation naturally affected the policy itself. The conclusion of the Tripartite Pact with Germany and Italy in September 1940 ended any possibility of easing tensions between Japan and the United States. The overwhelmingly powerful pro-German group in the government and military considered Japan's relations with the Axis allies more important and insisted that Japan change its Jewish policy. As a Japanese-American war became inevitable, the schemes of the "Jewish experts" became meaningless. The "experts" were soon expelled, and the Jewish settlement plan vanished. Yasue Norihiro and Inuzuka Koreshige's plan to exploit the Jews ironically saved the lives of many European Jewish refugees in Shanghai during the Second World War. Nevertheless, it was simply an accidental result since Colonel Yasue and Captain Inuzuka never had any intention of rescuing Jews. On the contrary, they regularly threatened that if the vulnerable refugees failed to cooperate with Japan, the Japanese would withdraw their "protection." This underscores that the "Jewish experts" did not save the Jews for humanitarian or ethical reasons, as their supporters claimed after the end of World War II, but did so out of expediency.

On the other hand, although many Shanghai survivors still have positive feelings toward and are grateful to the city, they escaped to China from the late 1930s to early 1940s because it was the only place to offer them sanctuary. They chose Shanghai because they had no other option. Polish rabbi Simkha Elberg made his way to the city via Lithuania and Japan. He wrote in 1941, "Three countries spat me out as a dead body is spat out by stormy seas."[48] The city took him in, along with many other European Jews, but it never became the final destination for the refugees. Nevertheless, the remnants of the Shanghai Jews continue to appreciate that the shambling metropolis at the mouth of the Yangtze offered them refuge that allowed them to survive while their families and relatives in Europe were consumed in the flames of the Holocaust.

NOTES

INTRODUCTION

1. See Maisie Meyer, *From the Rivers of Babylon to the Whangpoo: A Century of Sephardi Jewish Life in Shanghai* (Lanham, MD: University Press of America, 2003); and Tang Peiji, Xu Buzeng, Yan Huimin, Gu Borong, and Zheng Yiliu, *Shanghai Youtai ren* [The Shanghai Jews] (Shanghai: Sanlian shudian, 1992), 23–112.
2. See Zhang Tiejiang, *Jiekai Haerbin Youtai ren lishi zhimi = Reveal Enigmas of the Jewish History in Harbin* (Harbin: Heilongjiang renmin chubanshe, 2005); and Herman Dicker, *Wanderers and Settlers in the Far East: A Century of Jewish Life in China and Japan* (New York: Twayne, 1962), 17–60.
3. Saul Friedlander, *Nazi Germany and the Jews, Vol. I. The Years of Persecution, 1933–1939* (New York: HarperCollins, 1997), 177–179, 200–201, 224–225.
4. Sigmund Tobias, *Strange Haven: A Jewish Childhood in Wartime Shanghai* (Urbana: University of Illinois Press, 1999), 2–4; James R. Ross, *Escape to Shanghai: A Jewish Community in China* (New York: Free Press; Toronto: Maxwell Macmillan Canada; New York: Maxwell Macmillan International, 1994), 16.
5. Ross, *Escape to Shanghai*, 16.
6. Friedlander, *Nazi Germany*, 263–264.
7. Ibid., 248–249.
8. Ross, *Escape to Shanghai*, 3–18.
9. Ibid., 26–35.
10. Throughout the text, proper Chinese names are rendered in the pinyin style. The names of historical figures from the Nationalist period follow in parentheses in the older Wade-Giles spelling system, which maybe more familiar to Western readers. The names Sun Yat-sen and Chiang Kai-shek are always rendered in the more common Wade-Giles form.
11. Avraham Altman and Irene Eber, "Flight to Shanghai, 1938–1940: The Larger Setting," *Yad Vashem Studies* 28 (2000): 61–63.
12. David Kranzler, *Japanese, Nazis and Jews: The Jewish Refugee Community of Shanghai, 1938–1945* (New York: Yeshiva University Press, 1976), 174.
13. Ibid., 231–233.
14. Pamela Rotner Sakamoto, *Japanese Diplomats and Jewish Refugees: A World War II Dilemma* (Westport, CT: Praeger, 1998), 7.
15. Marcia Ristaino, *Port of Last Resort: The Diaspora Communities of Shanghai* (Stanford, CA: Stanford University Press, 2001), 280.
16. Ibid.

CHAPTER 1

1. Pan Guang, ed., *Youtairen zai Zhongguo* [The Jews in China] (Beijing: Wuzhou chuanbo chubanshe, 2001), 131.

2. On Sun Yat-sen and the Zionist Movement, see, for example, Zhou Xun, *Chinese Perceptions of the "Jews" and Judaism: A History of the Youtai* (Richmond, Surrey: Curzon Press, 2001); Sun Yat-sen, *Guo fu quan ji* [The Complete Works of Dr. Sun Yat-Sen] (Taipei: Zhongguo guo min dang zhong yang wei yuan hui dang shi wei yuan hui, 1973); and Audrey Wells, *The Political Thought of Sun Yat-sen: Development and Impact* (Houndmills, Basingstoke, Hampshire: Palgrave, 2001). On Chinese intellectuals and Jews, see, for example, Yu Songhua, "Youtairen yu Youtai de fuxing yundong [The Jews and the Jewish Zionist Movement]," *Dongfang zazhi* 24, no. 17 (1927): 27–28; Editorial, "Youtairen de kunan [The Sufferings of the Jews]," *Shenbao*, November 15, 1938, 4; and He Yiwen, "Youtai minzu wenti [The Jewish National Problem]," *Dongfang zazhi* 36, no. 12 (1939): 14–15.

3. Jonathan Goldstein, ed., *The Jews of China: Volume One, Historical and Comparative Perspectives* (Armonk, NY: M. E. Sharpe, 1999), xii.

4. Irene Eber, "Kaifeng Jews: The Sinification of Identity," in Jonathan Goldstein, ed., *The Jews of China: Volume One, Historical and Comparative Perspectives*, 23–24. For more on the Kaifeng Jews, see Donald Daniel Leslie, *The Survival of the Chinese Jews: The Jewish Community of Kaifeng* (Leiden: E. J. Brill, 1972.)

5. Xiao Xian, "An Overview of Chinese Impressions of and Attitudes toward Jews before 1949," in Jonathan Goldstein, ed., *The Jews of China: Volume Two, A Sourcebook and Research Guide* (Armonk, NY: M. E. Sharpe, 2000), 34.

6. Ibid., 35.

7. Ping-Kuen Yu, *Introduction to Tung-fang tsa-chih* [The Eastern Miscellany], Vols. 1–44 (Shanghai: Shangwu yinshu kuan, 1904–1948), microfilm; Leo Ou-fan Lee, *Shanghai Modern: The Flowering of a New Urban Culture in China, 1930–1945* (Cambridge, MA: Harvard University Press, 2001), 47; Xiao Xian, "Chinese Impressions," 35–36.

8. Xiao Xian, "Chinese Impressions," 36.

9. Zhang Xichen, "The Racial Problems in International Relations," *Dongfang zazhi* 9, no. 2 (1912): 5–8; Qian Zhixiu, "Jews and Chinese," *Dongfang zazhi* 8, no. 12 (1911): 39, both cited in Xiao Xian, "Chinese Impressions," 36.

10. Xiao Xian, "Chinese Impressions," 36.

11. Ibid., 37.

12. Zhou Xun, *Chinese Perceptions*, 56–57, 114.

13. Ibid., 114.

14. Jonathan Goldstein, "The Republic of China and Israel, 1911–2003," *Israel Affairs* 10, no. 1–2 (October–December 2004): 223.

15. Zhou Xun, *Chinese Perceptions*, 113; Goldstein, "The Republic of China and Israel," 224.

16. Goldstein, "The Republic of China and Israel," 225.

17. *Israel's Messenger*, November 24, 1927, quoted in Goldstein, "The Republic of China and Israel," 225.

18. The Archives of the Institute of Modern History, Academia Sinica, Taipei. Foreign Ministry Documents, 03-41-022-04, "Documents concerning the Jewish Zionism," February 23, 1919, Charles A. Cowen to Toneng Loh, Vice-Minister of Foreign Affairs.

19. Sun Yat-sen to N. E. B. Ezra, April 24, 1920, in *Guo fu quan ji* [The Complete Works of Dr. Sun Yat-Sen], Vol. 5, 426–427. Also see Zhou Xun, *Chinese Perceptions*, 57.
20. Wells, *Political Thought of Sun Yat-sen*, 61.
21. Sun Yat-sen and Zhang Qiyun, *Guo fu quan shu* [The Complete Works of the Founding Father] (Taipei: Guo fang yan jiu yuan, 1960), 187; Sun Yat-sen, translated by Frank W. Price, *The Principle of Nationalism* (Taipei: Chinese Cultural Service, 1953), 6.
22. Sun Yat-sen and Zhang Qiyun, *Guo fu quan shu*, 196; Sun Yat-sen, *Principle of Nationalism*, 20.
23. Sun Yat-sen and Zhang Qiyun, *Guo fu quan shu*, 198; Sun Yat-sen, *Principle of Nationalism*, 20–23.
24. Wells, *Political Thought of Sun Yat-sen*, 72.
25. "Tenth Anniversary of the Balfour Declaration—China and Japan Greet New Judea," *Israel's Messenger*, December 2, 1927, 4–5.
26. "A Leader of Chinese Nationalists Expresses Faith in Jewish Nationalism," *Israel's Messenger*, March 2, 1928, 17.
27. Ibid.
28. Tang Peiji et al., *Shanghai Youtairen*, 244.
29. Jung Chang and Jon Halliday, *Mme Sun Yat-Sen (Soong Ching-ling)* (Harmondsworth, Middlesex: Penguin Books, 1986), 75.
30. Ibid., 78.
31. Xiao Xian, "Chinese Impressions," 37.
32. Zhou Xun, *Chinese Perceptions*, 116–117.
33. Ibid.
34. Yu Songhua, "Youtairen yu Youtai de fuxing yundong," 27–28. Also see Xiao Xian, "Chinese Impressions," 38.
35. Editorial, "Youtairen de kunan," 4.
36. Li Zheng, "Guanyu paiyou [About Anti-Semitism]," *Yi bao zhou kan*, No. 9, December 7, 1938, 234–235.
37. He Yiwen, "Youtai minzu wenti," 14–15. Also see Xiao Xian, "Chinese Impressions," 40.
38. Xiao Xian, "Chinese Impressions," 39.
39. Eber, "Kaifeng Jews," 22–23.
40. William Kirby, *Germany and Republican China* (Stanford, CA: Stanford University Press, 1984), 167.
41. Ibid.
42. Ibid.
43. Ibid., 167–168.
44. Chung Dooeum, *Elitist Fascism: Chiang Kaishek's Blueshirts in 1930s China* (Aldershot; Burlington, VT: Ashgate, 2000), xi.
45. Ch'en P'u, "Min-tsu fu-hsing yu Chung-kuo cheng-chih" [The Revival of the Race and Chinese Politics], *Ch'ien-t'u* [The Future] 3, no. 6 (June 1935): 62, quoted in Kirby, *Germany and Republican China*, 168.
46. Lloyd E. Eastman, "Fascism in Kuomintang China: The Blue Shirts," *China Quarterly*, no. 49 (1972): 28–29.
47. Kirby, *Germany and Republican China*, 169.
48. Archives of the Japanese Ministry of Foreign Affairs, 1868–1945, S series, microfilms (hereafter AJMFA). "Copy, Translation of a Telegram from the Japanese Consul-General at Harbin," February 1935, S9460-3, 536.
49. David Goodman and Masanori Miyazawa, *Jews in the Japanese Mind: The History and Uses of a Cultural Stereotype* (New York: Free Press, 1995), 9; Pamela Rotner

Sakamoto, *Japanese Diplomats and Jewish Refugees: A World War II Dilemma* (Westport, CT: Praeger, 1998), 17.

50. Goodman and Miyazawa, *Jews in the Japanese Mind*, 9.
51. Ibid., 77.
52. This claim is repeated by the son of Yasue Norihiro, Yasue Hiroo, in *Dairen tokumu kikan to maboroshi no Yudaya kokka* [The Dairen Intelligence Agency and the Phantom Jewish State] (Tokyo: Yahata Shoten, 1989), 34. Similarly, Marvin Tokayer and Mary Swartz assert in *The Fugu Plan* that "along with the rifles and canteens, [White Russian General Gregorii] Semonov issued to each soldier a copy of *The Protocols of the Elders of Zion*." Marvin Tokayer and Mary Swartz, *The Fugu Plan: The Untold Story of the Japanese and the Jews during World War II* (New York: Paddington Press, 1979), 47. David Goodman likewise contends that "White Russian soldiers in Siberia were being issued with copies of The Protocols to familiarise them with the enemy they were supposedly fighting. Japanese soldiers also received copies." David Goodman, "Anti-Semitism in Japan: Its History and Current Implications," in Frank Dikotter, ed., *The Construction of Racial Identities in China and Japan: Historical and Contemporary Perspectives* (Honolulu: University of Hawaii Press, 1998), 181.
53. Yasue Hiroo, *Dairen tokumu kikan*, 34–35.
54. Ibid., 7.
55. Ibid., 25–28.
56. Ibid., 34–35.
57. Hō Kōshi [Yasue Norihiro], *Sekai kakumei no rimen* [Behind the World Revolution] (Tokyo: Niyū Meicho Kankōkai, 1924).
58. Ibid., 39.
59. Ibid., 53.
60. Inuzuka Kiyoko, *Yudaya mondai to Nihon no kōsaku* [The Jewish Problem and Japanese Maneuvering] (Tokyo: Nihon Kōgyō Shinbunsha, 1982), 65–68.
61. Ibid., 68–69.
62. Yasue Norihiro, *Yudaya minzoku no sekai shihai?* [The Jewish Control of the World?] (Tokyo: Kokon Shoin, 1933).
63. Inuzuka Koreshige, *Yudayajin no inbō to kokusai supai* [The Plot of the Jews and International Spies] (Tokyo: Naikaku Jōhōbu, 1938); Utsunomiya Kiyō [Inuzuka Koreshige], *Yudaya mondai to Nihon* [The Jewish Problem and Japan] (Tokyo: Naigai shobō, 1939).
64. "Yudaya mondai to Furī Mēson [The Jewish Problem and the Free Masons]," May 26, 1933. Selected archives of the Japanese Army, Navy and other government agencies, 1868–1945, the Library of Congress, microfilm collection, no. 5041, reel 93, F 19766–19848.
65. John Young, *The Research Activities of the South Manchurian Railway Company, 1907–1945: A History and Bibliography* (New York: East Asian Institute, Columbia University, 1966), 3.
66. Ibid., 4.
67. Itō Takeo, *Life along the South Manchurian Railway—the Memoirs of Itō Takeo*, translated by Joshua A. Fogel (Armonk, NY: M. E. Sharpe, 1988), 16.
68. Itō, *Life*, 3.
69. Young, *Research Activities*, 3.
70. Itō, *Life*, 152; Young, *Research Activities*, 6.
71. Young, *Research Activities*, 28.
72. Itō, *Life*, 116.

73. Liaoning sheng dangan guan [The Archives of the Liaoning Province], ed., *Man tie mi dang: Man tie yu qin Hua Ri jun* [Secret Documents from the South Manchurian Railway Company: The South Manchurian Railway Company and the Japanese Invading Army] (Guilin: Guangxi shifan daxue chubanshe, 1999), Vol. 18, 142. *Man tie mi dang* is a series of collections of rare documents from the South Manchurian Railway Company held by the Liaoning Provincial Archives. *Man tie yu qin Hua Ri jun* collected approximately fifteen hundred documents exchanged between the SMR and the Kwantung Army. These documents reflect the interdependent relationship between the SMR and the military authorities in China.

74. Xie Xueshi, *Ge shi yi si: ping Man tie diao cha bu* [Thoughts Left by the Last Generation: Reviewing the Research Department of the South Manchurian Railway Company] (Beijing: Renmin chubanshe, 2003), 616.

75. Imura Tetsuo, ed., *Mantetsu Chōsabu: kankeisha no shōgen* [The Research Activities of the South Manchurian Railway Company: The Reminiscences of the Research Staff] (Tokyo: Ajia keizai kenkyūjo: Hatsubaijo Ajia Keizai Shuppankai, 1996), 600.

76. Manchuria at the time was controlled by the "Manchurian Group" within the "Imperial Way clique" in the army. In foreign affairs, the "Imperial Way clique," especially the "Manchurian Group," emphasized "the 'Manchurian' panacea for Japan's ills of overpopulation and lack of natural resources," and Manchuria's position as a "natural buffer between the Japanese mainland and the Soviet Union." Therefore, they saw Manchuria as "the key to Japan's national defense hopes." David Kranzler, *Japanese, Nazis and Jews*, 187–192, 219. Kranzler is particularly informative about the "Imperial Way clique" and the "Manchurian Group." Also see chapter 3 for the Kwantung Army's strategic goals in Manchuria.

77. Imura, *Mantetsu Chōsabu*, 600.

78. Ibid. The current Dalian City Library formerly served as the SMR Library; it is also the biggest library and information center Japan established in China during the war. The Dalian City Library still houses collections left by the Special Research Team after Japan's surrender and has opened them to the public. The "Jewish Collection" comprises 1,023 items, including books, newspapers, and periodicals. It focuses on Jewish history, culture, religion, and literature. It also contains resources concerning Jews in the United States and European countries, and on Judaism, Palestine, Zionism, freemasonry, anti-Semitism, and "the Jewish Problem." The materials are in German, French, English, Russian, Italian, and Japanese. There are Hebrew dictionaries and grammar books, too. Interestingly, the collection includes not only anti-Semitic works, but also books by Jews, such as Rabbi Joachim Prinz's *We Jews* (Berlin: Verlegt Bei Erich Reiss, 1934), and influential American Jewish columnist George Sokolsky's *We Jews* (Garden City, NY: Doubleday, 1935).

79. The details about the reports and periodical are based on the author's research at the Library of Congress. Also see Young, *Research Activities*, 585–589; Xie, *Ge shi yi si*, 617; Ajia Keizai Kenkyūjo Tosho Shiryōbu, ed., *Kyū shokuminchi kankei kikan kankōbutsu sōgō mokuroku* [General Catalogue of the Publications of the Organizations Related to Former Colonies] (Tokyo: Ajia Keizai Kenkyūjo, 1973–1979), 565–567.

80. Imura, *Mantetsu Chōsabu*, 600–601.

81. Arnold Spencer Leese, "Jewish Influence in British Political World," translated by Ishidō Kiyotomo, *Yudaya mondai chōsa shiryō* [Research Materials on the Jewish Problem], No. 13 (The Special Research Team of the SMR, 1938), 01.

82. Narahashi Wataru, "Narahashi shi no kataru Ōbei Yudaya seiryoku to Mantetsu no kokusai teki chii [Narahashi's Lecture on Jewish Influence in Europe and the United States, and the International Status of the SMR]." The Special Research Team of the Research Department, the SMR, report No. 35, 1939, 1–2.

83. Ibid., 2.

84. Minami Manshū Tetsudō Kabushiki Kaisha Chōsabu, *Beikoku no Yudayajin shakai to sono dantai* [Jewish Community and Organizations in the United States] (Dairen-shi: Minami Manshū Tetsudō Kabushiki Kaisha, 1939), translation of Maurice J. Karpf, *The Jewish Community and Organization in the United States: An Outline of Types of Organizations, Activities, and Problems* (New York: Bloch, 1938.)

85. The Diplomatic Record Office of the Ministry of Foreign Affairs of Japan, Japan Center for Asian Historical Records (hereafter JACAR; this digital archive may be found at http://www.jacar.go.jp). Reference no. C01003705300, the Ministry of Army, "Regarding the Special Research Team of the South Manchurian Railway Company," July 1941.

86. Sakamoto, *Japanese Diplomats*, 26; Goodman and Miyazawa, *Jews in the Japanese Mind*, 94.

87. Inuzuka Kiyoko, *Yudaya mondai to Nihon no kōsaku*, 66–67.

88. JACAR, B04013207300, 0355–0357, "A Short Biography of Felix Frankfurter in the New York Jewish Journal 'American Hebrew,'" *Jewish Information*, no. 58, March 7, 1939.

89. AJMFA, "Summary of the Jewish Refugee Issue in Shanghai," *Top Secret Jewish Information*, no. 5, January 27, 1939. S9460-3, 960–963.

90. JACAR, B04013207300, 0370–0371, "Information about the Shanghai Jewish Club," *Top Secret Jewish Information*, no. 9, March 24, 1939.

91. Miyazawa Masanori, "Japanese Anti-Semitism in the Thirties," *Midstream* (March 1987): 23.

92. Ibid., 24.

93. Goodman and Miyazawa, *Jews in the Japanese Mind*, 89.

94. Ibid., 94, 96–97.

95. Yamagata Tokon [Nunokawa Magoichi], "Yudaya minzoku no seikaku ni tsuite" [Regarding the Characteristics of the Jewish People], *Teiyu rinrikai rinri koen shu*, February 1926, 87. Cited in Goodman and Miyazawa, *Jews in the Japanese Mind*, 97.

96. Nunokawa Seien [Nunokawa Magoichi], "Yudaya Himitsuryoku no Urakosaku" [The Secret Machinations of Covert Jewish Power], *Teiyu rinrikai rinri koen shu* (July 1938): 108. Cited in Goodman and Miyazawa, *Jews in the Japanese Mind*, 99.

97. Goodman and Miyazawa, *Jews in the Japanese Mind*, 100.

98. Ibid., 101–104; Miyazawa, *Midstream*, 26.

99. "Shimpuson Fujin, Nihon Eiga ni Kunrin suru Yudaya Kinken, Nichidoku Bokyo Kyotei Zadankai [Panel Discussion on Mrs. Simpson, The Jewish Money that Rules Over the Japanese Film Industry, and the Anti-Comintern Pact]," *Kokusai Himitsuryoku no Kenkyū*, no. 2, 147–148. Cited in Goodman and Miyazawa, *Jews in the Japanese Mind*, 104–105.

100. Miyazawa, *Midstream*, 26.

101. For a discussion of how the Japanese, especially the military officers, saved and protected the Jewish refugees in China during World War II, see Uesugi Chitoshi, *Yudaya nanmin to hakkō ichiu* [The Jewish Refugees and Hakkō Ichiu] (Tokyo: Tendensha, 2002); Inuzuka Kiyoko, *Yudaya mondai to Nihon no kōsaku*; and Yasue Hiroo, *Dairen tokumu kikan to maboroshi no Yudaya kokka*.

CHAPTER 2

1. "The Righteous of the Nations: Feng-shan Ho, China," Yad Vashem, http://www1
   .yadvashem.org/yv/en/righteous/stories/ho.asp, accessed July 7, 2011.
2. Academia Historica (the National Archives of Taiwan), Foreign Ministry
   Documents, 611.21/172–1/3046 (hereafter FMD). "The Executive Yuan to the
   Ministry of Foreign Affairs concerning the Establishment of a Jewish Settlement
   in Southwest China and the Drafting of Overseas Propaganda," March 14, 1939.
   Also see "President of the Legislative Yuan Sun Ke's Proposal concerning 'the
   Establishment of a Settlement in Southwestern China to Accommodate
   Destitute and Homeless Jewish People,'" March 2, 1939. Shao Minghuang, ed.,
   "Kangzhan shiqi guomin zhengfu rongliu Youtairen jihua dangan yizu"
   [Collection of Documents concerning the Nationalist Government's Plan to
   Accommodate Jews during the Sino-Japanese War]. *Jindai Zhongguo* [Modern
   China], no. 147 (February 25, 2002): 168; 170–171. Shao Minghuang is the
   director of the Archives of the Chinese Nationalist Party in Taiwan. His article
   introduced the background of the Nationalist government's settlement plan
   and eighteen documents from the Central Executive Council and the Highest
   National Defense Council. These records are housed in the Archives of the
   Chinese Nationalist Party.
3. Ibid.
4. See Suisheng Zhao, *Power by Design: Constitution-Making in Nationalist China*
   (Honolulu: University of Hawaii Press, 1996).
5. Academia Historica, Executive Yuan Documents, 271.12/1/62/1330 (hereafter
   EYD). "Minute of the 408th Meeting of the Executive Yuan," April 4, 1939. Also
   see "Drafted Memorandum Submitted to the Highest National Defense Council:
   Opinions of the Executive Yuan concerning the Jewish Settlement Plan," April 20,
   1939, in Shao, "Collection of Documents," 171–175.
6. In 1921, the newly established Bolshevik government annulled the citizenship of
   Russians living outside the Soviet Union. Ristaino explains that as a result the
   Russians, both Jews and non-Jews, in China "no longer had either independent
   legal jurisdiction . . . or the protection of representatives of a home government."
   Marcia Reynders Ristaino, *Port of Last Resort: The Diaspora Communities of Shanghai*
   (Stanford, CA: Stanford University Press, 2001), 37.
7. FMD, "Opinions of the Secretariat of the Executive Yuan [on the Jewish
   Settlement Plan]," No. 871, March 22, 1939. Also, although Germany and China
   officially severed diplomatic relations in July 1941, Germany had recalled its
   ambassador to China earlier, in June 1938. The Nationalist officials indicated
   clearly in the relevant Foreign Ministry and Executive Yuan documents that the
   Germans did not enjoy consular jurisdiction at the time. It appears that the
   Germans gave up such rights after Hitler recalled his ambassador to China.
   Nothing, in either the primary or secondary record, has been found that addresses
   this issue specifically.
8. Ibid., "Memorandum on a Jewish Settlement in China," prepared for the Executive
   Yuan by Dr. T. F. Tsiang in May 1939, noted that "In the process of building up our
   nation, we need the services of many specialists of different ranks and professions,
   such as scientists, engineers, medical doctors, and mechanics." FMD, Hollington
   K. Tong to Wang [Zhengting], May 10, 1939.
9. FMD, "Opinions of the Secretariat of the Executive Yuan [on the Jewish Settlement
   Plan]."

10. FMD, "From the Secretariat of the Executive Yuan to the Foreign Ministry: Opinions of the Ministries of Interior, Foreign Affairs, Military Affairs, Finance and Transportation concerning the Settlement of Jewish Refugees," March 15, 1939.
11. Guo Hengyu, "Sun Zhongshan yu Deguo" [Sun Yat-sen and Germany]. *Guoshiguan guankan* [Journal of the Academia Historica], no. 23 (1997): 83.
12. William C. Kirby, *Germany and Republican China* (Stanford, CA: Stanford University Press, 1984), 3.
13. Ibid., 253–254.
14. "Memorandum by Weizsacker," July 22, 1937, 917; "Dirksen to German Foreign Ministry," Tokyo, July 27, 1937, 918; "Memorandum by Heyden-Rynsch," October 19, 1937, 920; "Dirksen to German Foreign Ministry," Tokyo, November 8, 1937, 925; "Memorandum by Neurath," September 22, 1937, 926, all in Zhang Bofeng and Zhuang Jianping, eds., *Kang Ri zhan zheng* [The Anti-Japanese War] (Hereafter KRZZ), Vol. 4, no. 1 (Chengdu: Sichuan daxue chubanshe, 1997); Tao Wenzhao, ed., *Kang zhan shiqi Zhongguo waijiao* [Chinese Diplomacy during the Anti-Japanese War] (Chengdu: Sichuan daxue chubanshe, 1997).
15. Zhang Beigen, "1933–1941 nian de Zhong De guanxi" [The Sino-German Relations: 1933–1941], *Lishi Yanjiu*, no. 2 (1995): 116. Chen Renxia, *Zhong De Ri sanjiao guanxi yanjiu*, 1936–1938 [The Study of the Triangle Relations of China, Germany and Japan: 1936–1938] (Beijing: Sanlian shudian, 2003), 263–268.
16. "Germany Colluded with Japan: Germany Recognized 'Manchukuo,'" February 20, 1938, 191; "Germany Decided Not to Accept Military Trainees from China and Japan during the Conflict," March 3, 1938, 233; "Germany Withdrew Its Military Advisers in China," May 21, 1938, 484; "German and Italian Leaders Met in Roma and Decided to Strengthen Their Cooperation with Japan; Hitler Secretly Imposed an Arms Embargo on China," May 3, 1938, 442; "Germany Recalled Ambassador Oskar P. Trautmann," June 26, 1938, 598, all in Zhu Huisen, Lai Min, and He Zhilin, eds., *Zhonghua Minguo shishi jiyao chugao: 1938* [First Edition of the Records of Historical Events of the Republic of China, 1938] (Taipei: Guo shi guan, 1989).
17. Kirby, *Germany and Republican China*, 254.
18. KRZZ, Vol. 4, no. 1, "Chiang Kai-shek to Chen Jie," Changsha, November 11, 1939, "Chiang Kai-shek to Kong Xiangxi," Nanyue, November 24, 1939, 958; "Martin Fischer to German Foreign Ministry," Shanghai, December 9, 1939, 959–960.
19. Kirby, *Germany and Republican China*, 222–223.
20. Marcia Ristaino asserts that Jacob Berglas "presented his plan to the Chinese government" and "his request received support from Sun Fo." Ristaino, *Port of Last Resort*, 117. In fact, Sun Ke and Jakob Berglas formulated different plans. The Chinese League of Nations Union (*Zhongguo guoji lianmeng tongzhihui*) was a non-governmental organization established on February 11, 1919, in Beijing to support and promote the spirit of the League of Nations. Liang Qichao was elected its first president. See Zhou Qian and Chen Jimin, "Lun Beijing zhengfu shiqi Zhongguo dui guolian chengli de renshi he canyu (On China's Recognition and Participation in the Establishment of the League of Nations during the Period of the Beijing Government)," *Beihua daxue xuebao* (shehui kexue ban) 9, no. 1 (2008): 79–80.
21. "Berglas Plan for Yunnan Colony of 100,000 Europeans," American Consulate in Kobe, Japan to the Secretary of State, August 11, 1939. RG59, Confidential U.S.

State Department Central Files: China, Internal Affairs, 1930–1939 (hereafter CUSSDCF-China), 893.55/35, LM 182, Reel 96.

22. "Yunnan to Take Jewish Emigres: South-west to Absorb 100,000 Europeans in New Plan," *Shanghai Evening Post*, June 22, 1939.
23. "'Shō ni gomakasarenu' Unnan-shō 'Yudayajinkyō' no motojime shikin atsume ni tobei" ["Don't Be Fooled by Chiang [Kai-shek]": The Promoter of the "Jewish Settlement" in Yunnan on His Way to Collect Funds in the United States]," *Daichō Shimbun*, Shanghai, August 10, 1939.
24. FMD, "Jakob Berglas to H.H. Kung," June 6, 1939. Attachment, "Plan for the Immigration of Central European Immigrants into China."
25. Ibid.
26. "Proposal of the Jewish Immigration Plan from the Chinese League of Nations Union to the Central Executive Committee of the Chinese Nationalist Party," May 26, 1939, in Shao, "Collection of Documents," 176–177.
27. Ibid.
28. FMD, "Governor Long Yun's Proposal to Use Jewish Refugees to Cultivate Yunnan, Forwarded by the Secretariat of the Highest National Defense Council to the Ministry of Foreign Affairs," June 27, 1939.
29. "Secretary-General Zhu Jiahua to President Chiang Kai-shek: Comments on Advantages and Disadvantages of German Jew Berglas's 'Plan for the Immigration of Central European Jews into China' Forwarded by the Chinese League of Nations Union," June 22, 1939, in Shao, "Collection of Documents," 181–183.
30. EYD, Wei Tao-ming to Jakob Berglas, July 26, 1939.
31. Maurice William, *The Social Interpretation of History: A Refutation of the Marxian Economic Interpretation of History* (Long Island City, NY: Sotery, 1921). Maurice Zolotow, *Maurice William and Sun Yat-sen* (London: Robert Hale, 1948), 108–110.
32. Zolotow, *Maurice William*, 9.
33. James Shotwell, "Sun Yat-sen and Maurice William," *Political Science Quarterly* 47, no. 1 (1932): 20–22.
34. The Maurice William Archives (hereafter MWA), UCLA, the Center for Chinese Studies, http://www.international.ucla.edu/china/WilliamMauriceArchive/, A21.003. Maurice William to Herbert Hoover, August 4, 1928.
35. Zolotow, *Maurice William*, 112–113.
36. Ibid., 121.
37. Maurice William, *Sun Yat-sen versus Communism: New Evidence Establishing China's Right to the Support of Democratic Nations* (Baltimore: Williams & Wilkins, 1932).
38. MWA, A17.001, Maurice William to James Shotwell, July 6, 1932.
39. Ibid.
40. MWA, A7.001, Maurice William to Albert Einstein, January 30, 1934.
41. MWA, A7.002, Albert Einstein to Maurice William, February 13, 1934.
42. MWA, A7.004, Maurice William to Albert Einstein, February 19, 1934.
43. MWA, A7.013, Maurice William to Albert Einstein, February 27, 1935.
44. FMD, Chengting T. Wang to C.H., July 21, 1939.
45. Zolotow, 121.
46. A number of local committees were set up to attend to the growing number of Jewish refugees arriving in Shanghai. In 1934, the first such relief committee in Shanghai, the Relief Society for German and Austrian Jews, was established by German and Austrian Jews. In July 1938, a group of Jewish and non-Jewish

Europeans in Shanghai founded the "I.C.," the International Committee for European Refugees. The "I.C." was also commonly called the Komor Committee as Paul Komor, a Hungarian businessman, chaired the committee. In the full of 1938, the two committees combined as a new organization called the Committee for the Assistance of European Jewish Refugees in Shanghai. James R. Ross, *Escape to Shanghai: A Jewish Community in China* (New York: Free Press, 1994), 52–53.

47. Letter from M. Speelman to the American Consul General in Shanghai (Gauss), March 1, 1939, attached to "Jewish Refugees in Shanghai," letter from the American Consulate General in Shanghai to the State Department, March 8, 1939, CUSSDCF-China, 893.55 J/10.

48. Ibid.

49. EYD, "Text of a Telegraphic Message from the Ministry of Foreign Affairs, Chungking, May 6, 1939," attached to Hu Shih to Maurice William, May 18, 1939.

50. FMD, Hu Shih to the Ministry of Foreign Affairs, attention Hollington Tong, April 29, 1939.

51. Ibid.

52. Hu Shi, *Hu Shi koushu zizhuan* [The Oral Autobiography of Hu Shi], Tang Degang, ed. (Guilin: Guangxi shifan daxue chubanshe, 2005), 40.

53. EYD, "Text of a Telegraphic Message from the Ministry of Foreign Affairs, Chungking, May 6, 1939," attached to Hu Shi to Maurice William, May 18, 1939.

54. EYD, Maurice William's marginal comments on two newspaper articles from the *New York Herald Tribune*: "Colony in China Is Planned for 100,000 Exiles: Government Is Interested in German's Proposal for Yunnan Refugee Haven," June 20, 1939; "Chinese Official Rules Out Big Colony for Refugees: Says 'Few Thousand' Might Find Home, but Not 100,000," June 22, 1939.

55. FMD, Maurice William to Hu Shi, May 31, 1939.

56. FMD, second letter from Maurice William to Hu Shi, May 31, 1939.

57. Ibid.

58. Ibid.

59. Ibid.

60. FMD, Maurice William to Wang Zhengting, July 3, 1939.

61. FMD, Chengting T. Wang to C. H., July 21, 1939.

62. EYD, Sun Fo to Maurice William, August 15, 1939.

63. EYD, Wei Tao-ming to Maurice William, August 9, 1939.

64. EYD, "General Principles Governing the Working of the Plan for the Immigration of Jews into China," attached to Wei Tao-ming to Jakob Berglas, July 26, 1939.

65. EYD, Maurice William to H. H. Kung, August 28, 1939.

66. F. Tillman Durdin, "Roosevelt Spurs Chinese," *New York Times*, July 31, 1939.

67. EYD, Maurice William to Hu Shi, August 22, 1939.

68. Ibid.

69. Ibid.

70. EYD, Maurice William to H. H. Kung, August 28, 1939.

71. "Memorandum of Conversation," August 31, 1939, CUSSDCF-China, 893.55 J/21.

72. Maurice William to Albert Einstein, October 31, 1939, Albert Einstein Archives, the Jewish & National University Library, Jerusalem, Call No.: 54–623.00.

73. David S. Wyman, *Paper Walls: America and the Refugee Crisis 1938–1941* (New York: Pantheon Books, 1968, 1985), xiii.

74. Ibid., 213.
75. Saul Friedlander, *Nazi Germany and the Jews, Vol. I. The Years of Persecution, 1933–1939* (New York: HarperCollins, 1997), 248–249.
76. Wyman, *Paper Walls*, 210–211.
77. Richard Breitman and Alan M. Kraut, *American Refugee Policy and European Jewry, 1933–1945* (Bloomington: Indiana University Press, 1987), 232–233.
78. Ibid., 232.
79. Ibid., 232, 8–9.
80. See Vivian Jeanette Kaplan, *Ten Green Bottles: The True Story of One Family's Journey from War-Torn Austria to the Ghetto of Shanghai* (New York: St. Martin's Press, 2002), 93; Berl Falbaum, *Shanghai Remembered: Stories of Jews Who Escaped to Shanghai from Nazi Europe* (Royal Oak, MI: Momentum Books, 2005), 85, 98; Sidney B. Kurtz, *Marcel Singer: The Gentle Butcher of Hongkew* ([Philadelphia]: Xlibris Corporation, 2003), 20–23.
81. Sigmund Tobias, *Strange Haven: A Jewish Childhood in Wartime Shanghai* (Urbana: University of Illinois Press, 1999), 3–4; Ross, *Escape to Shanghai*, 18.
82. "Feng-Shan Ho, China," http://www1.yadvashem.org/yv/en/righteous/stories/ho.asp, accessed July 7, 2011.
83. "Consular Body Unable to Halt Refugees Flow from Europe to S'hai: Reply to Request from S.M.C. to Be Sent in a Day or Two; Home Governments to Be Asked to Dissuade Émigrés from Coming Here," *The Shanghai Times*, February 5, 1939.
84. B. S. Barbash & Co. to the Secretary of the SMC, August 15, 1939. Shanghai Municipal Archives Files, reel 4, U001/4/2972, File No. K38/1, 0544. In cooperation with the United States Holocaust Memorial Museum, the Shanghai Municipal Archives gathered all the Jewish-related documents it holds and transferred them onto five microfilms. These microfilms are currently in the possession of the United States Holocaust Memorial Museum. The above file is hereafter referred to as SMAF.
85. Visas 1, 2, and 3 were provided to the author by Shanghai Jewish survivors with whom she corresponded from 2004 to 2006. Visas 4 and 5 were obtained from the collections of the United States Holocaust Memorial Museum (USHMM), catalog no. 2005.24, "Lubinski Family Papers, USHMM: Gift of Susan Herlinger." Visa 6 is available on the website of the USHMM's Photo Archives, "Schenker Citizenship Document," http://www.ushmm.org/museum/exhibit/online/flight_rescue/search_results.php?type=2&q=&object_type=Object, accessed July 7, 2011.
86. EYD, the Foreign Ministry to the Secretariat of the Executive Yuan concerning Governor Long Yun's Proposal to Use Jewish Refugees to Cultivate Yunnan, July 4, 1939.
87. "Report from the Acting Consul General Yao Dingchen to the Foreign Ministry concerning the Activities of the Consulate General," May 22, 1940, Foreign Ministry Documents, 914.3/0238, housed in the archives of the Institute of Modern History, Taipei (hereafter FMD–IMH). Files of the Consulate General in Vienna.
88. "Files regarding Visas to Foreign Nationals." Telegram No. 63, January 13, 1941, from Sinoconsul in Amsterdam to the Foreign Ministry concerning Fuerstenberg's request for Visas to China; telegram from the Foreign Ministry to Sinoconsul Amsterdam (undated). FMD-IMH, 745.3.
89. He Fengshan, *Waijiao shengya sishi nian* [Forty Years of My Diplomatic Life] (Hong Kong: Zhongwen daxue chubanshe, 1990), 75–76.
90. Ibid., 76.

91. V. K. Wellington Koo, *The Wellington Koo Memoir* (New York: Columbia University, East Asian Institute, 1978), Vol. 4 (5), 750.
92. Ibid., p. 752; FMD, telegram from Ambassador Gu Weijun in Paris to the Foreign Ministry in Chongqing, No. 7879, June 22, 1939.
93. FMD, telegram from Ambassador Gu Weijun in Paris to the Foreign Ministry in Chongqing, No. 7879, June 22, 1939.
94. Koo, *The Wellington Koo Memoir*, 751; FMD, telegram from Gu Weijun to the Foreign Ministry, no. 8715, August 18, 1939.
95. FMD, the Foreign Ministry to the Chinese Embassy in France, no. 043204, August 21, 1939.
96. FMD-IMH, 745.3, "Files Regarding Visas to Foreign Nationals." February 7, 1941, from Vice-Consulate of the Republic of China in Antwerp, Belgium to the Foreign Ministry concerning "Requests for Entry Visas by Jews."
97. He, *Waijiao shengya sishi nian*, 76.

CHAPTER 3

1. "*Hakkō Ichiu*," or "[bringing] all eight corners of the world under one roof [meaning Japan]," was a phrase that imperial Japan employed during the Second World War to justify its invasion of East Asian countries. "*Hakkō Ichiu*" indicates Japan's dream of excluding European powers from Asia and creating a "Greater East Asia Co-prosperity Sphere" under its leadership.
2. JACAR: B04013204800, 0076–0077. *Top Secret Jewish Information*, No. 2, "Detailed Report on the First Far Eastern Jewish Conference," February 17, 1938; JACAR: B04013204800, 0085. *Top Secret Jewish Information*, No. 2, "Detailed Report on the First Far Eastern Jewish Conference," February 17, 1938; AJMFA, No. 1472, From Foreign Minister Konoe Fumimaro to consular offices in China and Manchukuo, "Colonel Yasue's Speech at the Meeting of the Committee on the Muslim and Jewish Problem," October 13, 1938, S9460-3, 750–766; Liaoning sheng dangan guan [The Archives of the Liaoning Province], ed. *Man tie mi dang: Man tie yu qin Hua Ri jun* [Secret Documents from the South Manchurian Railway Company: The South Manchurian Railway Company and the Japanese Invading Army] (Guilin: Guangxi shifan daxue chubanshe, 1999), Vol. 18, 303–308; Inuzuka Kiyoko, *Yudaya mondai to Nihon no kōsaku* [The Jewish Problem and Japanese Maneuvering] (Tokyo: Nihon Kōgyō Shinbunsha, 1982), 77; Yasue Hiroo, *Dairen tokumu kikan to maboroshi no Yudaya kokka* [The Dairen Intelligence Agency and the Phantom Jewish State] (Tokyo: Yahata Shoten, 1989), 109; JACAR: B04013208300, 0282, "Opinions concerning the Treatment of Jewish Refugees," Consul General Miura in Shanghai to Foreign Minister Arita, April 18, 1940; JACAR: B04013205700, 0068–0072. Foreign Minister Arita Hachirō to Japanese ambassadors to Germany, the United States and Manchukuo, and consulates in China concerning Jewish refugees, December 7, 1938.
3. JACAR: B04013210300, 0215–0235. Top secret, "Summary of Captain Inuzuka's Report at the Committee on the Muslim and Jewish Problem: Personal Opinions on Current Situation of and Measures Taken toward the Jewish Refugees in Shanghai," January 18, 1939.
4. JACAR: B04013204800, 0040–0044. *Secret Jewish Information*, No. 1, "Review of the Far Eastern Jewish Conference," January 18, 1938.

5. JACAR: B04013204800, 0072–0074. *Top Secret Jewish Information*, No. 2, "Detailed Report on the First Far Eastern Jewish Conference," February 17, 1938.
6. Zhang Tiejiang, *Jiekai Haerbin Youtairen lishi zhimi* = *Reveal Enigmas of the Jewish History of Harbin* (Harbin: Heilongjiang renmin chubanshe, 2005), 99–100.
7. Marvin Tokayer and Mary Swartz, *The Fugu Plan: The Untold Story of the Japanese and the Jews during World War II* (New York: Paddington Press, 1979), 53.
8. Ibid.
9. Ibid., 53–55. See also Marcia Reynders Ristaino, *Port of Last Resort: The Diaspora Communities of Shanghai* (Stanford, CA: Stanford University Press, 2001), 95–96.
10. Ibid.
11. Gandel Centre of Judic, Jewish Museum of Australia, *The Story of a Haven: The Jews in Shanghai : 21 October 1997–22 March 1998* (St Kilda, Vic.: Jewish Museum of Australia, 1997), 18.
12. Archives of the Japanese Ministry of Foreign Affairs, 1868–1945, S series, microfilms (hereafter AJMFA). Consul General Tsurumi Ken in Harbin to Foreign Minister Hirota Kōki, January 13, 1938. S9460-3, 630–631.
13. Ibid.
14. AJMFA, Consul General Tsurumi Ken in Harbin to Foreign Minister Hirota, December 21, 1937. S9460-3, 608–609; Ambassador to Manchukuo Ueda Kenkichi to Foreign Minister Hirota, December 22, 1937. S9460-3, 611; Consul General Tsurumi to Foreign Minister Hirota, December 22, 1937. S9460-3, 612.
15. JACAR: B04013204800, 0075. *Top Secret Jewish Information*, No. 2, "Detailed Report on the First Far Eastern Jewish Conference," February 17, 1938.
16. JACAR: B04013204800, 0076–0077. *Top Secret Jewish Information*, No. 2, "Detailed Report on the First Far Eastern Jewish Conference," February 17, 1938.
17. AJMFA, Consul General Tsurumi in Harbin to Foreign Minister Hirota, January 14, 1938. S9460-3, 632–633.
18. JACAR: B04013204800, 0085. *Top Secret Jewish Information*, No. 2, "Detailed Report on the First Far Eastern Jewish Conference," February 17, 1938.
19. JACAR: B04013204800, 0096–0099. *Top Secret Jewish Information*, No. 2, "Detailed Report on the First Far Eastern Jewish Conference," February 17, 1938.
20. Maisie J. Meyer, "The Interrelationship of Jewish Communities in Shanghai," *Immigrants and Minorities* 19, no. 2 (July 2000): 71–77.
21. Ibid., 73–74. See also Sarah Abrevaya Stein, "Protected Persons? The Baghdadi Jewish Diaspora, the British State, and the Persistence of Empire," *American Historical Review* 116, no. 1 (2011): 80–108.
22. Meyer, "The Interrelationship of Jewish Communities in Shanghai," 77.
23. Maisie J. Meyer, *From the Rivers of Babylon to the Whangpoo: A Century of Sephardi Jewish Life in Shanghai* (Lanham, MD: University Press of America, 2003), 36.
24. Ibid., 6, 35.
25. Ibid., 35–36.
26. Ristaino, *Port of Last Resort*, 24.
27. JACAR: B04013204800, 0064. Ambassador Tōgō Shigenori in Berlin to Foreign Minister Hirota Kōki, February 7, 1938.

28. JACAR: B04013204800, 0065–0066, Ambassador to Poland Sakō Syūichi to Foreign Minister Hirota, February 8, 1938.
29. Yale Candee Maxon, *Control of Japanese Foreign Policy: A Study of Civil-Military Rivalry, 1930–1945* (Westport, CT: Greenwood Press, 1973), v.
30. Ibid., 1.
31. Ian Nish, *Japanese Foreign Policy in the Interwar Period* (Westport, CT: Praeger, 2002), 180–181.
32. Fujiwara Akira, "Nihon rikugun to taibei senryaku" [The Japanese Army and Its Strategies toward the United States], in Hosoya Chihiro, Saitō Makoto, Imai Seiichi, and Rōyama Michio, eds., *Nichi-Bei kankeishi- kaisen ni itaru 10 nen (1931–41nen)* [The History of Japanese-American Relations: 10 Years to the Outbreak of the [Pacific] War (1931–41)], Vol. 2 (Tokyo: Tokyo Daigaku Shuppankai, 1971), 75–76.
33. Maxon, *Control of Japanese Foreign Policy*, 73–74.
34. Fujiwara, "Nihon rikugun to taibei senryaku," 6–7.
35. Ibid., 10–12.
36. JACAR: A01200631600. "General Plan to Unify Institutions in Manchuria" by Prime Minister Saitō Makoto, July 26, 1932.
37. Maxon, *Control of Japanese Foreign Policy*, 75–76; Imai Seiichi, "Naikaku to tennō jūshin" [The Cabinet, the Emperor and the Senior Statesmen], in Hosoya Chihiro, Saitō Makoto, Imai Seiichi, and Rōyama Michio, eds., *Nichi-Bei kankeishi- kaisen ni itaru 10 nen (1931–41nen)* [The History of Japanese-American Relations: 10 Years to the Outbreak of the [Pacific] War (1931–41)], Vol. 1 (Tokyo: Tokyo Daigaku Shuppankai, 1971), 8.
38. Asada Sadao, "Nihon kaigun to taibei seisaku oyobi senryaku" [The Japanese Navy and Its Policies and Strategies toward the United States], in Hosoya Chihiro, Saitō Makoto, Imai Seiichi, and Rōyama Michio, eds. *Nichi-Bei kankeishi- kaisen ni itaru 10 nen (1931–41nen)* [The History of Japanese-American Relations: 10 Years to the Outbreak of the [Pacific] War (1931–41)], Vol. 2 (Tokyo: Tokyo Daigaku Shuppankai, 1971), 89–94.
39. Maxon, *Control of Japanese Foreign Policy*, 91–92.
40. Imai, "Naikaku to tennō jūshin," 8–9.
41. Ibid., 17.
42. Ibid., 19.
43. Barbara Brooks argues that under pressure from many sources, including the army, the Foreign Ministry was gradually excluded from the decision making concerning Manchuria after September 18, 1931. In December 1938, the army fostered the creation of the Kō-Ain, or Asian Development Board, "a new China agency that almost completely usurped the duties" of the Foreign Ministry where China was concerned. Brooks contends that the establishment of Kō-Ain marked "the final ascendance of outside forces agitating against the Gaimushō [Foreign Ministry] and the existing management of China affairs." However, this chapter and the next will demonstrate that the Foreign Ministry continued to play a key role in formulating Japan's Jewish policy in occupied China. Barbara Brooks, *Japan's Imperial Diplomacy: Consuls, Treaty Ports, and War in China, 1895–1938* (Honolulu: University of Hawaii Press, 2000), 117, 160, 206–207.
44. Maxon, *Control of Japanese Foreign Policy*, 100.
45. Ibid.
46. Tang Peiji, Xu Buzeng, Yan Huimin, Gu Borong, and Zheng Yiliu, *Shanghai Youtairen* [The Shanghai Jews] (Shanghai: Shanghai San lian Shudian, 1992), 134.

47. HIAS ICA-Emigdirect was backed by the American Jewish Joint Distribution Committee, the Hebrew Sheltering and Immigrant Aid Society (HIAS), and the Jewish Colonization Society (ICA). Avraham Altman and Irene Eber, "Flight to Shanghai, 1938–1940: The Larger Setting," *Yad Vashem Studies* 27 (2000): 51–53.
48. Tang, Xu, Yan, Gu and Zheng, *Shanghai Youtairen*, 134.
49. JACAR, B04013204000, 0008–0010. Ambassador Kawai Hiroyuki in Warsaw to Foreign Minister Uchida Yasuya, March 20 and March 27, 1933; 0043–0051, Ambassador Nagai Matsuzō in Berlin to Foreign Minister Uchida, May 6, 1933; B04013204100, 0138–0149. Consul General Horinouchi Kensuke in New York to Foreign Minister Uchida, August 12, 1933; B04013204400, 0034–0042. Consul General Yokoyama Masayuki in Washington to Foreign Minister Hirota Kōki, August 27, 1934; B04013204700, 0330–0332. Consul General Yokoyama in Washington to Foreign Minister Arita Hachirō, September 11, 1936.
50. AJMFA, "The Reaction of the Head of Tokyo Muslim Association toward the Far Eastern Jewish Conference," January 17, 1938. S9460–3, 634–642. Consequently, according to Maruyama Naoki, the Japanese government decided that this "Muslim issue" required its attention along with Jewish matters. Two months later, the Committee on the Muslim and Jewish Problem was established. Although the committee members considered the Muslim issue an important one, they agreed that the Jewish matter was more significant. In fact, the committee mostly discussed Jewish-related issues. See Maruyama Naoki, *Taiheiyō Sensō to Shanhai no Yudaya nanmin* [The Pacific War and the Shanghai Jewish Refugees] (Tokyo: Hōsei Daigaku Shuppankyoku, 2005), 89.
51. JACAR: B04013204900, 0134–0135. Vice Minister of Foreign Affairs Horinouchi Kensuke to Vice Minister of Army Umezu Yoshijirō and Vice Minister of Navy Yamamoto Isoroku concerning the Committee on the Muslim and Jewish Problems, March 31, 1938.
52. AJMFA, Foreign Minister Konoe Fumimaro to consular offices in China and Manchukuo, "Colonel Yasue's Speech at the Meeting of the Committee on the Muslim and Jewish Problem," October 13, 1938. S9460–3, 750–766.
53. AJMFA, "[Report] Concerning the Jewish Issue in Shanghai," October 12, 1938. S9360–3, 746–749.
54. AJMFA, "Colonel Yasue's Speech at the Meeting of the Committee on the Muslim and Jewish Problem," October 13, 1938. S9460–3, 750.
55. AJMFA, "Minutes of the Meeting of the Committee on the Muslim and Jewish Problem," S9460–3, 739–745.
56. Ibid.
57. JACAR: B04013205200, 0149–0151, 0157–0158. From Foreign Minister Konoe Fumimaro to Japanese consular offices overseas concerning the entrance of the Jewish refugees, October 7, 1938.
58. Liaoning sheng dangan guan, ed., *Man tie mi dang*, Vol. 18, 303–308.
59. Ibid.
60. Ibid.
61. Ibid.
62. Ibid.
63. Sadako N. Ogata, *Defiance in Manchuria: The Making of Japanese Foreign Policy, 1931–1932* (Berkeley: University of California Press, 1964), 3–4.
64. Michael Barnhart, *Japan Prepares for Total War: The Search for Economic Security, 1919–1941* (Ithaca, NY: Cornell University Press, 2001), 18.

65. Ibid.
66. Ibid., 73, 77.
67. Ogata, *Defiance in Manchuria*, 9–11.
68. Ibid., 13–16.
69. Ibid., 41–44.
70. Haruo Iguchi, *Unfinished Business: Ayukawa Yoshisuke and U.S.-Japan Relations, 1937–1953* (Cambridge, MA: Harvard University Press, 2003), 32.
71. Cho Yukio, translated by Edgar C. Harrell, "An Inquiry into the Problem of Importing American Capital into Manchuria: A Note on Japanese-American Relations, 1931–1941," in Dorothy Borg and Shumpei Okamoto, eds., *Pearl Harbor as History: Japanese-American Relations, 1931–1941* (New York: Columbia University Press, 1973), 388.
72. Ibid., 377.
73. JACAR, B02030539300, 0448–0454. "The Army's Hopes regarding Current Foreign Policies," July 3, 1938.
74. Ishiwara Kanji and Tsunoda Jun, *Ishiwara Kanji shiryō: Kokubō ronsaku hen* [Historical Materials on Ishiwara Kanji: Theories of the National Defense] (Tokyo: Hara Shobō, 1967), 292.
75. Inuzuka Kiyoko, *Yudaya mondai to Nihon no kōsaku*, 77; Yasue Hiroo, *Dairen tokumu kikan*, 109.
76. JACAR: B04013208300, 0282, "Opinions concerning the Treatment of Jewish Refugees," Consul General Miura in Shanghai to Foreign Minister Arita Hachirō, April 18, 1940.
77. JACAR: B04013205700, 0068–0072. Foreign Minister Arita Hachirō to Japanese ambassadors to Germany, the United States, and Manchukuo, and consulates in China concerning Jewish refugees, December 7, 1938.
78. Ibid.
79. David Kranzler, *Japanese, Nazis and Jews: The Jewish Refugee Community of Shanghai, 1938–1945* (New York: Yeshiva University Press, 1976), 231–233.
80. JACAR: B04013210700, 0014–0016, Consul General Tsurumi in Harbin to Ambassador to Manchukuo Ueta Kenkichi, December 20, 1938; 0085, Consul General Tsurumi to Ambassador Ueta, January 27, 1939.
81. JACAR: B04013210700, 0012, Chief of Staff of the Kwantung Army to the Chief of Military Affairs, n.d. (between December 14 and December 16, 1938).
82. JACAR: B04013210700, 0022–0027. Consul General Tsurumi to Ambassador Ueta concerning "Report Submitted to the American Jewish Congress and the World Jewish Congress from the Chairman of the National Council of the Jews of the Far East," December 28, 1938.
83. JACAR: B04013210700, 0068. Consul General Tsurumi to Ambassador Ueta concerning "The Speech and Conduct of Influential Jews in Manchukuo and the United States," January 12, 1939.
84. JACAR: B04013210700, 0022–0023. Consul General Tsurumi to Ambassador Ueta concerning "Report Submitted to the American Jewish Congress and the World Jewish Congress from the Chairman of the National Council of the Jews of the Far East," December 28, 1938.
85. JACAR: B04013210700, 0046–0047. Yasue Norihiro, "Report on the Second Far Eastern Jewish Conference (Part Two)," December 30, 1938.
86. JACAR: B04013210700, 0031–0043. "Report on the Second Far Eastern Jewish Conference (Part One)," Yasue Norihiro, December 30, 1938.

87. Shanghai Municipal Police Files, 1894–1949, Records of the Central Intelligence Agency, Record Group 263, D5422(c) (hereafter SMPF). D5422(c), "Arrival of Jewish Refugees from Germany and Austria," December 8, 1938; D5422(c), "Arrival of Jewish Refugees from Germany and Austria," January 11, 1939; D5422 (c) "Arrival of Jewish Refugees from Germany and Austria," January 31, 1939.

88. JACAR: B04013206100, 0064–0067. Consul General Miura Yoshiaki in Shanghai to Foreign Minister Arita concerning "The Relief Issue of the Jewish Refugees in Shanghai," January 17, 1939.

89. Zhaojin Ji, *A History of Modern Shanghai Banking: The Rise and Decline of China's Financial Capitalism* (Armonk, NY: M. E. Sharpe, 2003), 205.

90. SMAF, reel 4, U001/4/2971, File No. K38/1, 0240–0245. G. Godfrey Phillips to the Chairman and the Secretary-General of the SMC on "Jewish Refugees," December 20, 1938.

91. SMAF, reel 4, U001/4/2971, File No. K38/1, 0223, Copy of cable sent to German Jewish Aid Committee in London, HIAS-ICA Emigration Association in Paris and American JOINT Distribution Committee in New York by G. Godfrey Phillips of the SMC, December 23, 1938.

92. JACAR: B04013205800, 0197–0199, Acting Consul General Gotō Itsuo in Shanghai to Foreign Minister Arita, December 27, 1938.

93. SMAF, reel 4, U001/4/2971, File No. K38/1, 0176. "Extract from the Council Minutes dated February 8, 1939"; 0179–0180. From the Consul General for Italy and Senior Consul L. Neyrone to C. S. Franklin, Chairman of the Shanghai Municipal Council, February 8, 1939; Reel 4, U001/4/2972, File No. K38/1, 0571–0572. From Godfrey Phillips, Secretary and Commissioner General of the SMC to the Acting Consul General for Germany, E. Bracklo, August 14, 1939.

94. AJMFA, Foreign Minister Arita to Acting Consul General Gotō in Shanghai concerning the SMC's measures to prevent the influx of Jewish refugees to Shanghai, December 30, 1938. S9460-3, 903–904.

95. Maruyama, *Taiheiyō Sensō*, 67–70.

96. AJMFA, Acting Consul General Gotō to Foreign Minister Arita, January 2, 1939. S9460-3, 908–909.

97. Inuzuka applied the term "Jewish *Zaibatsu*" mostly to the wealthy heads of the Baghdadi Jewish business enterprises.

98. JACAR: B04013210300, 0215–0235. "Summary of Captain Inuzuka's Report at the Committee on the Muslim and Jewish Problem: Personal Opinions on Current Situation of and Measures Taken toward the Jewish Refugees in Shanghai," January 18, 1939.

99. Ibid.

100. Ibid.

101. Inuzuka's comparison of handling the Jewish issue to eating fugu is most notably related in Tokayer and Swartz, *The Fugu Plan*. The captain's original speech is, perhaps, not as dramatic as it is described in the book.

102. JACAR: B04013210300, 0215–0235. "Summary of Captain Inuzuka's Report at the Committee on the Muslim and Jewish Problem: Personal Opinions on Current Situation of and Measures Taken toward the Jewish Refugees in Shanghai," January 18, 1939.

103. AJMFA, The Committee on the Muslim and Jewish Problem, "Memorandum on Agreed Items/ Matters Agreed Upon," March 20, 1939. S9460-3, 1102.

104. AJMFA, "Joint Report of the Investigation on the Jewish Issue in Shanghai," July 7, 1939. S9460-3, 1238.

105. Ibid., S9460-3, 1256–1260.

106. SMPF, D5422(c), Special Branch, "Jewish Refugees," June 3, 1939; AJMFA, Memorandum (original document in English), August 9, 1939. S9460-3, 1424–1426.

107. AJMFA, "Emergency Measures for Managing the Shanghai Jewish Refugees," July, 1, 1939. S9460-3, 1224–1226.

108. AJMFA, "Joint Report of Investigation on the Jewish Issue in Shanghai," July 7, 1939. S9460-3, 1235–1295.

109. Ibid., S9460-3, 1261–1267.

110. *Ibid.*

111. Ibid., S9460-3, 1276–1279.

112. Ibid., S9460-3, 1268–1274.

113. AJMFA, "Supplement to the Joint Report of Investigation on the Jewish Issue in Shanghai- Opinions of the Parties Concerned," July, 1939. S9460, 1339–1367.

114. AJMFA, Consul General Miura to Foreign Minister Arita, August 10, 1939. S9460, 1413–1418; JACAR: B04013207600, 0156–0158. "Emergency Measures for Managing the Shanghai Jewish Refugees," August, 10, 1939.

115. AJMFA, Memorandum (original document in English), August 9, 1939. S9460-3, 1424–1426; Consul General Miura to Foreign Minister Arita, August 10, 1939. S9460-3, 1406–1407.

116. AJMFA, Consul General Miura to Foreign Minister Arita, August 12, 1939. S9460-3, 1427–1430; SMAF, reel 4, U001/4/2972, File No. K38/1, 0560–0577, "European Refugees," letter from Godfrey Phillips, Secretary and Commissioner General of the SMC to all the members of the Consular Body and to three leading shipping companies, August 14, 1939.

117. SMAF, reel 4, U001/4/2972, File No. K38/1, 0544, B.S. Barbash & Co. to the Secretary of the SMC, August 15, 1939; K38/1, 0543, Secretary and Commissioner General of the SMC to B. S. Barbash & Co., August 16, 1939; K38/1, 0512, B. S. Barbash & Co. to the Secretary and Commissioner General of the SMC, August 22, 1939; K38/1, 0511, Assistant Secretary E. T. Nash of the SMC to B. S. Barbash & Co., August 22, 1939.

118. SMAF, reel 4, U001/4/2972, File No. K38/1, 0492–0493, Butterfield & Swire to the Secretary and Commissioner General of the SMC, August 16, 1939.

119. SMAF, reel 4, U001/4/2972, File No. K38/1, 0491, Secretary and Commissioner General of the SMC to Butterfield & Swire, August 16, 1939.

120. "Committee Formed for Jew Problem—First Meeting to Be Held Tomorrow; Many Questions to Be Raised," *North China Daily News*, August 19, 1939.

121. "Status of Refugees to Be Defined—Consuls, Council Reach Agreement Concerning Procedure," *North China Daily News*, August 18, 1939.

122. SMAF, reel 4, U001/4/2972, File No. K38/1, 0429, "Subject: Central European Refugees," Secretary and Commissioner General of the SMC to the members of Council, September 16, 1939.

123. For instance, see SMAF, reel 4, U001/4/2972, File No. K38/1, 0473–0477, "Prohibition of Entry of European Refugees into Shanghai" attached to the letter from E. T. Nash to E. Kann, August 23, 1939; K38/1, 0461–0463, "Suggested Regulations re Admittance into Shanghai of European Refugees,"

attached to the letter from E. Kann to E. T. Nash, August 25, 1939; K38/1, 0446, "Translation," date and provenance unknown.

124. AJMFA, Circular 272-G-VII, G. Brigidi, Acting Consul General for Italy, to Poul Scheel, Senior Consul of the SMC, August 16, 1939, attached to Consul General Miura to Foreign Minister Arita, August 19, 1939. S9460-3, 1470–1472; Circular 280-G-VII, E. Bracklo, Acting Consul General for Germany to G. G. Phillips, Secretary and Commissioner General of the SMC, August 19, 1939, attached to Consul General Miura to Foreign Minister Arita, August 29, 1939. S9460-3, 1483–1485.

125. SMAF, reel 4, U001/4/2972, File No. K38/1, 0377–0378. "Press Communiqué," October 22, 1939.

126. SMAF, reel 4, U001/4/2972, File No. K38/1, 0375, "Draft Statement regarding Entry into the Japanese Occupied Part of the International Settlement of Shanghai of Central European Refugees," October 21, 1939; 0362–0363, Japanese Consul General Miura to Ellis Hayim of the CAEJR, October 28, 1939.

127. "French Council to Have No Dealings with Germans: No Building Permits or Licenses of Any Kind to Be Granted in Concession to Holders of German Passports- Jews or Christians," *Shanghai Times*, October 13, 1939.

128. SMPF, D5422(c), "Admission into the French Concession of European Jewish Refugees—Decisions Made by the French Consul General on December 30, 1939," February 3, 1940; "Central European Jews—French Police Stop Issuing Immigration Permits," May 27, 1940.

129. SMPF, D5422(c)-10, "Central European Jews—French Police stop issuing immigration permits," May 27, 1940.

130. Kranzler, *Japanese, Nazis and Jews*, 273–274.

131. SMAF, reel 4, U001/4/2972, File No. K38/1, 0592–0601, "Central European Jewish Refugees–Immigration Affairs," May 2, 1940, attached to letter from R.W. Yorke of the Special Branch to the Commissioner of Police, May 3, 1940.

132. Ibid., K38/1, 0596–0597.

133. Ibid., K38/1, 0599.

134. Ernst L. Presseisen, *Germany and Japan: A Study in Totalitarian Diplomacy, 1933–1941* (The Hague: Martinus Nijhoff, 1958), 193.

135. Ibid., 191–192; Yoshii Hiroshi, *Shōwa gaikōshi* [The Diplomatic History of the Showa Era], 3rd ed. (Tokyo: Nansōsha, 1984), 85–86.

136. Presseisen, *Germany and Japan*, 56–57, 144–145.

137. Frank William Iklé, *German-Japanese Relations: 1936–1940* (New York: Bookman Associates, 1956), 68.

138. Ibid., 83–86.

139. Ibid., 81.

140. Yoshii, *Shōwa gaikōshi*, 86–87; Presseisen, *Germany and Japan*, 208.

141. Asada, "Nihon kaigun to taibei seisaku oyobi senryaku," 119.

142. Iklé, *German-Japanese Relations*, 94.

143. Presseisen, *Germany and Japan*, 216–217; for an extended treatment of the Nomonhan Incident, see also Alvin Coox *Nomonhan: Japan against Russia, 1939* (Stanford, CA: Stanford University Press, 1985).

144. Yoshii, *Shōwa gaikōshi*, 90–91.

145. Ibid., 93.

146. Iklé, *German-Japanese Relations*, 197.

147. JACAR: B04013207700, 0252–0254. "Jewish Refugee Issue in Shanghai," November 1, 1939.
148. Ibid., 0255–0257.
149. Ibid., 0258–0259.
150. Ibid., 0264–0265.
151. Ibid.
152. AJMFA, Consul Shimomura Hitsujirō in Suifenhe to Ambassador to Manchukuo Umezu "Concerning Situation of the Third Far Eastern Jewish Conference," January 17, 1940. S9460-3, 1743–1763.
153. AJMFA, Foreign Minister of Manchukuo to the Manchukuoan ambassador to Japan, "Concerning Manchukuo's Attitude toward the Travel of the Jews to Shanghai," January 19, 1940. S9460-3, 1786–1790.

CHAPTER 4

1. AJMFA, "The Secret Resolution of the (Third) Far Eastern Jewish Conference," Consul General Miura in Shanghai to Foreign Minister Nomura Kichisaburō, January 8, 1940. S9460-3, 1629–1630.
2. AJMFA, minutes of the meeting of the Committee on Muslim and Jewish Problem, January 26, 1940. S9460-3, 1826–1827.
3. Maruyama Naoki, *Taiheiyō Sensō to Shanhai no Yudaya nanmin* [The Pacific War and the Shanghai Jewish Refugees] (Tokyo: Hōsei Daigaku Shuppankyoku, 2005), 121–124.
4. Pamela Rotner Sakamoto, *Japanese Diplomats and Jewish Refugees: A World War II Dilemma* (Westport, CT: Praeger, 1998), 83–84.
5. N. E. B. Ezra to Shigemitsu, September 15, 1933, Z4/ 3225II, Central Zionist Archives (hereafter CZA), quoted in Maruyama, *Taiheiyō Sensō*, 121–122.
6. Ezra to Israel Cohen, September 17, 1933, Z4/ 3225II, CZA, quoted in Maruyama, *Taiheiyō Sensō*, 122.
7. Cohen to Ezra, October 17, 1933, Z4/ 3225II, CZA, quoted in Maruyama, *Taiheiyō Sensō*, 122–123.
8. Sakamoto, *Japanese Diplomats*, 21.
9. Maruyama, *Taiheiyō Sensō*, 123–124.
10. "Japan Opens Manchukuo to Refugees: Would Welcome 50,000 Reich Jews There, Says Diplomat," *Jewish Daily Bulletin*, August 6, 1934, 3c.
11. JACAR: B04013204400, 0032. Ambassador Nagai Matsuzō to Foreign Minister Hirota, August 16, 1934.
12. JACAR: B04013204400, 0030–0031. Foreign Minister Hirota to Ambassador Nagai, August 20, 1934.
13. AJMFA, N. E. B. Ezra to Shigemitsu, published in *Israel's Messenger*, September 14, 1934. S9460-3, 465.
14. *Israel's Messenger*, September 7, 1934, quoted in Maruyama, *Taiheiyō Sensō*, 124.
15. AJMFA, "Pro-Japanese Jew 'Zikman's' Proposal to Aid European Jewish Refugees," Deputy Consul General Taniguchi Suguru in Harbin to Ambassador Ueda Kenkichi in Manchukuo, April 4, 1939. S9460-3, 1155–1162. About Lew Zikman's Jewish settlement plan, see also Sakamoto, *Japanese Diplomats*, 83–84.
16. AJMFA, "Pro-Japanese Jew 'Zikman's' Proposal to Aid European Jewish Refugees," Ambassador Ueda in Manchukuo to Deputy Consul General Taniguchi in Harbin, April 24, 1939. S9460-3, 1172–1175.

17. Officially launched in December 1938, Kō-Ain was one of many Japanese research institutions on China established during the Sino-Japanese War of 1937–1945. Unlike other research institutions, Kō-Ain was a governmental agency. The prime minister was its president, and it enjoyed the same authority as other ministries. The Japanese government intended to use Kō-Ain to promote its administration in its occupied territories in China and to carry out the war with the Nationalist government. Honjō Hisako, Uchiyama Masao, and Kubo Tōru, eds., *Kō-Ain to senji Chūgoku chōsa: tsuketari kankōbutsu shozai mokuroku* [Kō-Ain and Research on China during the Sino-Japanese War] (Tokyo: Iwanami Shoten, 2002), 5, 8.

18. AJMFA, "Joint Report of the Investigation on the Jewish Issue in Shanghai," July 7, 1939. S9460-3, 1250–1252.

19. AJMFA, "Supplement to the Joint Report of the Investigation on the Jewish Issue in Shanghai—Opinions from the Ministries Concerned: Opinions from the Navy," June 16, 1939. S9460-3, 1359.

20. AJMFA, "Minutes of the Meeting of the Committee on Muslim and Jewish Problem concerning Kō-Ain's Opinions toward the Joint Report of the Investigation on the Jewish Refugee Issue in Shanghai," July 25, 1939. S9460-3, 1320–1322.

21. During Japan's invasion of China, the Japanese established many puppet regimes in their occupied territories and attempted to "use Chinese to rule Chinese." After Shanghai fell to Japan in late 1937, the Japanese authorities there established several successive puppet governments. Weixin zhengfu, or the Reform Government, administered central China from March 1938 to March 1940. Shanghai was ruled by the "Special Shanghai City Government" of the Weixin zhengfu. Zhang Peide, Yang Guoqiang, and Xiong Yuezhi, eds., *Shanghai tongshi, di qi juan, minguo zhengzhi* [History of Shanghai, Vol. 7, Politics in the Republican Era] (Shanghai: Shanghai Renmin Chubanshe, 1999), 356–369.

22. AJMFA, "Supplement to the Joint Report of the Investigation on the Jewish Issue in Shanghai—Opinions from the Ministries Concerned: From the Army," June 7, 1939. S9460-3, 1349–1350.

23. Ibid., S9460-3, 1351.

24. AJMFA, "Minutes of the Meeting of the Committee on Muslim and Jewish Problem concerning 'The Treatment of the Shanghai Jewish Refugees,'" July 18, 1939. S9460-3, 1305–1307.

25. Maruyama, *Taiheiyō Sensō*, 130.

26. Memorandum from Bernhard Kahn, "Conversation with Mr. Tamura," November 19, 1940. American Jewish Joint Distribution Committee Archives (hereafter AJJDC), AR 33/44, #723 Japan. United States Holocaust Memorial Museum Institutional Archives (hereafter USHMMIA), "Exhibitions Division: Records Relating to Developing the 'Flight and Rescue' Exhibition, 1998–1999," box 10.

27. AJMFA, Foreign Minister Nomura to Ambassador Horinouchi in the United States, November 16, 1939. S9460-3, 1557–1561.

28. JACAR: B04013207800, 0388–0389. Circular, the Committee on the Muslim and Jewish Problem, December 21, 1939.

29. JACAR: B04013207800, 0401–0404. The Ministry of Navy, "Concerning the Settlement of Jewish Refugees," December 26, 1939.

30. Memorandum, from Bernhard Kahn to Paul Baerwald, December 21, 1939. AJJDC, AR 33/44, #723 Japan, USHMMIA, "Exhibitions Division: Records Relating to Developing the 'Flight and Rescue' Exhibition, 1998–1999," box 10.

31. JACAR: B04013207800, 0403. The Ministry of Navy, "Concerning the Settlement of Jewish Refugees," December 26, 1939.
32. AJMFA, Foreign Minister Nomura to Ambassador Horinouchi in the United States, November 16, 1939. S9460-3, 1557–1561.
33. AJMFA, Ambassador Horinouchi in Washington to Foreign Minister Nomura, November 24, 1939. S9460-3, 1572–1574.
34. Memorandum from Bernhard Kahn, "Conversation with Mr. Tamura," November 19, 1940. AJJDC, AR 33/44, #723 Japan, USHMMIA, "Exhibitions Division: Records Relating to Developing the 'Flight and Rescue' Exhibition, 1998–1999," box 10; Sakamoto, *Japanese Diplomats*, 86–87.
35. JACAR: B04013207800, 0401–0402. "Concerning the Issue of Receiving Jewish Refugees," December 26, 1939.
36. AJMFA, Consul General Miura in Shanghai to Foreign Minister Nomura, December 29, 1939. S9460-3, 1615–1617; also see Maruyama, *Taiheiyō Sensō*, 134, and Sakamoto, *Japanese Diplomats*, 87.
37. Ibid.
38. AJMFA, Foreign Minister Nomura to Ambassador Horinouchi in Washington, January 6, 1940. S9460-3, 1635–1638.
39. AJMFA, "Delivering the SMR Reports on the Jews," Consul General in Shanghai to the Foreign Minister, June 21, 1940. S9460-3, 2124–25, 2146–51.
40. Ibid.
41. AJMFA, Consul Shimomura Hitsujirō in Suifenhe to Ambassador Umezu in Manchukuo, "The Current Situation of the Jewish Autonomous State," October 21, 1940. S9460-3, 2335–41.
42. AJMFA, Foreign Minister Nomura to Consul General Miura in Shanghai, January 13, 1940. S9460-3, 1686.
43. AJMFA, Inuzuka Koreshige, "Explanation of Several Questions on Maneuvers with Respect to American Jews," January 1940. S9460-3, 1701–1721.
44. JACAR: B04013208300, 0278–0297, "Opinions Concerning the Treatment of Jewish Refugees," Consul General Miura in Shanghai to Foreign Minister Arita, April 18, 1940.
45. Ibid.
46. Ibid.
47. Ibid.; "Local Jews Give Thanks to Japanese: Appreciation for Kindness Expressed," *North China Daily News*, February 29, 1940.
48. AJMFA, Consul General Miura in Shanghai to Foreign Minister Matsuoka Yōsuke, August 2, 1940. S9460-3, 1369–1378; Maruyama, *Taiheiyō Sensō*, 131–132.
49. AJMFA, Letter from Karl Kindermann to Mr. Niwa, June 7, 1940, attached to Consul General Miura to Foreign Minister Matsuoka, August 2, 1940. S9460-3, 1377.
50. AJMFA, Letter from Stephen Wise to Karl Kindermann, June 10, 1940, attached to Consul General Miura in Shanghai to Foreign Minister Matsuoka, August 2, 1940. S9460-3, 1378.
51. Ibid., S9460-3, 1373–1376.
52. Maruyama, *Taiheiyō Sensō*, 132.
53. Fujiwara Akira, "Nihon rikugun to taibei senryaku" [The Japanese Army and Its Strategies toward the United States], in Hosoya Chihiro, Saitō Makoto, Imai Seiichi, and Rōyama Michio, eds., *Nichi-Bei kankeishi- kaisen ni itaru 10 nen (1931–41nen)* [The History of Japanese-American Relations: 10 Years to the Outbreak of the [Pacific] War *(1931–41)*], Vol. 2 (Tokyo: Tokyo Daigaku Shuppankai, 1971), 3–5.

54. Asada Sadao, "Nihon kaigun to taibei seisaku oyobi senryaku" [The Japanese Navy and Its Policies and Strategies toward the United States], in Hosoya Chihiro, Saitō Makoto, Imai Seiichi, and Rōyama Michio, eds., *Nichi-Bei kankeishi- kaisen ni itaru 10 nen (1931–41nen)* [The History of Japanese-American Relations: 10 Years to the Outbreak of the [Pacific] War (1931–41)], Vol. 2 (Tokyo: Tokyo Daigaku Shuppankai, 1971), 87.
55. Ibid., 92–94, 100–107.
56. Ibid., 120–121; Frank William Iklé, *German-Japanese Relations: 1936–1940* (New York: Bookman Associates, 1956), 148–163.
57. Iklé, *German-Japanese Relations*, 150.
58. Ibid., 152.
59. Yoshii Hiroshi, *Shōwa gaikōshi* [The Diplomatic History of the Showa Era], 3rd ed. (Tokyo: Nansōsha, 1984), 106.
60. Ernst L. Presseisen, *Germany and Japan: A Study in Totalitarian Diplomacy, 1933–1941* (The Hague: Martinus Nijhoff, 1958), 246–249.
61. Ibid., 246.
62. Ibid., 279.
63. "Dairen Jewish Community Holds Banquet in Honor of Colonel Yasue," *Israel's Messenger*, January 24, 1941, 2.
64. David Kranzler, *Japanese, Nazis and Jews: The Jewish Refugee Community of Shanghai, 1938–1945* (New York: Yeshiva University Press, 1976), 325–326.
65. JACAR: B04013209000, 0292–0326. Inuzuka Koreshige, "The Handling of the [China] Incident and the Measures toward Jews," August 7, 1940.
66. Ibid.
67. British National Archives (hereafter BNA), FO 371/ 24684. Despatch no. 576, British Consul General A. H. George in Shanghai to the British Ambassador, September 5, 1940.
68. "Captain Inazuka's [*sic*] Radio Broadcast Speech," *Israel's Messenger*, December 20, 1940, 14–15.
69. Ibid.
70. Ibid.
71. Yoshii, *Shōwa gaikōshi*, 125.
72. JACAR: B04013209400, 0099–0100. Foreign Minister Matsuoka Yōsuke to the Japanese consular offices overseas, October 10, 1940.
73. AJMFA, "Reasons for Proposing the [New] Basic Policy toward Jews and Proposals for a [New] Basic Jewish Policy," November 14, 1940. S9460-3, 2357–2361.
74. Ibid.
75. Sugihara Yukiko, *Rokusennin no inochi no biza* [Six Thousand Visas for Life] (Tokyo: Asahi Sonorama, 1990), 6.
76. Sugihara Yukiko, *Rokusennin no inochi no biza*, 28. Also see Sakamoto, *Japanese Diplomats*, 102–103.
77. Sakamoto, *Japanese Diplomats*, 4.
78. AJMFA, Acting Consul General Sugihara Chiune in Prague to Foreign Minister Matsuoka, February 5, 1941. S9460-3, 2410; On February 28, 1941, Sugihara provided to the foreign minister a list of 2,132 names of people to whom he had issued visas in Kaunas. Sugihara to Foreign Minister Matsuoka, February 28, 1941, USHMMIA, "Exhibitions Division: Records Relating to Developing the 'Flight and Rescue' Exhibition, 1998–1999," boxes 9–10; Sakamoto, *Japanese Diplomats*, 163.
79. Sugihara Yukiko, *Rokusennin no inochi no biza*, 33–34, 48–49, 56; Sakamoto, *Japanese Diplomats*, 103–106.

80. The United States Holocaust Memorial Museum, *Flight and Rescue* (University of Washington Press, 2001), xvii–xviii; United States Holocaust Memorial Museum, "Polish Jewish Refugees in Lithuania, 1939–1940," *Holocaust Encyclopedia*, http://www.ushmm.org/wlc/en/article.php?ModuleId=10005586, accessed July 7, 2011.
81. *Flight and Rescue*, xviii; Avraham Altman and Irene Eber, "Flight to Shanghai, 1938–1940: The Larger Setting," *Yad Vashem Studies* 27 (2000): 81.
82. AJMFA, Acting Consul General Sugihara in Prague to Foreign Minister Matsuoka, February 5, 1941. S9460-3, 2410; Sugihara to Foreign Minister Matsuoka, February 28, 1941. USHMMIA, boxes 9–10.
83. Sugihara Yukiko, *Rokusennin no inochi no biza*, 16–25.
84. Yecheskel Leitner, *Operation: Torah Rescue: The Escape of the Mirrer Yeshiva from War-Torn Poland to Shanghai, China* (Jerusalem and New York: Feldheim, 1987), 49. Telshe Yeshiva was founded in 1875 in Telshe, Lithuania, and was one of the most famous yeshivas in Eastern Europe.
85. Sugihara Yukiko, *Rokusennin no inochi no biza*, 25.
86. JACAR: B04013208800, 0196. Consul Sugihara Chiune in Kaunas to Foreign Minister Matsuoka Yōsuke, July 28, 1940.
87. JACAR: B04013208900, 0220. Consul Sugihara in Kaunas to Foreign Minister Matsuoka, August 9, 1940.
88. JACAR: B04013208900, 0231. Foreign Minister Matsuoka to Consul Sugihara in Kaunas, August 13, 1940; Sakamoto, *Japanese Diplomats*, 110.
89. "List of Visa [sic], Given by the Consulate to Foreigens [sic], 1940, the Imperial Consulate in Kaunas." Acting Consul General Sugihara Chiune in Prague to Foreign Minster Matsuoka, February 28, 1941. File J 2.3.0. J/X 2–6. USHMMIA, box 9; Sakamoto, *Japanese Diplomats*, 110.
90. Efraim Zuroff, *The Response of Orthodox Jewry in the United States to the Holocaust: The Activities of the Vaad ha-Hatzala Rescue Committee, 1939–1945* (New York: Michael Scharf Publication Trust of the Yeshiva University Press; Hoboken, NJ: [Distributed by] KTAV, 2000), 84.
91. JACAR: B04013208900, 0235. Foreign Minister Matsuoka to Consul Sugihara in Kaunas, August 16, 1940.
92. JACAR: B04013208800, 0198. Consul Sugihara in Kaunas to Foreign Minister Matsuoka, August 1, 1940. The date of this cable is a mistake since Sugihara was responding to Matsuoka's telegram of August 16, 1940. Also, Sugihara's telegram of August 24, 1940 to Matsuoka was numbered 66 and this cable was numbered 67. Therefore, this cable must have been sent after August 24, 1940, not August 1, 1940; Sakamoto, *Japanese Diplomats*, 112.
93. JACAR: B04013208900, 0263. Foreign Minister Matsuoka to Consul Sugihara in Kaunas, September 2, 1940; Sakamoto, *Japanese Diplomats*, 112–113.
94. Sakamoto, *Japanese Diplomats*, 113.
95. Hillel Levine, *In Search of Sugihara: The Elusive Japanese Diplomat Who Risked His Life to Rescue 10,000 Jews from the Holocaust* (New York: Free Press, 1996), 271.
96. Levine, *In Search of Sugihara*, 282.
97. JACAR: B04013209100, 0419–0420. Ernst Baerwald of the Relief Aid Committee in Yokohama to the Imperial Japanese Department of Foreign Affairs. October 28, 1940.
98. JACAR: B04013209600, 0214–0218. "Situation of the European Refugees Arriving in Japan," April 15, 1941.
99. JACAR: B04013210100, 0149, the Jewish Community in Kobe, "Statement of Refugees Who Left from April 1, till April 15 1941 INCL."

100. Ibid., 0141, the Jewish Community in Kobe, "Information about Financial Means Received from Jewish Charitable Societies Abroad for the Assistance of Jewish Refugees in Japan, from July 1, 1940 till March 31, 1941."
101. Yoshii, *Shōwa gaikōshi*, 120–121.
102. Ibid., 129.
103. Marvin Tokayer and Mary Swartz, *The Fugu Plan: The Untold Story of the Japanese and the Jews during World War II* (New York: Paddington Press, 1979), 139–143; Sakamoto, *Japanese Diplomats*, 142.
104. JACAR: B04013209500, 0130–0132. "Regarding the Handling of European Refugees' Visas," Foreign Minister to the consular offices in Europe and the Soviet Union, March 14, 1941.
105. AJMFA, Ambassador Tatekawa Yoshitsugu in Moscow to Foreign Minister Konoe, March 20, 1941. S9460-3, 2468.
106. AJMFA, Acting Consul General Nei Saburō in Vladivostok to Foreign Minister Konoe, March 20, 1941. S9460-3, 2441–2442.
107. JACAR: B04013209500, 0156–0157. Foreign Minister Konoe to Ambassador Tatekawa in Moscow, March 25, 1941.
108. JACAR: B04013209700, 0323–0324. Foreign Minister Toyoda Tejirō to Consul General Horiuchi Tateki in Shanghai, August 20, 1941.
109. AJMFA, No. 55876, Consul General Horiuchi in Shanghai to Foreign Minister Toyoda, August 13, 1941. S9460-3, 2497–2498.
110. Kobe is the capital city of Hyōgo prefecture.
111. JACAR: B04013209700. 0323–0324. Foreign Minister Toyoda to Consul General Horiuchi in Shanghai, August 20, 1941.
112. AJMFA, no. 56101. Consul General Horiuchi in Shanghai to Foreign Minister Toyoda, August 21, 1941. S9460-3, 2504–2505.
113. SMAF, reel 4, U001/4/2974, File No. K38/1(part 4), 1001. The Committee for the Assistance of European Jewish Refugees in Shanghai to Captain K. Inuzuka, September 6, 1941; 1002–1005. Ellis Hayim to G. Godfrey Phillips, Secretary and Commissioner-General of the Shanghai Municipal Council, September 4, 1941.
114. BNA, FO 371/ 29235. Memorandum, Enclosure in Shanghai Despatch to H. M. Ambassador, no. 333, Consul General A. H. George in Shanghai to the British Ambassador, October 2, 1941.
115. SMAF, reel 4, U001/4/2974, File No. K38/1(part 4), 1002–1005. Ellis Hayim to G. Godfrey Phillips, Secretary and Commissioner-General of the Shanghai Municipal Council, September 4, 1941.
116. Ibid.
117. Ibid.
118. Sakamoto, *Japanese Diplomats*, 151.
119. BNA, FO 371/ 29235. Memorandum, Enclosure in Shanghai Despatch to H. M. Ambassador, no. 333, Consul General A.H. George in Shanghai to the British Ambassador, October 2, 1941.
120. Ibid.
121. AJMFA, Foreign Minister Tōgō to consular offices in China and Manchukuo, January 17, 1942. S9460-3, 2516–2518.
122. AJMFA, "Measures toward Treatment of Jews under Current Situation," Foreign Minister Tōgō to consular offices in China, March 13, 1942. S9460-3, 2519–22, 2557–2562.
123. Ibid.

124. AJMFA, Ambassador Ōshima in Berlin to Foreign Minister Tōgō, May 7, 1942. S9460-3, 2527.
125. AJMFA, Consul General Yano Seiki in Shanghai to Aoki Kazuo, Minister of Greater East Asia, November 18, 1942. S9460-3, 2554–2556.
126. AJMFA, Consul General Yano to Minister Aoki, February 9, 1943. S9460-3, 2563–2566.
127. "Proclamation Concerning Restriction of Residence and Business of Stateless Refugees," *Shanghai Times*, February 18, 1943, 1; AJMFA, Consul General Yano to Minister Aoki, February 9, 1943. S9460-3, 2563–2566.
128. Ibid., AJMFA, S9460-3, 2563–2566.
129. Maruyama, *Taiheiyō Sensō*, 195.
130. Maruyama, *Taiheiyō Sensō*, 194–196; Kranzler, *Japanese, Nazis and Jews*, 477–479; Marcia Reynders Ristaino, *Port of Last Resort: The Diaspora Communities of Shanghai* (Stanford, CA: Stanford University Press, 2001), 179–181.
131. Kranzler, *Japanese, Nazis and Jews*, 478.
132. Laura Margolis, "Report of Activities in Shanghai, China, from December 8, 1941, to September 1943." AJJDC, Shanghai File, #463. USHMMIA, "Exhibitions Division: Records Relating to Developing the 'Flight and Rescue' Exhibition, 1998–1999," box 10.
133. Kranzler, *Japanese, Nazis and Jews*, 477–479; Ristaino, *Port of Last Resort*, 179–181.
134. Margolis, "Report"; Ristaino, *Port of Last Resort*, 181; Kranzler, *Japanese, Nazis and Jews*, 479.

EPILOGUE

1. Anna Ginsbourg, "Thousands of Shanghai's German-Jewish Refugees Lead Lives of Disillusionment, Despair," *China Weekly Review* 96, no. 8 (April 26, 1941): 252.
2. Ibid., 253.
3. Ibid.
4. Berl Falbaum, *Shanghai Remembered: Stories of Jews Who Escaped to Shanghai from Nazi Europe* (Royal Oak, MI: Momentum Books, 2005), 1–2.
5. See David Kranzler, *Japanese, Nazis and Jews: The Jewish Refugee Community of Shanghai, 1938–1945* (New York: Yeshiva University Press, 1976); James R. Ross, *Escape to Shanghai: A Jewish Community in China* (New York: Free Press, 1994).
6. Tang Peiji Xu Buzeng, Yan Huimin, Gu Borong, and Zheng Yiliu, *Shanghai Yutairen* [The Shanghai Jews] (Shanghai: Sanlian shudian, 1992), 133.
7. R. Shoshana Kahan, *In fayer un flamen: togbukh fun a yidisher shoyshpilerin* [In Fire and Flames: Diary of a Jewish Actress] (Buenos Aires: Tsentral farband fun poylishe yidn in Argentine, 1949), 283, reproduced in Irene Eber ed., *Voices from Shanghai: Jewish Exiles in Wartime China* (Chicago: University of Chicago Press, 2008), 1. Eber's slender volume presents a collection of short pieces, some in verse, some in prose, written in various languages by European Jews who had taken refuge in Shanghai. They vividly underscore the complex emotions their new home inspired in the displaced Jews. Eber points out that many Polish refugees who relocated to China from Japan, like Kahan, "had taken an instant dislike to Shanghai." Eber explains that "they had been treated generously in Kobe, but then they had been the only refugees there." Eber, *Voices from Shanghai*, 17.

8. Eber, *Voices from Shanghai*, 1.
9. William Schurtman, "Report on: The Jewish Refugee Community in Shanghai," unpublished term paper, City College of New York, January 1954, 22, author's collection.
10. M, "I Love You, Shanghai," *Future* 1, no. 12 (January 1948): 19.
11. *The Year of Survival: 1946 Annual Report of the American Jewish Joint Distribution Committee* (New York: American Jewish Joint Distribution Committee, 1947), 13.
12. *Ibid.*
13. Tang Peiji et al., *Shanghai Yutairen*, 148.
14. Falbaum, *Shanghai Remembered*, ?
15. Pan Guang, and Li Peidong, eds., *Youtairen yi Shanghai* [Jews Remember Shanghai] (Shanghai: Shanghai shi zheng xie wen shi zi liao bian ji bu, 1995), 234.
16. Tang Peiji et al., *Shanghai Yutairen*, 148.
17. Schurtman, "Report," 16.
18. Ernest Heppner, *Shanghai Refuge: A Memoir of the World War II Jewish Ghetto* (Lincoln: University of Nebraska Press, 1995), 163.
19. *Future*, 1.
20. *Ibid.*, 22, 27.
21. Schurtman, "Report," 1–2.
22. Schurtman, "Report," 19; see also Heppner, *Shanghai Refuge*, 64.
23. Felix Gruenberger, "The Jewish Refugees in Shanghai," *Jewish Social Studies* 12, no. 4 (October 1950): 331.
24. Ibid., 332.
25. Falbaum, *Shanghai Remembered*, 103.
26. Pan Guang and Li Peidong, eds., *Youtairen yi Shanghai*, 163.
27. Ursula Bacon, *Shanghai Diary: A Young Girl's Journey from Hitler's Hate to War-Torn China* (Milwaukie, OR: Milwaukie Press, 2004), 57–58.
28. Ibid.
29. Israel Kipen, *A Life to Live . . . : An Autobiography* (Burwood, Victoria: Chandos, 1989), 126.
30. Heppner, *Shanghai Refuge*, 59–60.
31. Ibid., 61.
32. Ibid., 62.
33. Falbaum, *Shanghai Remembered*, 92–93.
34. Henry Culman, *Growing up on Three Continents*, the United States Holocaust Memorial Museum Archives, Accession No. 2006.5, 33–34.
35. Schurtman, "Report," 21.
36. Ross, *Escape to Shanghai*, 235–236; see also N. A. Pelcovits, "European Refugees in Shanghai," *Far Eastern Survey* 15, no. 21 (October 23, 1946): 321.
37. Maruyama Naoki, *Taiheiyō Sensō to Shanhai no Yudaya nanmin* [The Pacific War and the Shanghai Jewish Refugees] (Tokyo: Hōsei Daigaku Shuppankyoku, 2005), 251.
38. Ross, *Escape to Shanghai*, 240.
39. Maruyama, Taiheiyō Sensō, 222, 225, 240; Ross, Escape to Shanghai, 241.
40. Tang Peiji et al., *Shanghai Yutairen*, 164.
41. Pan Guang and Wang Jian, *Yi ge ban shi ji yi lai de Shanghai Youtairen: Youtai minzu shi shang de dongfang yi ye* [Shanghai Jews of a Century and a Half: The Oriental Page in Jewish History] (Beijing: Shehui kexue wenxian chubanshe, 2002), 247.
42. Ross, *Escape to Shanghai*, ix.
43. See Falbaum, *Shanghai Remembered*.

44. Ross, *Escape to Shanghai*, ix.
45. Pan Guang and Wang Jian, *Yi ge ban shi ji yi lai de Shanghai Youtairen*, 251.
46. Sigmund Tobias, *Strange Haven: A Jewish Childhood in Wartime Shanghai* (Urbana: University of Illinois Press, 1999), 133.
47. Ibid., 155.
48. "Three Country Spat Me Out" in Eber, *Voices from Shanghai*, 59–60.

BIBLIOGRAPHY

PRIMARY SOURCES

Archival Sources
People's Republic of China
Shanghai Municipal Archives, Shanghai
  U1: Files of the Shanghai Municipal Council of the International Settlement
  U1-3: Files of the Secretariat
  U1-14: Files of the Public Works Department, Puppet Shanghai Special Government under Japanese Occupation
  U1-16: Files of the Public Health Department, Puppet Shanghai Special Government under Japanese Occupation
  U38: Files of the French Concession
  U38-1: Files of the Municipal Council of the French Concession
  U38-5: Files of the French Concession Public Health Department
  Q1: Files of the Shanghai Municipal Government, 1927–1948
  Q6: Files of the Shanghai Social Affairs Bureau
  Q127, Q131, Q150: Files of the Shanghai Municipal Police Offices
  Q190: Files of the Shanghai Lawyers Association
  Q20: Files of the Shanghai Chamber of Commerce
  Q284: Files of the Land Bank of China
  R1: Files of the Puppet Shanghai Government under Japanese Occupation
  R36: Files of the Shanghai Police Department under Japanese Occupation
The Second Historical Archives of China, Nanjing
  Records of the Executive Yuan of the Republic of China

Taiwan
Academia Historica (The National Archives of Taiwan), Taipei
  Records of the Foreign Ministry of the Republic of China
  Records of the Executive Yuan of the Republic of China
The Archives of the Institute of Modern History, Academia Sinica, Taipei
  Records of the Foreign Ministry of the Republic of China
The Archives of the Chinese Nationalist Party, Taipei
  Records of the Central Executive Council and the Highest National Defense Council, Republic of China

Japan
The Diplomatic Record Office of the Ministry of Foreign Affairs of Japan, Japan Center for Asian Historical Records (This digital archive may be found at http://www.jacar.go.jp)

Records of the Ministry of Foreign Affairs: Series I, Cultural Society—Category 4, Labor and Social Issues—Miscellaneous Documents Relating to Issues Concerning Ethnic Groups/The Jewish Issue

United States

United States Holocaust Memorial Museum, Washington, D.C.
  Selected Files of the Shanghai Municipal Archives (microfilm)
  Selected Oral History Interview Recordings
  Institutional Archives, Exhibitions Division: Records Relating to Developing the "Flight and Rescue" Exhibition, 1998–1999
United States National Archives and Records Administration, College Park, MD
  RG 59—General Records of the Department of State
  RG 84—Records of the Foreign Service Posts of the Department of State
  RG 226—Office of Strategic Services Archives
The Library of Congress, Washington, D.C.
  Selected Archives of the Japanese Army, Navy and Other Government Agencies 1868–1945 (microfilm)
  Archives of the Japanese Ministry of Foreign Affairs, S series (microfilm)
  Reports of the South Manchurian Railway Company relating to Jewish Matters
The Shanghai Municipal Police Files (microfilm), holdings of Alderman Library, University of Virginia
The Maurice William Archives, UCLA Center for Chinese Studies, Los Angeles, CA (http://www.international.ucla.edu/china/William MauriceArchive/)

United Kingdom

British National Archives, Kew
  FO 371—Foreign Office, General Correspondence

Israel

The Albert Einstein Archives, the Jewish & National University Library, Jerusalem
  Correspondence with Maurice William, 1939, piece numbers 54-623–54-625

Memoirs

Bacon, Ursula. *Shanghai Diary: A Young Girl's Journey from Hitler's Hate to War-Torn China*. Milwaukie, OR: M Press, 2004.

Eisfelder, Horst. *Chinese Exile: My Years in Shanghai and Nanking*. Bergenfield, NJ: Avotaynu Foundation, 2003.

He, Fengshan. *Waijiao shengya sishi nian* [Forty Years of My Diplomatic Life]. Hong Kong: Zhongwen daxue chubanshe, 1990.

Headley, Hannelore Heinemann. *Blond China Doll: A Shanghai Interlude, 1939–1953*. St. Catharines, ON: Blond China Doll Enterprises, 2004.

Heppner, Ernest G. *Shanghai Refuge: A Memoir of the World War II Jewish Ghetto*. Lincoln: University of Nebraska Press, 1993.

Itō, Takeo. *Life along the South Manchurian Railway: The Memoirs of Itō Takeo*. Translated by Joshua A. Fogel. Armonk, NY: M. E. Sharpe, 1988.

Iwry, Samuel, and L. J. H. Kelley. *To Wear the Dust of War: From Bialystok to Shanghai to the Promised Land: An Oral History*. New York: Palgrave Macmillan, 2004.

Kaplan, Vivian J. *Ten Green Bottles: The True Story of One Family's Journey from War-Torn Austria to the Ghettos of Shanghai*. New York: St. Martin's Press, 2004.

Kipen, Israel. *A Life to Live...: An Autobiography*. Burwood, Victoria: Chandos, 1989.

Koo, V. K. Wellington. *The Wellington Koo Memoir*. New York: Columbia University, East Asian Institute, 1978.

Krasno, Rena. *Strangers Always: A Jewish Family in Wartime Shanghai*. Berkeley, CA: Pacific View Press, 1992.

Kurtz, Sidney B. *Marcel Singer: The Gentle Butcher of Hongkew*. Philadelphia: Xlibris, 2003.

Lincoln, Anna. *Anna Lincoln Views China*. Shanghai: Shanghai renmin chubanshe, 2001.

Riess, Hans L. *My Middle Name Is Israel: A Wartime Memoir of Berlin, London and Shanghai*. Bloomington, IN: 1st Books Library, 2001.

Ross, James R. *Escape to Shanghai: A Jewish Community in China*. New York: Free Press, 1994.

Rubin, Evelyn Pike. *Ghetto Shanghai*. New York: Shengold Books, 1993.

Saionji, Kinmochi, and Harada Kumao. *The Saionji-Harada Memoirs [1930–1940]: Civil Intelligence Section Special Report*. Tokyo: General Headquarters, Far East Command, Military Intelligence Section, General Staff, 1946, 1978.

Sugihara, Yukiko. *Rokusennin no inochi no biza* [Six Thousand Visas for Life]. Tokyo: Asahi Sonorama, 1990.

Tobias, Sigmund. *Strange Haven: A Jewish Childhood in Wartime Shanghai*. Urbana: University of Illinois Press, 1999.

Miscellaneous

Aid to Jews Overseas: Report on the Activities of the American Jewish Joint Distribution Committee, for the Year 1938. American Jewish Joint Distribution Committee, New York, 1939.

Aiding Jews Overseas: Report of the American Jewish Joint Distribution Committee, Inc. for 1940 and the First 5 Months of 1941. American Jewish Joint Distribution Committee, Inc., New York.

China Handbook. Compiled by the Chinese Ministry of Information. New York: Macmillan, 1943.

Report. American Jewish Joint Distribution Committee, New York, 1934–1941, 1945–1946.

Sun Yat-sen, *Prescriptions for Saving China: Selected Writings of Sun Yat-sen*. Edited by Julie Lee Wei, Ramon Hawley Myers, and Donald G. Gillin. Stanford, CA: Hoover Institution Press, 1994.

The Year of Survival: 1946. Annual Report of the American Jewish Joint Distribution Committee. New York: American Jewish Joint Distribution Committee, Inc., 1947.

Newspapers and Journals

China Weekly Review
Dongfang zazhi [Eastern Miscellany]
Israel's Messenger
Kokusai Himitsuryoku no Kenkyū [Studies on International Secret Power]
Minguo Dangan [Archives of the Republic of China]
North China Daily News
Shanghai Evening Post and Mercury
Shanghai Jewish Chronicle
Shanghai Times
Shen Bao [Shanghai News]

Yudaya Kenkyū [Jewish Studies]
Yudaya Mondai Jihō [Jewish Issue Periodical]

SECONDARY SOURCES
Chinese Sources

Awen. *Hatong quanzhuan* [The Biography of Hardoon]. Beijing: Zhongguo renshi chubanshe, 1997.

Bi, Chunfu, ed. "Chongqing guomin zhengfu anzhi taowang Youtairen jihua chouyi shimo" [The Chongqing Nationalist Government's Plan to Settle Jewish Refugees]. *Minguo dangan* [Archives of the Nationalist Period] no. 3 (1993): 17–21.

Chen, Hongmin, ed. *Zhonghua Minguo shi xinlun: jingji, shehui, sixiang wenhua juan* [New Theory on the History of the Republic of China: Economy, Society, Thoughts and Culture]. Beijing: Sanlian shudian, 2003.

Chen, Qianping, ed. *Zhonghua Minguo shi xinlun: zhengzhi, zhongwai guanxi, renwu juan* [New Theory on the History of the Republic of China: Politics, Domestic and International Relations, and Peoples]. Beijing: Sanlian shudian, 2003.

Chen, Renxia. *Zhong De Ri sanjiao guanxi yanjiu (1936–1938)* [The Study of the Triangular Relations between China, Germany and Japan: 1936–1938]. Beijing: Sanlian shudian, 2003.

Fang, Jianchang. "Ben shiji san ci shi niandai Zhongguo gedi Youtairen gaimao" [General Picture of the Jews in China in the 1930s and the 1940s]. *Jindaishi Yanjiu* [Studies of Modern History], no. 3 (1997): 48–80.

———. "Erzhan qijian Deji Youtai nanmin zai Shanghai" [German Jewish Refugees in Shanghai during World War II]. *Deguo Yanjiu* [Deutschland-Studien] 13, no. 3 (1998): 40–44.

———. "Shanghai he Harbin Youtai shengyishe shu lue" [About the B'nai B'rith in Shanghai and Harbin]. *Shilin* [Historical Review], no. 2 (1997): 101–106.

Gao, Hong, and Dan Fuliang. "Lun Riben erzhan shiqi de duiyou zhengce" [Japan's Policy toward the Jews during World War II]. *Shijieshi Yanjiu Dongtai* [Trends of World History Studies], no. 3 (1990): 14–20.

Ge, Zhuang. *Zongjiao yu jindai Shanghai shehui de bianqian* [Religion and the Transformation of Modern Shanghai Society]. Shanghai: Shanghai shudian chubanshe, 1999.

Guo, Hengyu. "Sun Zhongshan yu Deguo" [Sun Yat-sen and Germany]. *Guoshiguan guankan* [Journal of the Academia Historica], no. 23 (1997): 83–110.

Guo, Hengyu, and Mechthild Leutner, eds. *Deguo waijiao dangan, 1928–1938 nian zhi ZhongDe guanxi* [German Foreign Office Archives: Sino-German Relations, 1928–1938]. Translated by Xu Linfei and Sun Shanhao. Taipei: Zhongyang yanjiuyuan jindaishi yanjiusuo, 1991.

He, Yiwen. "Youtai minzu wenti" [The Jewish National Problem]. *Dongfang zazhi* [Eastern Miscellany] 36, no. 12 (1939): 9–16.

Kaminski, Gerd, ed. *Zhongguo de da shi dai: Luoshengte zaihua shouji, 1941–1949* [Jacob Rosenfeld's China Diary]. Translated by Du Wentang. Beijing: Zhongguo shehui kexue chubanshe, 2003.

Li, Tiangang. *Wenhua Shanghai* [The Culture of Shanghai]. Shanghai: Shanghai jiaoyu chubanshe, 1998.

Li, Zheng. "Guanyu paiyou" [About Anti-Semitism]. *Yi bao zhou kan* [Yibao Weekly], no. 9 (1938): 234–235.

Liaoning sheng dangan guan [The Archives of the Liaoning Province], ed. *Man tie mi dang: Man tie yu qin Hua Ri jun* [Secret Documents from the South Manchurian

Railway Company: The South Manchurian Railway Company and the Japanese Invading Army]. Guilin: Guangxi shifan daxue chubanshe, 1999.

Liu, Bing. "Guomin zhengfu guanyu yuanjiu Youtairen dangan jiemi" [Revealing the Archives concerning the Nationalist Government's Plan to Save Jews]. *Dangan yu shixue* [Archives and Historical Studies], no. 2 (2001): 53–55.

Ma, Zhendu. *Zhong De waijiao mi dang, 1927 nian–1947 nian* [Secret Diplomatic Archives between China and Germany, 1927–1947]. Guilin: Guangxi shifan daxue chubanshe, 1994.

Pan, Guang, ed. *Youtairen zai Shanghai* [The Jews in Shanghai]. Shanghai: Shanghai huabao chubanshe, 1995

———. *Youtairen zai Zhongguo* [The Jews in China]. Beijing: Wuzhou chuanbo chubanshe, 2001.

Pan, Guang, and Li Peidong, eds. *Youtairen yi Shanghai* [Jews Remember Shanghai]. Shanghai: Shanghai shi zheng xie wen shi zi liao bian ji bu, 1995.

Pan, Guang, and Wang Jian. "Jiefanghou Shanghai de Youtairen yu 'Youlian'" [Jews and the Council of the Jewish Community in Shanghai after 1949]. *Ouya guancha* [Eurasia Review], no. 2 (1999): 31–33.

——— *Yi ge ban shi ji yi lai de Shanghai Youtairen: Youtai minsu shi shang de dongfang yi ye* [Shanghai Jews of a Century and a Half: The Oriental Page in Jewish History]. Beijing: Shehui kexue wenxian chub anshe, 2002.

Pan, Guang, Yu Jianhua, and Wang Jian. *Youtai minzu fuxing zhilu* [The Revitalization of the Jewish People]. Shanghai: Shanghai shehui kexue yuan chubanshe, 1998.

Pan, Guang, and Yu Weidong. "Guanyu jiu Shanghai Youtairen fuguo yundong de lishi kaocha" [Research on the Jewish Zionist Movement in Old Shanghai]. *Xueshu jikan* [Academic Periodical], no. 1 (1992): 160–169.

Pan, Guangdan. *Zhongguo jingnei Youtairen de ruogan lishi wenti: Kaifeng de Zhongguo Youtairen* [On Several Historical Issues Concerning the Jews in China: the Kaifeng Jews]. Beijing: Beijing daxue chubanshe, 1983.

Qin, Xiaoyi, ed. *Zhonghua Minguo zhongyao shiliao chubian—dui Ri kangzhan shiqi. Di 3 bian, zhanshi waijiao* [First Edition of Important Historical Materials of the Republic of China—the Anti-Japanese War Period, Vol. 3, Diplomacy during the War]. Taipei: Zhongguo guomindang zhongyang weiyuanhui dangshi weiyuanhui: Jing xiao zhe zhongyang wenwu gong ying she, 1981.

Rao, Lihua. *"Shanghai Youtai jishibao" yanjiu* [The Study of the Shanghai Jewish Chronicle]. Beijing: Xinhua chubanshe, 2003.

Shao, Minghuang, ed. "Kangzhan shiqi guomin zhengfu rongliu Youtairen jihua dangan yizu" [Collection of Documents concerning the Nationalist Government's Plan to Accommodate Jews during the Sino-Japanese War]. *Jindai Zhongguo* [Modern China], no. 147 (2002): 168–189.

Shi, Fukang, ed. *Shanghai shehui daguan* [General View of the Shanghai Society]. Shanghai: Shanghai shudian chubanshe, 2000.

Sun, Yat-sen. *Guo fu quan ji* [The Complete Works of Dr. Sun Yat-Sen]. Taipei: Zhongguo guomindang zhongyang weiyuanhui dang shi weiyuanhui, 1973.

———. *The Principle of Nationalism*. Translated by Frank W. Price. Taipei: China Cultural Service, 1953.

Sun, Yat-sen, and Zhang Qiyun. *Guo fu quan shu* [The Complete Works of the Founding Father]. Taipei: Guo fang yan jiu yuan, 1960.

Tang, Peiji. "Youtairen zai Shanghai" [The Jews in Shanghai]. *Shanghai yanjiu conglun* [Shanghai Studies], no. 8 (1993): 313–323.

Tang, Peiji, Xu Buzeng, Yan Huimin, Gu Borong, and Zheng Yiliu. *Shanghai Youtairen* [The Shanghai Jews]. Shanghai: Sanlian shudian, 1992.

Wang, Jian. "Hu shen yuan shou: Erzhan shiqi de Zhong You youyi" [Extending a Helping Hand to Each Other: The Sino-Jewish Friendship during World War Two]. *Shehui kexue* [Social Sciences], no. 6 (2000): 67–71.

———. "Jindai Shanghai Youtai yimin ji qi shetuan zuzhi" [Jewish Immigrants and Their Organizations in Modern Shanghai]. *Ouya guancha* [Eurasia Review], no. 3 (1998): 18–29.

———. "Shi lun dier ci shijie dazhan shiqi de Zhongyou guanxi" [The Relationship between the Chinese and Jewish Peoples during World War II]. *Xiya feizhou* [West Asia and Africa], no. 4 (1997): 44–50.

———. "Shilun Youtairen yu jindai Shanghai jingji" [Jews and Modern Shanghai Economy]. *Shilin* [Historical Review], no. 2 (1999): 1–15.

———. "Youtairen yu jindai Shanghai wenhua" [Jews and Modern Shanghai Culture]. *Ouya guancha* [Eurasia Review], no. 1 (1999): 25, 26–33.

Wang, Minghui. *Hongkou qu zhi* [Record of the Hongkou District]. Shanghai: Shanghai shehui kexue yuan chubanshe, 1999.

Wang, Qingyu. "Jiu Shanghai de Youtairen" [Jews in Old Shanghai]. *Xueshu jikan* [Academic Periodical], no. 2 (1987): 165–172.

Xie, Xueshi. *Ge shi yi si: ping Man tie diao cha bu* [Thoughts Left by the Last Generation: Reviewing the Research Department of the South Manchurian Railway Company]. Beijing: Renmin chubanshe, 2003.

Xiong, Xuezhi. ed. *Shanghai tongshi* [Comprehensive History of Shanghai]. Shanghai: Shanghai renmin chubanshe, 1999.

Xiong, Yuezhi, Ma Xueqiang, and An Kejia, eds. *Shanghai de waiguo ren, 1842–1949* [Foreigners in Shanghai, 1842–1949]. Shanghai: Shanghai gu ji chubanshe, 2003.

Xu, Buzeng. "Nacui tudao xia de tousheng she: ji er ci dazhan zhong binan lai hu de Youtairen" [Escape from the Nazi Massacre: Jewish Refugees in Shanghai during World War II]. *Shanghai dangan* [Shanghai Archives], no. 1 (1989): 37–43.

Xu, Che, and Xu Yue. *Zhang Zuoling zhuan* [The Biography of Zhang Zuolin]. Tianjin: Baihua wenyi chubanshe, 2004.

Xu, Xin. "20 shiji 50 niandai houqi zai Hua Youtairen zhuangkuang jianshu" [Brief Description of the Situation of the Jews in China in the Late 1950s]. *Shehui kexue* [Social Sciences], no. 4 (2000): 72–76.

Xue, Liyong. *Jiu Shanghai zujie shihua* [The Historical Narratives of the International Settlement in Old Shanghai]. Shanghai: Shanghai shehui kexue yuan chubanshe, 2002.

Yi, Xianshi. *"Jiu yi ba" shibian Shi* [The History of the "September 18 Incident"]. Shenyang: Liaoning renmin chubanshe, 1981.

Yu, Songhua. "Youtairen yu Youtai de fuxing yundong" [The Jews and the Jewish Zionist Movement]. *Dongfang zazhi* [Eastern Miscellany] 24, no. 17 (1927): 21–28.

Zhang, Beigen. "1933–1941 nian de Zhong De guanxi" [Sino-German Relations: 1933–1941]. *Lishi yanjiu* [Historical Studies], no. 2 (1995): 107–119.

Zhang, Bofeng, and Zhuang Jianping, eds. *Kang Ri zhan zheng* [The Anti-Japanese War]. Chengdu: Sichuan daxue chubanshe, 1997.

Zhang, Tiejiang. *Jiekai Haerbin Youtairen lishi zhimi = Reveal Enigmas of the Jewish History of Harbin*. Harbin: Heilongjiang renmin chubanshe, 2005.

Zhang, Zhongli, and Chen Cengnian. *Shaxun jituan zai jiu Zhongguo* [The Sasoons in Old China]. Beijing: Renmin chubanshe, 1985.

Zhou Qian, and Chen Jimin. "Lun Beijing zhengfu shiqi Zhongguo dui guolian chengli de renshi he canyu" [On China's Perception of and Participation in the Establishment of the League of Nations during the Beijing Government]. *Beihua daxue xuebao* (shehui kexue ban) [Bulletin of the Beihua University (on Social Sciences)] 9, no. 1 (2008): 78–83.

Zhu, Huisen, Lai Min, and He Zhilin, eds. *Zhonghua Minguo shishi jiyao chugao: 1938* [First Edition of the Records of Historical Events of the Republic of China, 1938]. Taipei: Guo shi guan, 1989.

English Sources

Ahlers, John. "The Proposal to Send 100,000 German Jewish Refugees to Yunnan Province." *China Weekly Review* (July 22, 1939): 226–227.

Altman, Avraham, and Irene Eber. "Flight to Shanghai, 1938–1940: The Larger Setting." *Yad Vashem Studies* 27 (2000): 51–86.

Barnett, Robert W. "Shanghai's German Refugees Face Uncertainties." *Far Eastern Survey* 8, no. 21 (1939): 251–253.

Barnhart, Michael. *Japan Prepares for Total War: the Search for Economic Security, 1919–1941*. Ithaca, NY: Cornell University Press, 2001

Blumenthal, W. Michael. "Shanghai: The Persistence of Interest." *Points East* 11, no. 1 (1996): 1, 3–4.

Borg, Dorothy, and Shumpei Okamoto, eds. *Pearl Harbor as History: Japanese-American Relations, 1931–1941*. New York: Columbia University Press, 1973.

Breitman, Richard, and Alan M. Kraut. *American Refugee Policy and European Jewry, 1933–1945*. Bloomington and Indianapolis: Indiana University Press, 1987.

Brooks, Barbara. *Japan's Imperial Diplomacy: Consuls, Treaty Ports, and War in China, 1895–1938*. Honolulu: University of Hawaii Press, 2000.

Chang, Jung, and Jon Halliday. *Mme Sun Yat-Sen (Soong Ching-ling)*. Harmondsworth, Middlesex: Penguin Books, 1986.

Chung, Dooeum, *Élitist Fascism: Chiang Kaishek's Blueshirts in 1930s China*. Aldershot: Ashgate, 2000.

Crowley, James B. "Japanese Army Factionalism in the Early 1930's." *Journal of Asian Studies* 21, no. 3 (1962): 309–326.

———. *Japan's Quest for Autonomy: National Security and Foreign Policy, 1930–1938*. Princeton, NJ: Princeton University Press, 1966.

Dicker, Herman. *Wanderers and Settlers in the Far East: A Century of Jewish Life in China and Japan*. New York: Twayne, 1962.

Eastman, Lloyd E., "Fascism in Kuomintang China: The Blue Shirts." *China Quarterly*, no. 49 (Jan.–Mar., 1972): 1–31.

Eber, Irene, ed. *Voices from Shanghai: Jewish Exiles in Wartime China*. Chicago: University of Chicago Press, 2008.

Falbaum, Berl. *Shanghai Remembered: Stories of Jews Who Escaped to Shanghai from Nazi Europe*. Royal Oak, MI: Momentum Books, 2005.

Fiszman, Joseph R. "The Quest for Status: Polish Jewish Refugees in Shanghai, 1941–1949." *Polish Review* 43, no. 4 (1998): 441–460.

Fox, John P. *Germany and the Far Eastern Crisis 1931–1938: A Study in Diplomacy and Ideology*. Oxford: Clarendon Press; New York: Oxford University Press, 1982.

Friedlander, Saul. *Nazi Germany and the Jews, Vol. I. The Years of Persecution, 1933–1939*. New York: HarperCollins, 1997.

Future: Farewell Issue 1947–1948. Shanghai: Shanghai Jewish Youth Community Center, 1948.

Gandel Centre of Judaic, Jewish Museum of Australia. *The Story of a Haven: The Jews in Shanghai: 21 October 1997–22 March 1998*. St Kilda, Victoria: Jewish Museum of Australia, 1997.

Gao, Bei. "The Chinese Nationalist Government's Policy towards European Jewish Refugees during World War Two." *Modern China* 37, no. 2 (2011): 202–237.

Gao, Wang-Zhi. "The Contributions of the Jewish Communities in Shanghai Viewed in Their Sino-Judaic Perspective." *Points East* 2, no. 1 (1987): 1, 4–8.

Ginsbourg, Anna. *Jewish Refugees in Shanghai*. Shanghai: China Weekly Review, 1940.

———. "Thousands of Shanghai's German-Jewish Refugees Lead Lives of Disillusionment, Despair." *China Weekly Review* 96, no. 8 (1941): 252–253.

Goldstein, Jonathan, ed. *The Jews of China: Volume One, Historical and Comparative Perspectives*. Armonk, NY: M. E. Sharpe, 1999.

———, ed. *The Jews of China: Volume Two, A Sourcebook and Research Guide*. Armonk, NY: M. E. Sharpe, 2000.

———. "The Republic of China and Israel, 1911–2003." *Israel Affairs* 10, no. 1–2 (2004): 223–253.

———. "Shanghai Consular Records about Jewish Refugees: Visits to Polish, Russian and United States Consulates—1992." *SHAFR Newsletter* 24, no. 2 (June 1993): 19–23.

Goodman, David G., and Miyazawa Masanori. *Jews in the Japanese Mind: The History and Uses of a Cultural Stereotype*. New York: Free Press, 1995.

Gruenberger, Felix. "The Jewish Refugees in Shanghai." *Jewish Social Studies* 12, no. 4 (1950): 329–348.

Hirsch, Claus W. "The Shanghai Jewish Ghetto, 1940–1947." *Dorot* 15, no. 3 (1994): 7–10.

Iguchi, Haruo. *Unfinished Business: Ayukawa Yoshisuke and U.S.-Japan Relations, 1937–1953*. Cambridge, MA: Harvard University Press, 2003.

Iklé, Frank William. *German-Japanese Relations: 1936–1940*. New York: Bookman Associates, 1956.

Iwasaki, Uichi. *The Working Forces in Japanese Politics: A Brief Account of Political Conflicts, 1867–1920*. New York: Columbia University, 1921.

"Jews in the Far East." *Jewish Affairs* 1, no. 6 (1942): 1–7.

Jones, Francis Clifford. *Japan's New Order in East Asia: Its Rise and Fall, 1937–45*. London: Oxford University Press, 1954.

King, Wunsz (Jin, Wensi). *China at the Washington Conference, 1921–1922*. New York: St. John's University Press, 1963.

Kirby, William C. *Germany and Republican China*. Stanford, CA: Stanford University Press, 1984.

Kranzler, David. *Japanese, Nazis and Jews: The Jewish Refugee Community of Shanghai, 1938–1945*. New York: Yeshiva University Press, 1976.

———. "Restrictions against German-Jewish Refugee Immigration to Shanghai in 1939." *Jewish Social Studies* 36, no. 1 (1974): 40–60.

Kremer, Roberta S. *Diplomat Rescuers and the Story of Feng Shan Ho*. Vancouver: Vancouver Holocaust Education Centre, 1999.

Lee, Leo Ou-fan. *Shanghai Modern: The Flowering of a New Urban Culture in China, 1930–1945*. Cambridge, MA: Harvard University Press, 2001.

Leitner, Yecheskel. *Operation: Torah Rescue: The Escape of the Mirrer Yeshiva from War-Torn Poland to Shanghai, China*. Jerusalem, New York: Feldheim, 1987.

Leslie, Donald Daniel. *The Survival of the Chinese Jews: The Jewish Community of Kaifeng*. Leiden: E. J. Brill, 1972.

Levine, Hillel. *In Search of Sugihara: The Elusive Japanese Diplomat Who Risked His Life to Rescue 10,000 Jews from the Holocaust.* New York: Free Press, 1996.

Lu, Hanchao. *Beyond the Neon Lights: Everyday Shanghai in the Early Twentieth Century.* Berkeley: University of California Press, 1999.

Margolis, Laura L. "Race against Time in Shanghai." *Survey Graphic* 33, no. 3 (1944): 168–171, 190–191.

Mars, Alvin. "A Note on the Jewish Refugees in Shanghai." *Jewish Social Studies* 31, no. 4 (1969): 286–291.

Maxon, Yale Candee. *Control of Japanese Foreign Policy: A Study of Civil-Military Rivalry, 1930–1945.* Westport, CT: Greenwood Press, 1973.

Meskill, Johanna Margarete Menzel. *Hitler & Japan: The Hollow Alliance.* New York: Atherton Press, 1966.

Meyer, Maisie J. *From the Rivers of Babylon to the Whangpoo: A Century of Sephardi Jewish Life in Shanghai.* Lanham, MD: University Press of America, 2003.

———. "The Interrelationship of Jewish Communities in Shanghai." *Immigrants & Minorities* 19, no. 2 (2000): 71–90.

Miyazawa, Masanori. "Japanese Anti-Semitism in the Thirties," *Midstream* 33, no. 3 (March 1987): 23–27.

Mochizuki, Ken, and Dom Lee. *Passage to Freedom: The Sugihara Story.* New York: Lee & Low Books, 1997.

Morley, James William, ed. *Deterrent Diplomacy: Japan, Germany, and the USSR, 1935–1940: Selected Translations from Taiheiyo Senso e no Michi, Kaisen Gaiko Shi.* New York: Columbia University Press, 1976.

Nish, Ian. *Japanese Foreign Policy in the Interwar Period.* Westport, CT: Praeger, 2002.

Ogata, Sadako N. *Defiance in Manchuria: The Making of Japanese Foreign Policy, 1931–1932.* Berkeley: University of California Press, 1964.

Pelcovits, N. A. "European Refugees in Shanghai." *Far Eastern Survey* 15, no. 21 (1946): 321–325.

Presseisen, Ernst L. *Germany and Japan: A Study in Totalitarian Diplomacy, 1933–1941.* The Hague: Martinus Nijhoff, 1958.

Ristaino, Marcia Reynders. *Port of Last Resort: The Diaspora Communities of Shanghai.* Stanford, CA: Stanford University Press, 2001.

Royama, Masamichi. *Foreign Policy of Japan: 1914–1939.* Westport, CT: Greenwood Press, 1973.

Sakamoto, Pamela Rotner. *Japanese Diplomats and Jewish Refugees: A World War II Dilemma.* Westport, CT: Praeger, 1998.

Sekiguchi, Yasushi. "The Changing Status of the Cabinet in Japan." *Pacific Affairs* 11, no. 1 (1938): 5–20.

Shotwell, James. "Sun Yat-sen and Maurice William." *Political Science Quarterly* 47, no. 1 (1932): 19–26.

Spang, Christian W., and Rolf-Harald Wippich, eds. *Japanese-German Relations, 1895–1945: War, Diplomacy and Public Opinion.* London: Routledge, 2006.

Stein, Sarah Abrevaya, "Protected Persons? The Baghdadi Jewish Diaspora, the British State, and the Persistence of Empire." *American Historical Review* 116, no. 1 (2011): 80–108.

Sun, Yat-sen. *The Teachings of Sun Yat-sen.* Compiled and introduced by Nagendranath Gangulee. Foreword by V. K. Wellington Koo. London: Sylvan Press, 1945.

Tokayer, Marvin, and Mary Swartz. *The Fugu Plan: The Untold Story of the Japanese and the Jews during World War II.* New York: Paddington Press, 1979.

United States Holocaust Memorial Museum. *Flight and Rescue.* Tacoma, WA: University of Washington Press, 2001.

Warhaftig, Zorach. *Refugee and Survivor: Rescue Efforts during the Holocaust.* Jerusalem: Yad Vashem, 1988.

Wells, Audrey. *The Political Thought of Sun Yat-sen: Development and Impact.* Basingstoke: Palgrave Macmillan, 2001.

Wilbur, Martin. *Sun Yat-sen: Frustrated Patriot.* New York: Columbia University Press, 1976.

Winston, Ada, and Josie Toochin. "Two Jewish Girls in Wartime Shanghai." *Rhode Island Jewish Historical Notes* 13, no. 1 (1999): 55–67.

Wyman, David S. *Paper Walls: America and the Refugee Crisis 1938–1941.* New York: Pantheon Books, 1968, 1985.

Young, Arthur N. *China and the Helping Hand, 1937–1945.* Cambridge, MA: Harvard University Press, 1963.

Young, John. *The Research Activities of the South Manchurian Railway Company, 1907–1945: A History and Bibliography.* New York: East Asian Institute, Columbia University, 1966.

Zhao, Suisheng. *Power by Design: Constitution-Making in Nationalist China.* Honolulu: University of Hawaii Press, 1996.

Zhou, Xun. *Chinese Perceptions of the "Jews" and Judaism: A History of the Youtai.* Richmond, Surrey: Curzon Press, 2001.

Zolotow, Maurice. *Maurice William and Sun Yat-sen.* London: Robert Hale, 1948.

Zuroff, Efraim. *The Response of Orthodox Jewry in the United States to the Holocaust: The Activities of the Vaad ha-Hatzala Rescue Committee, 1939–1945.* New York: Michael Scharf Publication Trust of the Yeshiva University Press; Hoboken, NJ: [Distributed by] KTAV, 2000.

Japanese Sources

Bandō, Hiroshi. *Nihon no Yudayajin seisaku, 1931–1945: Gaikō Shiryōkan bunsho "Yudayajin mondai" kara* [Japan's Jewish Policy, 1931–1945: Documents from the Diplomatic Record Office concerning "the Jewish Issue"]. Tokyo: Miraisha, 2002.

Honjō Hisako, Uchiyama Masao and Kubo Tōru eds., *Kō-Ain to senji Chūgoku chōsa: tsuketari kankōbutsu shozai mokuroku* [Kō-Ain and Research on China during the Sino-Japanese War]. Tokyo: Iwanami Shoten, 2002.

Hosoya, Chihiro, Saitō Makoto, Imai Seiichi, and Rōyama Michio, eds. *Nichi-Bei kankei-shi- kaisen ni itaru 10 nen (1931–41nen)* [The History of Japanese-American Relations: 10 Years to the Outbreak of the War (1931–41)], Vol. 1. Tokyo: Tokyo Daigaku Shuppankai, 1971.

———. *Nichi-Bei kankeishi- kaisen ni itaru 10 nen (1931–41nen)* [The History of Japanese-American Relations: 10 Years to the Outbreak of the War (1931–41)], Vol. 2. Tokyo: Tokyo Daigaku Shuppankai, 1971.

Imura, Tetsuo, ed. *Mantetsu Chōsabu: kankeisha no shōgen* [The Research Activities of the South Manchurian Railway Company: The Reminiscences of the Research Staff]. Tokyo: Ajia keizai kenkyūjo: Hatsubaijo Ajia Keizai Shuppankai, 1996.

Inuzuka, Kiyoko. *Yudaya mondai to Nihon no kōsaku* [The Jewish Problem and Japanese Maneuvering]. Tokyo: Nihon Kōgyō Shinbunsha, 1982.

———. "Yudayajin wo hogo shita teikoku kaigun" [The Imperial Navy Protected Jews]. *Jiyū* [Freedom] (February 1973): 236–245.

Inuzuka, Koreshige. "Nihon no 'Aushubittsu' wa rakuen datta" [Japanese "Auschwitz" Was a Paradise]. *Jiyū* [Freedom] (February 1973): 228–235.

———. *Yudayajin no inbō to kokusai supai* [The Plot of the Jews and International Spies]. Tokyo: Naikaku Jōhōbu, 1938.

——— (Utsunomiya, Kiyō). *Yudaya mondai to Nihon* [The Jewish Problem and Japan]. Tokyo: Naigai Shobō, 1939.

Iriye, Akira, and Aruga Tadashi, eds. *Senkanki no Nihon gaikō* [Japanese Diplomacy during the War]. Tokyo: Tokyo Daigaku Shuppankai, 1984.

Ishiwara, Kanji, and Tsunoda Jun. *Ishiwara Kanji shiryō: Kokuhō ronsaku hen* [Historical Materials on Ishiwara Kanji: Theories of the National Defense]. Tokyo: Hara Shobō, 1967.

Kase, Hideaki. "Nihon no naka no Yudayajin" [Jews in Japan]. *Chūō Kōron* [The Central Review] 86, no. 6 (1971): 234–247.

Maruyama, Naoki. *Taiheiyō Sensō to Shanhai no Yudaya nanmin* [The Pacific War and the Shanghai Jewish Refugees]. Tokyo: Hōsei Daigaku Shuppankyoku, 2005.

Miyazawa, Masanori. *Yudayajin ronkō: Nihon ni okeru rongi no tsuiseki* [Debate concerning the Jews: Tracking the Arguments in Japan]. Tokyo: Shinsensha, 1982.

Oyama, Takeo. *Tōa to Yudaya mondai* [East Asia and the Jewish Problem]. Tokyo: Chuo Kōronsha, 1941.

Sakai, Katsuisa. *Sekai no shōtai to Yudayajin* [The Truth of the World and the Jews]. Tokyo: Naigai Shobō, 1924.

Sasaki, Yoshihiko, ed. *Aikawa Yoshisuke Sensei tsuisōroku* [Essays in Honor of Aikawa Yoshisuke]. Tokyo: Aikawa Yoshisuke Sensei Tsuisōroku Hensan Kankōkai, 1968.

Yasue, Hiroo. *Dairen tokumu kikan to maboroshi no Yudaya kokka* [The Dairen Intelligence Agency and the Phantom Jewish State]. Tokyo: Yahata Shoten, 1989.

Yasue, Norihiro. (Hō, Kōshi.) *Kakumei undō o abaku: Yudaya no chi o fumite* [Revealing the Revolution: On the Land of Judea]. Tokyo: Shōkasha, 1931.

———. *Sekai kakumei no rimen* [Behind the World Revolution]. Tokyo: Niyū Meicho Kankōkai, 1924.

———. *Yudaya minzoku no sekai shihai?* [The Jewish Control of the World?]. Tokyo: Kokon Shoin, 1933.

———. *Yudaya no hitobito* [The Jewish People]. Tokyo: Gunjin Kaikan Shuppanbu, 1937.

Yoshii, Hiroshi. *Shōwa gaikōshi* [The Diplomatic History of the Showa Era], 3rd ed. Tokyo: Nansōsha, 1984.

DISSERTATIONS
Silverman, Cheryl A. "Jewish Emigrés and Popular Images of Jews in Japan." Ph.D. diss., Columbia University, 1989.

Wiedemann, Susanne. "Transnational Encounters with 'Amerika': German Jewish Refugees' Identity Formation in Berlin and Shanghai, 1939–1949." Ph.D. diss., Brown University, 2006.

UNPUBLISHED MATERIALS
Culman, Henry. *Growing up on Three Continents*. United States Holocaust Memorial Museum Archives, Accession No. 2006.5.

Schurtman, William. "Report on: The Jewish Refugee Community in Shanghai." City College of New York, 1954 [author's collection].

INDEX

CPSIA information can be obtained at www.ICGtesting.com
Printed in the USA
BVOW02s1417230716

456330BV00001B/3/P